LINKS
OF
HEAVEN

A complete guide to
GOLF JOURNEYS IN IRELAND

LINKS OF HEAVEN

A complete guide to
GOLF JOURNEYS IN IRELAND

BY RICHARD PHINNEY AND SCOTT WHITLEY

BALTRAY BOOKS • OGDENSBURG, NY • OTTAWA

Published by Baltray Books
Corporate Center, 812 Proctor Ave., Ogdensburg NY 13669
Box 4902, Station E, Ottawa, Ont., K1S 2J1

Excerpts from *Following Through*, by Herbert Warren Wind (published by HarperCollins) reprinted by kind permission of the author. Copyright © 1995 by Herbert Warren Wind.

Printed in the United States of America
Design: Reactor Art+Design   Illustrations: Bill Russell
Cover Photograph (Royal County Down): Courtesy of Northern Ireland Tourist Board

Published simultaneously in Canada

Disclaimer: The publisher and authors have done their best to ensure the accuracy of all the information in this book. However, they can accept no responsibility for errors, inaccuracies, omissions or any other inconsistency herein, or for any loss, injury or inconvenience sustained by any traveler as a result of information or advice contained in this book. Any slights against people or organizations are unintentional. Conditions and prices can change rapidly: readers should consult their travel agent as well as airlines, hotels, embassies and golf clubs for up-to-the-minute information.

Library of Congress Catalog Card Number: 95-81020

Publisher's Catologing in Publication
(Prepared by Quality Books Inc.)

Phinney, Richard
    Links of heaven : a complete guide to golf journeys in Ireland /
by Richard Phinney and Scott Whitley.
    p. cm.
    Includes bibliographical references and index.
    ISBN: 1-888132-02-7.
    1. Golf—Ireland—Guidebooks. 2. Golf—Northern Ireland—
Guidebooks. 3. Ireland—Guidebooks. 4. Northern Ireland—
Guidebooks. I. Whitley, Scott. II. Title.
    GV985.I7P45 1996   796.352'068'415
                                        QB195-20658

To our parents and families
and to Eddie Hackett

GOLFER'S MAP
OF IRELAND

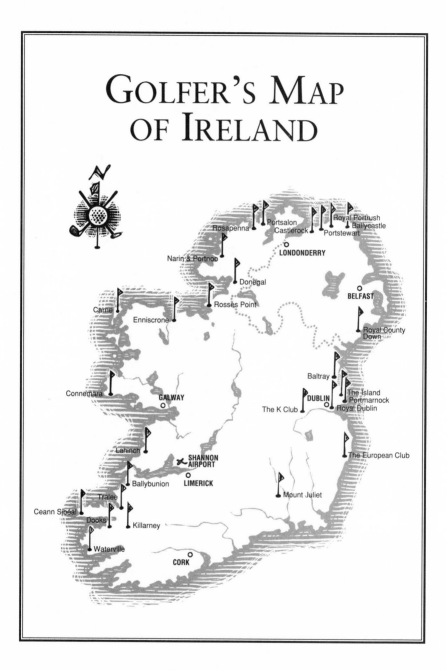

Rosapenna
Portsalon
Castlerock
Royal Portrush
Ballycastle
Portstewart
Narin & Portnoo
LONDONDERRY
Donegal
BELFAST
Carne
Rosses Point
Enniscrone
Royal County Down
Baltray
Connemara
GALWAY
The Island
Portmarnock
DUBLIN
The K Club
Royal Dublin
Lahinch
The European Club
SHANNON AIRPORT
Ballybunion
LIMERICK
Tralee
Ceann Sibéal
Mount Juliet
Dooks
Killarney
Waterville
CORK

TABLE OF CONTENTS

1   INTRODUCTION
    7   The Joy of Links

13   THE SOUTHWEST: THE CLASSICS
    15   *Ballybunion: An Oral History*
    22   *The Dreamers*

    34   Ballybunion Old
    37   Ballybunion New
    40   Waterville
    45   Killarney
    49   Lahinch
    53   Tralee
    58   Ceann Sibéal
    62   Dooks
    66   Diversions: The Southwest

71   THE NORTHWEST: THE GREAT ADVENTURE
    73   *Of Princes and Peasants:*
           Donegal's Rediscovered Golf Treasures
    78   *King of the Links*
    85   *A Miracle at Connemara*

    97   Rosapenna
    100   Portsalon
    102   Donegal
    106   Narin and Portnoo
    110   County Sligo (Rosses Point)
    114   Carne
    122   Enniscrone
    126   Connemara
    128   Diversions: The Northwest

131 THE EAST: FIVE GREAT LINKS (AND DUBLIN, TOO!)

133 *Moondance with Portmarnock*
139 *The Golf Theme Parks*

143 The Island
147 Portmarnock
152 County Louth (Baltray)
157 Mount Juliet
160 The Kildare Hotel and Country Club
162 Royal Dublin
168 The European Club
173 Diversions: Dublin and the Southeast

177 NORTHERN IRELAND: HIDDEN TREASURES

179 *Golfing Through the Troubles*

184 Royal Portrush
189 Portstewart
193 Ballycastle
197 Castlerock
200 Royal County Down
205 Diversions: Northern Ireland

209 CONTEXTS

210 Equal Partners? *Women's Golf in Ireland*
215 Try the Bread: *A Golfer's Survival Guide to Irish Cuisine*
220 Guinness is Good for You: *A Guide to Drinking in Ireland*
226 A Golfer's History of Ireland

237 PLANNING YOUR JOURNEY

239 When To Go
239 Getting There
239 Getting Around
240 Advance Starting Times
241 What To Take

241 What It Costs
242 Communications
243 Some Suggested Journeys
251 Accommodation

265 ONE HUNDRED MORE GOLF COURSES

285 LISTS
286 Ireland's Best 18 Holes
289 Tournaments Open to Visiting Golfers
293 Golfer's Glossary
297 Golfer's Reading List and Bibliography

301 Index

A man would think that the game of golf originated here.

TOM WATSON, *about Ballybunion*

Some of the Irish links, I was about to write, stand comparison with the greatest courses in the world. They don't. They are the greatest courses in the world, not only in layout but in scenery and "atmosphere" and that indefinable something which makes you relive again and again the day you played there.

HENRY LONGHURST

THE MAGNIFICENT SEASIDE LINKS of Ireland have stirred the imagination of the golfing traveller since Old Tom Morris, in 1894, pronounced Lahinch to be the greatest course of all. In the twilight of Queen Victoria's reign, the well-heeled golfing world flocked to Ireland—by boat, train, and horse and carriage—to taste the golfing pleasures offered at the golf resorts at Lahinch, Portrush, Portsalon and Rosapenna. The famous Triumvirate of professionals—Vardon, Taylor and Braid—were regular visitors, and the membership at Portrush included the two best women golfers in the world.

In the first quarter of the twentieth century everything began to change. The British aristocracy declined, the locus of the golf world moved to America, and Ireland entered a period of civil strife, partial independence and reconstruction. Golf travel to Ireland dwindled and remained dormant for half a century, although the reputation of its courses was fervently defended by a line of writers that stretched from Bernard Darwin to Henry Longhurst to Herbert Warren Wind.

Only in the 1970s and 1980s did golf travellers return in substantial numbers, encouraged by the ease of jet travel and the ringing endorsements of a new generation of golf celebrities such as Tom Watson. What they found was an unbeatable combination of breathtaking natural scenery, thrilling links golf and unparalleled hospitality. With the beginnings of a peace process in Ulster, the number of visiting golfers from North America, Britain and Europe is reaching unprecedented levels. With a little effort, however, it is still possible to enjoy some of the finest courses on the planet in blessed tranquillity.

There is, quite simply, no better place to play golf.

One obvious reason is that Ireland is blessed with the finest stretches of true, natural linksland in the world. To golf along Ireland's rugged coastline is to encounter a succession of spectacular views, each more astounding than the last. And it doesn't hurt that nature's gifts have been refashioned by some of golf's most distinguished architects. Old Tom Morris, Alister Mackenzie, Tom Simpson (and his assistant Molly Gourlay), H. S. Colt, Robert Trent Jones and Jack Nicklaus have all left their signature on Irish soil. The remarkable Eddie Hackett, Ireland's "national architect," has in more recent times added a stirring string of seaside courses of the highest caliber.

Just as intriguing are the mysterious origins of the great links of Portmarnock, Royal County Down and the incomparable Ballybunion. Like St. Andrews, they just evolved, caressed and molded by club members who spent a lifetime playing on their sandy soil. These courses—of no one age, and of no one hand—convey a sense of timelessness that cannot be recreated by bulldozers carrying out an architect's plan.

But there is a further dimension to the Irish golf experience that would make a golf holiday to Ireland worthwhile even if the courses were as flat and unappealing as day-old stout. Scratch the surface of even the most exclusive Irish golf club and you will find a genuine spirit of hospitality, and an eagerness to share tales (over a whiskey or a Guinness) about a game that the Irish have come to love with a passion equalled only in Scotland. Clubhouses in smaller communities are as friendly and egalitarian as any Irish pub.

It was not always so. Ireland's most famous clubs were founded by the ancestors of British aristocrats who supplanted Irish peasants on their own land. It was well after the Second World War before golf became, by any definition, a sport of the people. The transformation has been remarkable. What were once the playgrounds of the gentry are now lovingly managed by the descendants of tenant farmers. Golf courses have even been built to provide jobs for the poor. It is a transformation not only of class, but also of race—the proud use of Irish at the Ceann Sibéal golf club on the Dingle Peninsula was unthinkable only eighty years ago.

Politically, Ireland remains divided, but the Golfing Union of Ireland governs the game in *all* thirty-two counties and that "indefinable something" that sets Irish golf apart can be felt on both sides of the border. The popularity of golf has exploded in Northern Ireland and in the Republic, ignited by television coverage and the increasing affluence of an island where income levels were, until recently, much lower than the European average. Today more than 300,000 Irish men and women play golf, twice the number of only a few years ago, and thousands more compete for their Christmas turkeys on the pitch-and-putt courses that dot the island.

It would be a travesty, of course, to think of Ireland—North and South—as merely a golf destination. It is a place with an ancient and complex culture, its own language, and a tumultuous and often tragic history. Although Ireland is changing rapidly, the rooted quality of Irish life can still be startling (accents can be different in towns only a few miles apart). Each time you play golf in Ireland you encounter a new community with its own way of speaking and thinking about the world —and its own story. It is these encounters that make a golf journey to Ireland so fascinating. You will be sifting through layers of time as you marvel at unspoiled countryside, experience the charm of a village pub, and sample the attractions of vibrant and historic cities. And you will be collecting a bouquet of memories that will linger for a lifetime, and perhaps even help you face the challenges you left behind at home.

We hope that this book will assist anyone who is embarking on the journey for the first time, rekindle the memories of those who have already been, and be of interest to anyone with a love for the game of golf.

ABOUT THIS BOOK

This book has been seven years in the making. Our objective has been to write a different kind of golf travel book—one that is thoroughly and independently researched, contains useful practical advice, and yet conveys something of the rich tapestry that is Irish golf.

The core of the book is divided into four geographic sections—the Southwest, the Northwest, the East and Northern Ireland—corresponding to Ireland's great golfing regions. Within each section are in-depth chapters on each course that we believe you should seriously consider playing during your journey to Ireland. We have described the distinct qualities of each course and club, and filled in any historical background that we think will enrich your experience.

At the beginning of each geographical section you will find special chapters on specific subjects and themes. It is here that you will meet some of the people that make golf in Ireland so special—the aristocrat who wanted to broadcast Beethoven over Killarney; the oldest member of Ballybunion; the finest links designer of our time; and the participants in the zaniest and most satisfying golf tournament of them all.

In case you do not wish to golf *every* day on your journey, we have also provided a summary of outstanding sightseeing *diversions* that are available near Ireland's major golfing regions. These chapters may also be a source of ideas for the non-golfing spouse or friend. More detailed tourist information can be obtained from the resources listed at the back of the book.

The Contexts section has chapters on the fascinating saga of women and golf in Ireland, the overall historical context, and Irish food and drink.

There is also an entire section entitled Planning Your Journey, which will help you get the most out of limited time and budgets. Here you will find suggested day-by-day trip schedules, information about how to book starting times, what to take and what to expect during your journey. There is also an accommodation guide geared to the golf destinations we have recommended.

Finally, we offer a series of Lists, and an annotated listing of one hundred more golf courses. While not all are of championship caliber, a visit to any of these courses will rarely go unrewarded, and if the club is off the beaten track the welcome will be doubly warm.

We have taken a long journey of our own in writing this book, and at first we were acutely aware, as they say in County Kerry, of being "blow-ins." But over time we have come to consider this an advantage. It is perhaps inevitable that the Irish often take their glorious golf courses and their fascinating island for granted. Whenever possible we have tried to share the sense of wonder and discovery we felt in our Irish travels. Most of the people you will meet in this book did not think that their stories were in any way remarkable. We are confident that you will disagree.

As a small gesture of appreciation for the enjoyment we have derived from writing this book, we are delighted to be able to donate a portion of each book sold to the Golfing Union of Ireland to assist in junior golf coaching.

A NOTE ABOUT AUTHORSHIP

While this book has been a joint effort in terms of conception, research and editing, the bulk of the narrative has been written by Richard Phinney, and he must therefore take the bulk of responsibility for any shortcomings, errors and omissions. He is also the "I" in first person narratives. Exceptions include the Planning Your Journey section, the chapters on diversions and the guide to drinking in Ireland, which Scott Whitley has written. Ireland's Best 18 Holes were decided jointly and scientifically over several pints of Guinness, none of which, in Scott's view, were quite warm enough.

ACKNOWLEDGEMENTS

This book has been made possible by the generosity of scores of Irish golfers who offered us so much of their time and good humor. We would like to especially thank those who are profiled in some detail in the book, including Michael Mangan, John Moriarty, Pat Ruddy, Peter Waldron and Eddie Hackett. They provided inspiration as well as insight. We would also like to thank Tony Boner, Maurice Buckley, Frank Casey, William Condon, Jay Connolly, Noel Cronin, John Dalzell, Ivan Dickson, Michael Howard, Denis Kane, Joseph Kennedy, Peter Lyons, Liam McAndrew, Jim McKenna, Alison Metcalfe, Bob Mulholland, Gary Partington, Michael O'Brien, Jim O'Regan, Tom Prendergast, William Rocke, Cathal Toland, Simon Tormey and Pat Turvey.

We are also indebted to the dozens of historians, writers and club members who have produced the many exceptional club centenary books that have appeared during the last ten years. Taken together they represent a remarkable record of the social history of Ireland, as well as the development of some of the golf world's great treasures (they also make handsome mementos). We have benefitted greatly as well from William Gibson's *Early Irish Golf* and from the histories of the Golfing Union of Ireland (by William Merton) and of the Irish Ladies' Golf Union (by Dermot Gilleece and John Redmond). There is a full bibliography in the appendix.

Finally, we would like to thank everyone at Baltray Books, our editor Barbara Wade Rose, and Ron Bala, David Brice, Caroline Connell, Vicki Connolly, Neil Davies, Linda Finnigan, Jane Geddes, Susan Haight, Margaret Harding, Carole Houlihan, Roland Kuhn, Sophia Lam, Jerry Lee, George Lesnick, Christina Mairin, Maureen O'Grady, Janice Pasky, Jennifer Pepall, Beth Phinney, Brenda Phinney, Jonathan Rose, Adil Sayeed, Sean Slowey, Shari Spier, Jacques de Spoelberch, Tim and Jane Venus, Bonnie Weisz, Mark Whitley, Alain Wilson, David Wilson, Carolyn Wood and Susan Wright.

Portions of this book have appeared, in slightly different form, in the *St. Petersburg Times*, the *Rocky Mountain News* and the *Portland Oregonian*.

THE JOY OF LINKS

On a links there is so much that is natural, and it has taken centuries to get that look and feel, so you'd be a lunatic to tamper with it more than is necessary.

PAT RUDDY, *Irish writer and golf architect*

ALTHOUGH IRELAND HAS more than 300 golf courses of all descriptions, its great legacy to the sport are the thirty-five seaside links that form a bracelet of dazzling golfing gems along the island's craggy coastline. These courses are found on the same type of treeless, fiercely undulating terrain, linking the sea and farmland, that inspired the game's inventors. As the sandy soil was of no use save for sheep grazing, the ingenious Scots created a game that could be played on this unproductive ground. All golf courses built since are imitations, however abstract, of these original layouts and the natural features they incorporated—the sand pits where sheep sheltered against the wind, the dunes, and the areas of heather and fescue grass that came to be known as "rough."

To play a classic links is to play the genuine article, and return to the origins of the game. For some, the combination of stunning coastal scenery, bracing natural elements and the scent of history can make it something of a spiritual journey. (Michael Murphy's *Golf in the Kingdom*, a mystical voyage to an ancient links in Scotland, remains one of the best-selling golf books of all time.)

Another reason links golf is so special is that there isn't very much of it. Less than one half of one percent of golf courses are links, almost all of them in the British Isles, and virtually all of the world's linksland has been used up for golf courses and human settlement. During the last forty years only Ireland has seen a significant number of new links created, and European Community conservation laws may prevent the building of any more.

The eminent American golf writer Herbert Warren Wind has

described the unique qualities of a true links with his usual precision and grace:

> At first glance, even the most distinguished linksland courses look utterly ordinary to the man who has never played them before. If a golfer stands on the terrace at the Augusta National Club, say, and takes in the wide panorama of lush fairways swinging through tall pines, he senses at once that an authentic championship layout awaits him—an experience that also occurs at most of the world's renowned inland courses. But let him stand on the first tee at St. Andrews or Ballybunion, and all he sees is a treeless sweep of billowing pale-green land with a few dun-colored sand hills in the distance—a most unpromising vista. A fragment of fairway is visible here and another fragment there, and a few numbered flags are blowing in the breeze, so what he is looking at is evidently a golf course, but it might as easily be pastureland. It is only when the golfer gets out onto a linksland course that he discovers, to his amazement, that it is filled with great golf holes, all the more appealing since their strategic features were molded by nature instead of by the bull-dozer.

One of the most common misconceptions about links courses is that they are all the same. At Ballybunion, centuries of erosion and silting have pushed the linksland together, creating huge dunes and dramatic plateau greens that to many people represent Irish links. But the gently rolling terrain at Portmarnock—an equally great links—is entirely different.

On a links, the architect's job is less to create something new than to tease out the golf holes that are already there. When Tom Simpson advised the members at County Louth on how they could improve the course in the 1930s, he scolded the original designers for failing "to observe and/or take advantage of the glorious possibilities that the ground afforded."

For all its rewards, links golf can take some getting used to. Bobby Jones stomped off St. Andrews in frustration halfway through his first tournament there, in 1921, though he later came to love the world's oldest course with a passion.

The classic links courses were not, of course, designed for "target golf"—the high, precise and spinning shots, made easier with improvements in equipment, that can make hazards obsolete. Anyone who has watched the British Open on television knows that wind and hard greens can be a great equalizer, forcing competitors to use the imaginative low shots of an earlier time. But on a fine day, the great subtleties of even St. Andrews are lost in the relentless aerial attack of the top professionals.

For the average player—who drives the ball something less than 250 yards and whose 3 irons do not soar to the heavens—links golf is a won-drous, fascinating challenge every day of the week, and one in which brute strength is not the imperative it is on many inland courses. The absence of trees, the rollicking fairways, the unimpeded ocean winds, and the unpredictable placement of deep fairway bunkers mean that holes can be played any number of different ways. The corners of doglegs can be breached (or not) and a variety of lines of approach to the greens are possible. The ever-changeable wind adds more complexity. Depending on the wind's direction and velocity, even Bobby Jones had three different ways to play the Long Hole at St. Andrews. For the mere mortal there are countless more.

SOME SURVIVAL TIPS

It has become a cliché to say that one needs to master a pitch-and-run shot to survive on links. This used to be the case in the old days, when the sandy soil on links greens would dry out quickly in the summer and become as hard as a bowling alley. With the widespread introduction of watering systems, however, greens are much more receptive to high pitch shots, except on days that are extremely windy.

For the average player it is the *drive* that requires the most severe revision of thinking. Because of the absence of trees, there is an entirely misleading sense of space on links courses. Golfers who would retreat to a long iron off the tee on narrow, tree-lined fairways at home can be found whaling away on Royal County Down, which has some of the most exacting rough in the world. On a breezy summer day in Ireland, when the rough is at its fiercest and the fairways their hardest, there is an enormous premium to be gained from staying out of the rough. Not only do you avoid losing your ball in a gorse bush, you have the enjoyment of seeing your drive bound unexpected distances.

Links golf is not primarily about strength. On inland courses, it is often necessary to drive the ball a considerable distance in order to make the rest of the hole playable. The alternative is an embarrassing lay-up in front of the lake that the designer wants you to fly with a Corey Pavin 4 wood, or an irritating wedge to get around the neck of a dogleg. On links courses, indignities are more likely caused by miscalculation than a lack of strength. Disaster strikes because you have let the wind carry your ball like a kite into the rough, or bounced your chip clear over the green, or tried to be more ambitious than you should have out of a pot bunker.

"Without the wind, it would be like playing snooker," is how an Irish playing companion describes golf. Far from considering wind a nuisance, he thinks of it as the spice that brings out the full flavor of a links course, and the game.

It's an attitude worth cultivating, for a links course demands the skills of a sailor. You have to find ways to let the wind help you when it can, and resist the urge to fight it when it can't. There is no more helpless feeling than seeing your ball snatched by an Atlantic breeze and deposited into a great field of gorse. On extremely windy days you feel out of control and disoriented. Even putting is a new experience.

The wind can make par a very abstract term. Getting a six on an upwind par 4 can be more difficult than on a downwind par 5. The wise approach is to forget about par and concentrate on each stroke. Sometimes even par 3s are better played as two-shot holes. In the 1951 British Open at Royal Portrush, defending champion Bobby Locke refused to aim for the green at the famous Calamity hole, preferring the safety of a hollow to the left of the putting surface, which is perched on the edge of a great chasm.

Finally, there are the unpredictable lies. Tom Morris and other nineteenth-century Scots would be appalled at the thought of flat, immaculate fairways. The essence of links golf was to take the good bounce with the bad.

"We have been so anxious, in the sacred name of fair play, to take all the element of luck out of the game, that we have to a proportionate extent destroyed its value as a test of each man's ability to stand up to bad luck," lamented the golf historian Robert Browning in 1955. "Modern golf is a stiffer test of a player's skill, but it has robbed the game of something of its charm as an adventure of the spirit."

The adventure of the spirit is still very much alive on Irish links. It is to the credit of the ubiquitous Irish architect Eddie Hackett, who has designed more links courses than any man alive, and modern American architects such as Arnold Palmer (at Tralee) and Robert Trent Jones (at Ballybunion New) that they have respected the unpredictable nature of links golf. "Anything that is in nature is not wrong," Hackett says of the sometimes frustrating swales found on the fairways and greens of his best courses. Hackett rarely inserts artificial mounds, but he also hates taking out natural ones.

In the end, playing links golf is not about changing one's game, but about changing one's *attitude*. When Bobby Jones stomped off St. Andrews, it wasn't because he didn't have the game for the strange new conditions (he was the greatest player of his age by far). He just wasn't in the right frame of mind. Jones came to love links golf, as did the likes of Palmer, Watson and Daly after him. Chances are you will too. Soon you will be disappointed when the weather is too calm, critical when the rough is too benign, and positively insulted when sand traps around the green are too shallow. You will discover that there are few greater thrills than making a good recovery out of a deep pot bunker, belting a blind tee shot directly over the sandhill you were aiming at, or fashioning just the pitch-and-run needed to stay "underneath" an ocean wind.

At its best, links golf is both charmingly old-fashioned and thoroughly modern. For some it is addictive, an intoxicating mixture of elemental surroundings and multi-faceted strategy that no other kind of golf can duplicate. At the very least it is likely you will find the experience of golfing on the timeless links of Ireland to be a provocative and arousing departure from your normal routine, and one that will enrich your appreciation of the sport wherever you may play it.

THE
CLASSICS
(and more!)

GOLF ON THE RUGGED COAST OF COUNTIES Kerry and Clare is a uniquely Irish experience—huge dunes, crashing sea and remote, hospitable communities. The Southwest offers Ireland's most magnificent coastal scenery— including the famed Ring of Kerry and Dingle Peninsula—and the golf courses share in the splendor. While it was Old Tom Morris's original layout at Lahinch that first brought golfers to the region, it is now Ballybunion that quite rightly defines Irish golf in foreign eyes. Its remarkable history is recounted by its oldest surviving member, John Moriarty, on the following pages. But there is much more to admire in the Southwest, including links courses designed by Arnold Palmer and Robert Trent Jones, and what may be the greatest of all modern links, Waterville. There are also a variety of less well-known but enchanting links that on a sunny day will have you looking at local real estate prices. And to top it all off there is Killarney—as different to Ballybunion as it is possible to be—and yet just as intensely Irish. If you golf in only one region of Ireland, this has to be it.

Ballybunion:
An Oral History

THE INCOMPARABLE LINKS in the village of Ballybunion is Ireland's most famous golf destination. Virtually unknown twenty-five years ago, Ballybunion now attracts almost as many visitors as St. Andrews and is universally recognized as one of golf's treasures.

The Ballybunion legend was for a long time embellished by its role as golf's archetypal *undiscovered* treasure. Due to its isolation in a poor and inaccessible part of Ireland, Ballybunion was known to few foreigners, save for a handful of intrepid golf writers. Like some seventeenth-century Spanish explorer, they would periodically send word back to the "civilized" golf world of the amazing riches they had found.

It started as early as 1934. "Never have I been more surprised," wrote Viscount Castlerosse (who would later design the celebrated course at Killarney) in his widely read London newspaper column. "Ballybunion is the best course I have ever played on. It is better than St. George's or Princes or Rye. I except St. Andrews, but then that is not a golf course. It is a miracle."

Despite the occasional journalistic raptures, Ballybunion remained obscure. As late as 1971, Herbert Warren Wind, the greatest of American golf writers, could proceed almost by accident to Ballybunion and be astonished by what he discovered.

"To put it simply, Ballybunion revealed itself to be nothing less than the finest seaside course I have ever seen," he wrote in the *New Yorker*.

Not everyone reads the *New Yorker*, of course, and it was not until Tom Watson took up the torch in the early 1980s that visitors began arriving in great numbers.

Today Ballybunion is no longer a secret. In the summer it seems that *everyone*—at least in New Jersey and Florida—has heard of it. Foursomes tee off every ten minutes, and the club has built an enormous fortress/clubhouse to accommodate them. To recapture the thrill of discovery that the early "explorers" must have experienced you will have to visit Ballybunion in the off-season. On a weekday in November the course reclaims its splendid isolation.

Though Ballybunion may look ancient, it is not in fact so very old. But its mystique isn't hurt by the fact that its origins are oddly unclear. No one really knows who created the links; the theories run from Old Tom Morris, to James Braid, to a local hotel owner. It is known that the original eighteen holes were laid out by someone hired by the local railway company, which thought a golf course would attract more passengers. The links later shrank to nine holes and then were extended once more in 1927—again, no one is sure who was responsible. Everyone does agree that Tom Simpson—one of the best designers of the period—was engaged to make renovations in 1936.

Simpson was shocked by what he saw. "The beauty of the terrain surpasses that of any golf course we know, not excepting Pine Valley in America," he wrote in his report to the club. "Never for one moment did we imagine, or expect to find, such a really great course or such a glorious piece of golfing ground."

Simpson was perceptive enough to leave well enough alone. He and his associate Molly Gourlay, one of golf's few female architects, replaced two greens, inserted a few bunkers, and went home.

It could well be that the most important architects were the club members themselves, especially Patrick McCarthy (who worked for the railway) and his two sons, William and Paddy. Between them they filled the position of secretary at Ballybunion almost continuously from 1897 to 1952.

That such a famous club can trace its history with such little certainty may seem strange, until one realizes that for half a century the members of Ballybunion could fit comfortably into the tin shed that served as a clubhouse. There were no more than fifty full members (almost half of them women) when Simpson and Gourlay made their finishing touches.

In researching this book we decided to track down the longest-standing member we could find. We didn't have to look far. Eighty-year-old John Moriarty lives only about a mile from the links. Retired after a distinguished career as a bookmaker for horse and dog racing (bookmaking is a profession of some stature in Ireland), Moriarty has been a member of Ballybunion for sixty years, and a trustee for forty-six. In a living room full of soft easy chairs, lace-covered side tables and framed photographs, he painted a vivid picture of a time when Ballybunion shared its charms with a lucky few.

My Sixty Years at Ballybunion
By John Moriarty

MONEY WAS VERY SCARCE IN THE COUNTY WHERE I WAS born, and the feeling was "how can that boy be playing golf at Ballybunion when he owes me two pound." The telephone wasn't much in use then but there was much more gossip. Mick knew what Teddy was doing, and Teddy knew what Michael was doing. They didn't know the golf was there. Some of them thought we were mad.

I was born in 1914 on a farm in Lyracrumpane [fifteen miles from Ballybunion] that was mostly gorse land and heather—scrub land. We had twenty cattle and some sheep and pigs. We had chickens, turkeys, ducks and geese as well. We had all the bacon we wanted, plus turnips and cabbage. All we had to buy was flour, tea, sugar, and if you were smoking, a bit of tobacco. The country women used snuff, their one bit of luxury. When the month of September came on the farm you had no income until June arrived again, so you'd sell the batch of pigs, and eat the birds. I ate so much duck I never wanted to eat another. It was the same all over Ireland, though the shopkeepers were very good—they gave them credit until June until the cows were milking again, and that's how they survived.

When we came to town to a store, I was classified as a country boy. A country boy was classified as not being smart at all—in brains or in athletics. In other words the town boy was a step ahead of him, which of course was completely wrong. Now there's no such thing. Now the country people have more money that the town people. It's completely reversed.

Golf and the Uppity-ups
I didn't stick to school too long. I stayed with cousins in Listowel [ten miles from Ballybunion] and served my time in the timber and hardware business.

My cousin Eddie, who was also my boss, was very keen at the golf, but I didn't know the first thing about it at the time. I was a clerk, an estimator, and was only earning a couple quid a week. I started coming out to Ballybunion as a caddie for Eddie. One day he made me take a club and the next thing I had the bug. And he says why don't you join up. I was a bit shaky about it at first because I was just an ordinary working chap and golf was an uppity-up kind of game at the time. I remember coming up the eighteenth and if I saw pals of mine I'd turn my back because I didn't want them to see me, because of the image of golf. That is the truth.

But I ended up joining. It cost me one pound, ten shillings for the year. Golf was thought to be a big man's game, always classified as "upper upper" if you know what I mean. Most people wouldn't dream of paying a pound or two a year to play golf. Because of the price, and because of the gossip of the neighbors. They'd say it's only a mug's game anyway trying to hit a white ball into a little hole. "Did you hear he joined the golf club?" they'd say. "He must be an awful bloody mug altogether to join the golf club."

And there was a little bit of stigma too—"Oh, he's gone and joined the big fellows." And the next thing would be, "Where did he get the bloody money from?" And it would go on and on. You must realize at that time you had no electricity in this country, you had no running water, you had no toilets like you have today.

Early Days at Ballybunion

If I were asked tomorrow morning who laid out the course, I would say Simpson, yes, it's his business, but I would give credit to locals, and mostly to Willie McCarthy. And with the exception of two men it was all voluntary labor.

We hadn't anything like the machinery you have today, but the greenkeepers and the staff there were marvelous, they didn't work by the clock at all. The sun was their clock. Ballybunion was a part of their life. The greens were always very good, haven't really changed much. I never saw anything wrong with them.

We had a terrible scourge of rabbits, thousands and thousands of them. We had a rule you could drop out of a rabbit burrow. We tried everything, tried trapping them, tried gas, and eventually the answer was a form of poison. Not a nice sight to see them dying. No one knew who introduced it, but it had to be done.

There were only about twenty or thirty regular members. You'd be talking about the McCarthys of Ballybunion who owned the hotel, well-to-do business people in Listowel—lots of bankers! It was the upper class that played golf, usually plus-fours they wore. But there was no religious element in Ballybunion, all very friendly, never saw politics enter Ballybunion.

At that time you'd go down on a Sunday to the rusty old tin shed that was the clubhouse, with one bench inside and two lockers. If you wanted you could get a bit of timber and build one for yourself. God be with Tom Allan, he was the caddie-master there. He had a smile and a shake-hands for everybody. He helped you out if you were short of a club, or broke a club. Tom was the man to go to. The caddies got two shillings for a round of golf, and I usually gave them sixpence of a tip, fairly good. He always told the caddies, no bad language. His word was law with them.

THE WAR YEARS

When the war came you had no transport [petrol was rationed] so the club just barely ticked over at that time.

During the war everything came to a semi-standstill. If you had a good golf ball it was worth any kind of money. You just couldn't get one. Balls which we would throw away normally we would stick together. Everyone had his own paint to put on them. But wouldn't you know it the paint ran out too because paint is made of lead. And so that disappeared because of the war too. You'd use glue if you had any.

I'll never forget the day that we were playing for ten shillings—a lot of money at the time—and we were two down with four to go. So the chap we were playing against takes out a new ball, and hits it up the fairway. Well, a crow came along—this is not a yarn, you know—and picked up the ball and flew away. Freddy Hanlan, who I was playing with, said it was an Act of God. They were great times, great friendly times all right.

THE GOLDEN YEARS

After the war I went into bookmaking. They were great times. We had an open home. Never such a thing as a lock on the door at night. And that atmosphere was in the club up to about twenty-five years ago. A great sense of community feeling about it. But at that time you could count membership on your hands and fingers at Ballybunion. They were great times. You could still just go down and just tee off, nobody there. You'd see each other on weekends—a Members' Cup in the morning and then a fourball in the afternoon.

We built a new clubhouse in 1951 for four thousand pounds and we thought we would never get out of debt. We thought it was an amazing achievement. I opened it in 1952 with the Lord Mayor of Dublin and at that time the membership started increasing. There was a special room for men drinking only. It was unfair—sort of like highland sheep and lowland sheep. Three years later women eventually won the battle and broke into it. Personally, I was delighted.

I got my handicap down to six. But then my business got very busy when the dog racing started. After playing eighteen holes you wouldn't be inclined to drive fifty miles to the dog track.

THE AMERICANS ARE COMING

When I joined I had no idea about the quality of the course. We never appreciated it, since it came so soft to us, you see. We took it for granted. Then as time went on and you visited smaller clubs you could see the almighty difference and you began to realize slowly what a beautiful course it was. But I sure never thought I'd see the day where people would be falling over each other to come here.

The first "PR Man" for Ballybunion was Jimmy Bruen, a great player from Cork [Bruen won the British Amateur in 1946]. He had a funny swing, a figure-of-eight at the top of it, but he could hit the ball a terrible distance. Jimmy always said that Ballybunion was the best golf course in Ireland. Jimmy never got the credit for the publicity he gave the course. He brought a lot of golfers from Cork and Limerick up.

But the crowning cap was Tom Watson, as far as America is concerned. Tom Watson gave it a terrible big plug in America. Now they're flocking in, the Americans. They've helped us in a big way.

The course gives a good bit of employment in season, say from the first of June until the end of September. Buses come here to Ballybunion, full of golfers, they have to eat and they have to sleep. Even if they don't eat here, they'll eat at the golf course and the produce will have to be bought someplace. The money goes around in a circle.

Not many local people play golf. Ballybunion has only four months to make a living. The people in Ballybunion are like a brown bear, they hibernate in the winter. There's a great beach here, though.

CHANGING TIMES

I've travelled a bit. I went to Australia to see the dog racing, and to the United States. I was elected to the Board of Governors of greyhound racing in 1959 and that's what brought me to those countries.

I only played one round of golf in America, at an expensive club in Miami when I was visiting relatives. It was a hundred thousand dollars to be a member, that was in 1976. I like Americans because they talk very big. The course was polished like that table, but if you tried to lose a ball you couldn't. We played for a hundred dollars each, and I won all right.

It's nice to be a trustee of such a famous club, but at my age you lose a bit of an interest in it, and the person which tells you otherwise is telling you a bit of a lie. I'm eighty years of age, and the prestige is gone out of it for me. I've had three bypass operations. I take every day as it comes.

I suppose you must go with the times. They just knocked down the last clubhouse and built the new building. But then the green fees are just rolling in. I went to a meeting the other night and they said they were a million pounds in debt. I said that's a lot of money and they laughed at me. But times change. In the old days someone owed a pound and they were going to send the solicitors after them.

I still go down to the club. But the people who are kids today are men tomorrow. I don't recognize them.

The "shake-your-hand-how-are-you-Teddy?" is gone. Some of the friendliness and the companionship has disappeared. It's a great thing for young people and for girls, though. Golf has caught the imagination of the younger generation better than any other sport I could name.

There's no doubt in the world that television did bring it on, but the trend was there before. At one time a boy playing golf was considered a bit of a Nancy boy. He didn't have the physique to play Gaelic football or soccer or hurling. It's a bit of a slang word. Now you're called a chicken. But today you have everyone from the laboring man to the top man playing golf. No matter what he does, whether he toils with his hands, or his mind, he's playing golf today. The class thing is gone.

The Dreamers

There is something in the Irish atmosphere that occasionally makes the impossible possible.

DERVLA MURPHY

THE PROCESSION CARRYING Jack Mulcahy's ashes was led by a lone piper up the wooden steps to the small rectangle that held the seventeenth tee, the hole known as Mulcahy's Peak. It is the highest point on the great Waterville Links, and on this windy and chilly November morning the view was stirring, if tinged with sadness and nostalgia. A glorious confusion of shaggy green-and-yellow hills could be seen in all directions, with twisting ribbons of cut grass meandering between them—all bounded by the sea. Crashing Atlantic waves provided a low rumbling counterpoint to the high reedy sounds of the bagpipes as the casket was placed in a grave dug in the side of the tee box. The parish priest gave a glowing eulogy and a flask of Redbreast whiskey—the favorite brand of the deceased—was passed around by the club captain.

The mourners then started back along the eighteenth fairway next to the beach, to the clubhouse bar where much of the little west-coast town of Waterville would gather to remember Uncle Jack, the gregarious, generous Irish-American who had chased an impossible dream.

One week later on the other coast of Ireland, in a comfortable Dublin suburb, Pat Ruddy is discussing his plans for the European Club, a new links he has built south of the city. He has been talking non-stop for two hours, but his enthusiasm shows no signs of flagging.

"There are two types of golf courses," he says. "One is the drop-from-heaven type—you get fifteen million dollars, stir it around in a bowl, throw it on a field and you have instant golf. It may not be great golf but it's very impressive—like a lady painted to the nines in a miniskirt, it looks good. But in most cases it's not as good as it looks. It's commercially driven, not *dream driven*. A trading post in golf, not a *golf place*.

"What I'm trying to do at the European Club is accelerated evolution. To do what St. Andrews did in 400 years, what Royal Dublin and Portmarnock did in 100 years, and do it in fifteen."

How Ruddy's words would have warmed the heart of the last Earl of Kenmare!—although one suspects that Lord Castlerosse, as the Earl was known before inheriting his father's title, would have preferred the more formal and ornate language of his era, and his class.

"I have never cared for the second class and I want to leave something behind that will be paramount," Lord Castlerosse wrote from the family estate in Killarney, a few years before Pat Ruddy was born. Castlerosse may have ended a dynasty that had lasted 350 years, but he left behind a golf course that many considered the most beautiful in the world.

The grand projects of Castlerosse, Mulcahy and Ruddy flew in the face of Irish golfing tradition. Most of Ireland's golf courses have been built and managed collectively. In the early days golfing enthusiasts from the Protestant elite formed clubs, set up committees, and oversaw the development of some of the world's most classic links. Over time clubs broadened their membership to include other religions and classes, and in the 1970s several courses were actually built as community development projects—non-profit attempts to attract the tourist trade. But for more than a century the cooperative nature of most Irish golf clubs has remained in place.

There are, however, three heroic exceptions to this rule, three magnificent courses created by men whose lives, in most respects, could not be more different—a true aristocrat, a rags-to-riches Irish-American immigrant, and a thoroughly middle-class Dublin newspaperman. They were united by a crazy and insistent dream that took over their lives—to build one of the best damn golf courses in all the world. Here are their stories.

DREAM #1—LORD CASTLEROSSE AND KILLARNEY

It must have been a remarkable sight in the drab, economically depressed country that was Ireland in the late 1930s. A hulking, rotund man in pink plus-fours stalking around a golf course making mental notes, on land that his family had owned since the time of Elizabeth I.

Known to his friends by his given name, Valentine, Lord Castlerosse was one of the best-known and outlandish men of his time, the writer of a famous gossip column in a London newspaper, and a notorious glutton and womanizer. Some of his plans for the golf course at Killarney were suitably eccentric. He planned to plant acres of flowers and shrubs so that every hole would bloom in a different color. He wanted to introduce a sound system that would play the comforting sounds of Beethoven's Ninth Symphony across the golf course at noon each day. He also hoped to build a radio tower big enough to promote the attractions of Killarney all the way to America.

Although Castlerosse died before the more bizarre aspects of his vision were realized, he did manage the miraculous feat of building a golf course of international renown in the midst of a global depression, and helped to revive tourism in Ireland in the process. In the twilight years of the rural gentry, and his own family line, Castlerosse was consumed by an unlikely burst of authoritarian, aristocratic energy. In the space of about seven years he fulfilled much of his dream for Killarney. When he died in his sleep in 1943, the local newspaper called it a "national tragedy . . . a catastrophe which cannot be measured."

To say that Castlerosse was born into a life of privilege would be like saying that Killarney is a nice-looking spot. The Sixth Earl of Kenmare, Castlerosse's father, *owned* Killarney, or 118,000 acres of it. Unusual for the landed gentry in Ireland, the family was devoutly Catholic. One feels that Lord Castlerosse could have stepped right out of the pages of Evelyn Waugh's *Brideshead Revisited*.

"All I had to do was flash my title and I got unlimited credit," is how Castlerosse remembered his carefree years at Cambridge before the First World War. "I discovered that when you are a Viscount you not only do not need to pay your bills but that people were positively insulted if you attempted to do so."

The noted historian David Cannadine (*The Decline and Fall of the British Aristocracy*) considers Castlerosse's life to be a vivid illustration of the demise of the aristocracy generally. At university, Cannadine says, Castlerosse was "idle, unambitious, gluttonous, ran up many debts, and had many affairs."

The First World War took a horrific toll on the British aristocracy, which had considered it their duty to lead their country into battle. Though wounded, Castlerosse escaped the worst and joined the social whirl of London with reckless abandon. The family estate in Ireland was feeling the pinch from land reform, and his father was not about to bail

Castlerosse out of his growing debts. He was saved by the Canadian-born media magnate, Lord Beaverbrook. In return for £3,000 a year plus expenses, Castlerosse wrote the "Londoner's Log" in Beaverbrook's *Sunday Express*.

To become a gossip journalist was a humiliating comedown for a man of Castlerosse's pedigree. He took growing solace in the time spent at the family estate in Killarney, which he truly loved, and where he often escaped when funds ran low.

It seems that in his later years Castlerosse genuinely wanted to make some amends for a life of little achievement. At some point in the mid-1930s he hit upon the idea of building a grand new tourist resort in Killarney, with a new golf course as the "central jewel." As he explained to local Irish officialdom, visiting Americans were "shocked" by hotels in Ireland, and "returning visitors complain that in Ireland there is nothing to do and that a lethargy pervades the countryside." The golf resort, he predicted, "will be my bait to bring Americans to Ireland."

By coincidence, the local golf club was planning to expand anyway, on lands it had leased from Castlerosse's father since 1893. With a single-minded sense of purpose, Castlerosse took over the project and, not surprisingly, it became the grandest of schemes. The new course would be 7,400 yards, laid out on the difficult terrain on the edge of Lough Leane by respected British architect Sir Guy Campbell. Castlerosse also enlisted the help of his close friend Henry Longhurst, a golf writer for the *Times* of London, whose gravelly voice would later become known to millions of television viewers on both sides of the Atlantic.

Castlerosse had no money of his own, but he was well connected. Shares in the club were sold to local merchants and some of his London friends, and he somehow persuaded his skeptical father to take an equity position. Work began on the course in 1937.

Miraculously, the course was completed more or less on time, and opened in October 1939 as the war in Europe began. Castlerosse, who was an excellent golfer, made constant changes, building five entirely new holes, and changing eight. In 1941, he became the sixth Earl of Kenmare on his father's death, but he would only live for two more years himself. With no children of his own, his death effectively marked the end of the Kenmare line.

Although he did not live long enough to introduce his more original ideas, Castlerosse's vision for Killarney proved fundamentally accurate. For fifty years Killarney has been synonymous with Irish golf in the eyes of many foreigner travellers. The Irish tourist board built a second course on the same site in 1971 and today the courses attract more than 40,000 visitors each year, pumping millions of pounds into the local economy.

DREAM # 2—JACK MULCAHY AND WATERVILLE

When Irish-born Jack Mulcahy returned from America in the 1960s looking for a project to bring him back to Ireland he was the American Dream incarnate. Mulcahy had made millions in the chemical industry and was a friend of presidents and movie stars. The contrast with the economic fortunes of the villagers of Waterville couldn't have been more stark.

"He was a real gentleman—a new thing in this area," remembers Noel Cronin, now Secretary Manager of the Waterville Golf Links, who used to drive Mulcahy around in his taxi in the early days. "The course meant so much to the community, and he was responsible, bless his heart, for a lot of employment. This place was pretty depressed when he came. Workmen got wages that they never saw before. The standards of hotels and restaurants really rose."

Waterville had enjoyed a period of relative prosperity as a cable station for the first transatlantic cables in the 1880s. The urban-style row houses of the Commercial Cable Company on the outskirts of the village are a queer, out-of-place reminder of the period. Among the British upper classes, Waterville was also known for its fishing. In the catchment area behind the village, the salmon and trout fishing was extraordinary, making it a favorite holiday spot for Charlie Chaplin, among others. In 1968 the estate containing the fishing rights was purchased by Mulcahy, who also bought an enormous manor house for his own use in County Clare.

Mulcahy must have seemed heaven-sent for the residents of Waterville. A year after he arrived the Troubles began in Northern Ireland, and fishing visitors soon dwindled to almost nothing. Suddenly, Mulcahy's dream of building a first-class golf and fishing resort became one of the few sources of income in town. Inevitably, some people took advantage.

"Everything was multiplied by five," remembers Eddie Hackett, who designed the links and oversaw its construction. "'Jack,' I said,—he insisted on me calling him Jack—'I'm not going to certify accounts for these engineers that are here. You of course can do what you like, but I won't certify them.' And so he come over from America, and they were all put out."

At first, the golf course received less than Mulcahy's full attention. He still spent much of his time in America (where he was also a notable philanthropist), and when in Ireland he was often busy entertaining the global elite. Among the visitors to the manor in County Clare was the President of the United States (Mulcahy was the second most generous contributor to Richard Nixon's 1972 re-election campaign). He was also distracted by the design and construction of the Waterville Hotel, the luxury hotel that would sit on the other side of the village, overlooking Lough Currane.

Eddie Hackett—who had only designed two golf courses in his life at that point—was put in full charge of constructing the links. He reported on progress by phone to Mulcahy in the United States.

"He didn't know what sort of course he was going to get," says Hackett. "When the course was finished, he came over and he was mesmerized. It had turned out great you see, with the dunes, as it is now. Except it wasn't green—it was all soil, all black with the rain.

"We walked around, and he was delighted. He couldn't get over what he had. That night in the house over dinner I said 'Jack, if you're keen, you have a course out there that has the potential of being as good as any in the world, if you want to.'

"And from that day he changed. He came in April and stayed until October. He supervised, he was at the meetings every week. He wanted it manicured. That's when Mulcahy's Peak came into being. He christened it his tee. He was that kind of a man. And why not?—it was his money that made it."

Now that he realized he had a great golf course on his hands, Mulcahy spared no effort to let other people know about it. He planned a grand opening for early 1973, with celebrities such as Sam Snead on hand. Hackett became alarmed.

"He wanted the course ready in six months, but I needed topsoil and we were going into winter. I called him up at his house where Nixon stayed, and he said get topsoil from Limerick, and I said I would only be carting water.

"We had to bulldoze an awful lot of dunes, you see, and to stop the sand from blowing I had to put something on it. So I brought peat dust from a bog around Waterville instead. Eight shillings a load. That was all I paid. I brought in the peat dust, the peat turf, and spread it all around to contain the sand and used it on the greens instead of topsoil. It wasn't good quality, but I couldn't do it the orthodox way because there was no topsoil in winter. The greens now are wonderful, but it made maintenance difficult and the greens weren't 100 percent for quite a long time. But I got the course made for him."

Throughout the 1970s Mulcahy promoted the course with all his ingenuity. It was a Herculean task. Ireland was still not on the golfing map as far as North Americans were concerned, there were no nearby tournaments to tempt professionals in the area, and the Troubles put a crimp in the tourist trade. He hosted professional tournaments of his own invention and brought in a steady stream of celebrities. One of Noel Cronin's more treasured possessions is a photograph with Telly Savalas, a pint in his hand, and Tip O'Neill, then Speaker of the House of Representatives.

"The moments that I remember the most would be when he brought Bob Hope, Jack Lemmon and Telly Savalas over," he says. "As young lads we had watched Kojak on television, and to see him here in reality, it meant so much."

Gradually, Waterville's fame began to seep into the consciousness of the golf world. Professionals such as Snead, Doug Ford, Ken Venturi, Gary Player and Raymond Floyd were persuaded to play what was, after all, the first major new links course since Turnberry was redesigned just after the Second World War. Floyd would later write that Waterville was one of his five favorite courses—the others being Pebble Beach, Augusta, Cypress Point and St. Andrews. As golf writers made their way to Waterville, the links began to gain the recognition it so richly deserved. In its annual rankings *Golf World* magazine now rates Waterville higher than any course built in Great Britain and Ireland since 1947.

As Mulcahy grew older he didn't have the energy to maintain Waterville in peak condition. He decided to sell the complex in 1987, though he continued to live near the village. The new owners were also Irish-Americans, with a similar passion for the game and a respect for the local community.

Talk about Jack Mulcahy around Waterville and it is his informality that people seem to remember the most. That the friend of the rich and famous should ask them to call him Jack still elicits a shaking of the head.

"He was the kind of man who would always talk to you," says Noel Cronin. "A lovely man and a pure gentleman. He'd bring in presidents and the like—he could work at that level—but he would also talk to the common man. He'd see you swing and say 'Let me fix that,' and work with you for hours on it.

"Not long before he died a bunch of the young lads took him out to dinner and presented him with a green jacket. He had tears in his eyes, that these lads would do that for him. After all he did for them.

"He lived and loved the golf course, I'll tell you that."

DREAM #3—PAT RUDDY AND THE EUROPEAN CLUB

Golf in Ireland probably hit its nadir during the early 1950s. The Protestant merchants, military officers and aristocrats who had started the game in Ireland had declined in numbers and wealth, and the sport held few attractions for the average farmer or working man. In the small market town of Ballymote in County Sligo it was a struggle just to maintain a nine-hole golf course.

"There would have been thirty golfers max at good times, a hard core of ten addicts," remembers Pat Ruddy, whose family moved to Ballymote when he was ten. Ruddy is a garrulous man who likes a good laugh and who tends to look at the bright side of life. His memories of childhood have a glow about them—a lovely non-stop adventure with golf at its center.

"Dad used to come and pull me out of school when they were stuck for someone to play the fourball," he says. "And I found it a wonderful substitute for mathematics or English or Irish or Latin. The clubhouse was made of corrugated iron, no toilets, just hang up your coat and go golfing. They stacked up a bit of dirt in little rectangles two feet high to make a tee.

"They talk now about the rough being tough, but back then the fairway would be fifteen paces wide and the only way you could find the ball when it went into the rough was to watch it like a hawk and line up the fourball and scuffle up and down with your feet."

As an adult, Pat Ruddy would become a one-man writing and publishing machine, so it is little surprise that books had a special place for him as a youth.

"Henry Cotton's golfing album, a beautiful book, influenced me a lot in my life. He took a camera and wrote little essays pertaining to the picture showing the King of Belgium swinging the club and down in Monte Carlo hitting balls into the sea. And I thought God almighty, if only I had a dozen balls—and here they are hitting them into the sea. Amazing stuff!

"So I started to carry a camera, started to write. I used to sit in the back seat at school drawing plans of golf courses. On the side of all of the books I had written 'Pat Ruddy, Master Golfer'."

After deciding against pursuing a playing career, Ruddy bought a typewriter and wrote to the *Evening Herald* in Dublin. He was only nineteen, but like Castlerosse and Mulcahy he had an instinct for promotion.

"Dublin seemed a million miles away, I'd been there once or twice ever. So I wrote to this paper and said I was a genius and knew everything about golf, and they said they would give me a guinea a week for a column on golf in the west of Ireland. That was riches to me."

Before long, Ruddy had married, joined the staff of the *Herald*, and was writing more words about golf than just about any man alive. At one point, he wrote a full broadsheet page *a day* on golf and freelanced for magazines around the world. One of Ruddy's proudest moments at the *Herald* came when he spearheaded the movement to build a publicly funded golf course. Using the paper to relentlessly publicize the plight of what he coined the "Homeless Golfers," Ruddy helped shame politicians into allocating the necessary funds. The golf course proved an immediate success.

Working for others was never going to satisfy the irrepressible Ruddy, and in 1973 he quit his job to found and write his own golf magazine. He was often engaged to promote tournaments, and one of his favorite tactics involved attempts to get into the *Guinness Book of World Records*.

"I wanted Liam Higgins [an Irish professional] to hit the longest drive down an airport runway. So I got a couple of hundred Spalding balls—they were the sponsor of the tournament—and looked for a runway. I thought you could rent one just like that by phoning Dublin airport. But I was wrong. Luckily the minister of defence was a golfer and he got a military airport, and Liam managed to make the record hit!"

There is an Irish twinkle in Ruddy's eyes when he finishes such a story, and the laughter that ensues is often punctuated by exclamations of "Do you like it? Do you like it?" One of his most fondly remembered stunts was cancelled at the last moment.

"I was going to do the longest par 3, you see. I had Liam Higgins training parachute jumping, and we were going to fly over Royal Dublin, putt the ball out of the airplane, and then jump out and putt out."

For the next ten years Ruddy continued to be a publisher, writer and general golfing impresario ("in one little corner of the planet roaring my head off about golf"). He got to travel to Augusta and other famous golf shrines and inevitably began to wonder how he might turn his childhood dream of building a golf course into reality. He bought some land near Ballymote but the project was a disaster.

"I went to the university of stupidity and got an honors degree," says Ruddy with a huge grin. "It was the wrong ground, there wasn't enough money, people were stealing machinery when I was away. So I backed off."

A few years later, however, Ruddy and a friend won the chance to design a new parkland course near the Dublin airport. St. Margaret's was well received and other assignments followed; Ruddy's publishing enterprise continued to thrive, and he had a little money in the bank again.

Then in 1987 Ruddy spotted an advertisement in the property section of a Dublin newspaper that would change his life.

It was for a stretch of seaside land fifty miles south of Dublin at a place called Brittas Bay. The advertisement said it might be suitable for a caravan park or a golf course. He didn't have enough money to buy the property, but he was curious enough to take a helicopter ride down the east coast to see how it looked from the air. He was stunned. It was a fantastic, heaving piece of linksland, with huge dunes reminiscent of Ballybunion. It was also the only undeveloped linksland on the entire east coast.

Like Castlerosse before him, the lack of money didn't deter Ruddy. He trusted his own vision, turned to some banking friends for support, and bought the land.

"It was only after I had been there a while that the enormity of the ground grew on me," Ruddy remembers. "I went in there for days on end with grass over my head.

"It is awe-inspiring. You see such a multiplicity of golf holes on a links compared to parkland. Normally I can go to a golf site and take a week of walking in broad outline. You can visualize it. But this one took six months of intense study."

Ruddy knew he had found his life's project. But he also knew how little he had in the bank. He would have to work slowly, doing most of the work himself with the help of his children.

"We built this ourselves, 90 percent," he says with obvious pride. "I can drive every machine. No guy can tell me that a job isn't do-able on a golf course—I've done it. The money was being gobbled up, every penny. I re-mortgaged my home, sold my insurance policy, drove an old car, did everything to do this. You can't define that in money terms, the feeling you have for the place afterwards. The bond is so tight."

Just when he needed it most, Ruddy was struck with a bolt of good fortune. For the first time in twenty years, Bord Fáilte started giving out tourism grants to golf course development projects. The European Club received its share, which made it possible to speed up construction considerably. Still, it was five long years before the course opened on St. Stephen's Day in 1992. Ruddy could then use his promotional talents with unrestrained zeal. He brazenly promoted the course in his own publications and created a course guide that sets new standards of hyperbole. The first hole, the course guide points out, is a "classical opener," the third is "one of the most picturesque par 5s in golf," the seventh is "one of the most secluded and beautiful holes in golf," the twelfth is "possibly the most classical hole on the links," the thirteenth is a "magnificent par 5," the fourteenth is "a dramatic par 3," and the seventeenth is "one of the most dramatic par 4s in golf."

It is impossible to know whether Ruddy's prose or the undeniable quality of the links is responsible, but the European Club has been an instant hit. The club attracted twenty thousand visitors in 1994, even though the cautious Ruddy had not yet built a clubhouse. Guests had to change in temporary trailers.

Critical acclaim has followed. "A worthy addition to Britain's seaside golfing heritage," opined *Golf World* magazine when it named the European Club one of the ten best new courses in Great Britain and Ireland. Another writer suggested that it could hold the Ryder Cup some day. Only time will tell, but the European Club has the "bones" of a classic links. Its mixture of stirring holes through high dunes, punctuated by fine holes along the ocean, reminds one of Ballybunion and Waterville, and that is very fine company to be in.

"If I can just get in among the herd of greats it will be magic," Ruddy says.

Do our Dreamers have anything in common besides their preoccupation with golf and talent for promotion? Born a generation apart, they are in many ways archetypal Irishmen of their times—Castlerosse, the aristocrat in decline; Mulcahy, the Irish emigrant who finds a fortune in America; Ruddy, the product of a more confident, prosperous Ireland, a man of the information age.

They certainly all believed in posterity, comforted by the thought of their golf courses becoming their legacy to the world. Castlerosse left behind a revitalized golf club at Killarney that would maintain and later expand on his vision. Mulcahy found remarkably like-minded men to take over his dream, and asked to be buried under his beloved seventeenth tee. Ruddy is grooming his children to take over what is turning into a highly profitable enterprise.

Finally, all three men thought that there was something intrinsically good about golf. None thought the game should be restricted to the privileged few. Depressed about what he had come to see as a dissolute life, Castlerosse took great solace in what he had achieved for the townspeople of Killarney. Jack Mulcahy, dinner companion of presidents, was happy to help a taxi driver with his golf swing. And it is impossible to imagine Ruddy, the champion of the homeless golfer, ever letting the European Club become a bastion of privilege.

"Everywhere I go I see folks with hugely different attainments, hugely different political views, different religions, but they can all talk golf, and that's what it's about," Ruddy says.

Such sentiments aren't uniquely Irish. But they do lie at the heart of what makes Irish golf so enjoyable. It is also what sets the Dreamers' courses apart from the hundreds and thousands of "instant golf courses" sprouting up around the world. As much as the Dreamers may have enjoyed the acclaim, they also took great satisfaction from bringing some measure of contentment to others.

At the end of his life Lord Castlerosse finally became the Earl of Kenmare. In the security of the manor (indebted though it was), he wrote the following letter to Henry Longhurst:

My dear Henry, the success of the scheme has been surprising. There are still two new greens to be made but by the end of the month they should be completed. . . . I have been through quite a deal of war, and I am certain that the time will come when men's souls will cry for peace and not peace as opposed to war— but real peace, where the beat of an engine is not to be heard nor the loud-speaker nor the radio. I do not know how long I have for this world, but I should like the work to go on. I would like to make it a home for men who love these things. I wish you were here.

Goodbye, Valentine

BALLYBUNION (Old Course)

Founded: 1893
Designed by: Unknown (refined by William McCarthy, Tom Simpson and Molly Gourlay)

To put it simply, Ballybunion revealed itself to be nothing less than the finest seaside course I have ever seen.

HERBERT WARREN WIND

Almost unknown thirty years ago, Ballybunion is now a legend, receiving almost as many visitors as St. Andrews. They don't come for the history or the luxurious surroundings—no great tournaments have been played here, and you wouldn't want to send anyone a postcard of the clubhouse. The attractions of Ballybunion are found entirely on the links, which weaves its way through some of golf's most stirring terrain. It is not just the size or the wild look of the famous Ballybunion sand dunes, or the beauty of the seaside holes—it is the way the links fits so superbly into what nature has provided. Many golf courses are blessed with fine natural settings, but at Ballybunion one feels that the gods have also designed the holes.

PREPARING TO TEE OFF AT THE FIRST HOLE OF BALLYBUNION Old can be a bit disheartening. In the high season, you may be herded into foursomes by staff whose ingrained Irish hospitality has developed a veneer of officiousness. Despite the not inconsiderable green fee you have paid, you may be forced to play the forward tees, and the new clubhouse (architecturally a cross between Star Trek and Stalin) will cast a less than graceful shadow. But somehow the graveyard changes everything.

Not a metaphorical graveyard mind you, as in "Rae's Creek at Augusta National is the graveyard of many golfer's hopes." No sir, this is the real thing.

It doesn't matter if you've already heard about it, or played Ballybunion before, there is still something deliciously unsettling about navigating around the remains of departed souls on your opening drive. Make no mistake about it, the tombstones do come into play. Next to St. Andrews, the mystique of Ballybunion may cause more nervous shanks off the first tee than any course in the world.

Who on earth would have the nerve to place a tee so close to a cemetery? At Ballybunion no one knows for sure. We like to think the answer will turn up in the Old Testament somewhere. Okay, Ballybunion isn't *that* old. But its much commented-on sense of timelessness is wonderful to experience first hand just the same. At Ballybunion, one feels that one is playing the primordial links, that this is *Golf Before Man*.

If the cemetery is the first signal that Ballybunion is not your average track, the second hole confirms it. A quintessential Ballybunion hole, it is a ferocious par 4 into shaggy sand dunes that requires a perfectly played second to a green set high on an exquisite natural plateau. It's the kind of heroic shot you rarely find on the more subdued links of Scotland and England. Ballybunion is full of them.

What is amazing is that the dramatic golf one finds at Ballybunion evolved entirely without the benefit of bulldozers—every pathway through these magnificent hills was put there by nature. It is a fantastic and inspiring place to play.

Not all the holes are as good as the second. The following three holes—a par 3 and two par 5s—are solid links holes, but rather out of character with the rest of the course (they used to be the finishing holes, until a new clubhouse necessitated a much better routing). Although also on relatively flat land, the sixth is a terrific, nerve-racking par 4 that challenges you to bite off the corner of a dogleg, then tantalizes you with a humpy green that backs right onto the edge of a seaside cliff. The line of the seventh used to be thrillingly close to the cliff edge, but erosion has necessitated a dogleg route inland. Fortunately, an international fundraising campaign to help the club combat erosion has saved the wonderful cliff-side green (one of the changes introduced by Tom Simpson).

The very short eighth is Ballybunion's "postage stamp." It seems dead simple on first glance, but the skinny green, set charmingly in a bowl of dunes, is plagued by violent undulations and fierce pot bunkers. The ninth is a long par 4 that, like the second, requires a difficult approach shot to an elevated green.

It is all very wonderful, yet what sets the course apart are the holes still to come. The front nine flirts with the most rugged stretch of linksland, but the back nine is swallowed up by it.

Herbert Warren Wind's famous piece in the *New Yorker* helped put Ballybunion on the golfing map. He believed that the secret to Ballybunion's charm was that "sand-hill ridges do not run parallel to the shore but at a decided traverse. This opens all sorts of possibilities—dogleg holes of every description sculptured through the choppy land, and straightaway holes where the sand hills patrol the entrance to the green like the Pillars of Hercules."

Almost all of the holes on the back nine at Ballybunion are extraordinary, and to pick out individual holes is really beside the point. Suffice to say that you hit a variety of thrilling, often downhill tee shots through the dunes and precise approach shots to fabulously sited natural greens. Around each corner is a view more stunning than the last. At under 6,600 yards Ballybunion is not extraordinarily long, but it is both difficult and fair. Despite the large number of heroic shots required, you never feel unjustly punished. And you always want another go. British journalist and television commentator Henry Longhurst summed up the feeling of playing Ballybunion very well, indeed:

> Its simple, elemental quality sweeps away the cobwebs of golfing theory and brings home to you once more the original fact that golf is a business not of pivots, hip turns, wrist formation and the rest but of grasping an implement firmly in two hands and banging the ball with it.

Appropriately enough, the course that begins with a cemetery ends with an archeological site. According to the club, the massive sandtrap known as the "Sahara" that lies across the eighteenth fairway contains a "curious mixture of sand, shell, ashes, stones and bones, the source of which could date to the late Iron Age, around the fifth century A.D." Apparently they hadn't invented the sand wedge back then.

Location:	On Sandhill Road, just south of Ballybunion; sixty-five miles from Shannon Airport and forty miles from Killarney.
Green Fee:	£35 (one round); £50 for both Old and New Course
Restrictions:	Visitors permitted weekdays only; write well in advance
Manager:	Jim McKenna
Address:	Ballybunion, Co. Kerry
	phone: (068) 27146 fax: (068) 27387

BALLYBUNION (New Course)

Built: 1984
Designed by: Robert Trent Jones

This God given piece of land, with its tumbling undulating free flowing rhythm of line is beauty beyond description—a piece of land with the ocean on one side of it, river on the other . . . . There are no weak holes on the course. Each is a spectacular gem.

ROBERT TRENT JONES

If you haven't a caddie it is a murderous thing.

JOHN MORIARTY, *oldest surviving member of Ballybunion*

Ballybunion New is not just a second course at Ballybunion, it is a theatrical event all its own, and a highlight of any golfing visit to Ireland. Considered by Trent Jones to be one of his master-pieces, Ballybunion New is like a daring film that is loved by some critics but less appreciated by the masses. It is the Apocalypse Now *of links golf—controversial, occasionally self-indulgent, big budget (by Irish standards) and full of splashy set pieces. But the overall effect is the opposite of what is conveyed by the magical Old Course next door. At Ballybunion New, the whole seems somehow less than the sum of its dazzling parts.*

~

BALLYBUNION NEW HAS BEEN ONE OF IRELAND'S MOST talked-about courses since the day it opened in 1984, and the debate shows no sign of letting up. Things probably would have gone more smoothly had the club decided to go with the layout originally drawn up by Eddie Hackett, the Irish architect who had already designed several outstanding links courses on the west coast of Ireland. But instead the club approached Robert Trent Jones, the most celebrated and influential architect of his generation.

37

From the beginning Trent Jones saw Ballybunion New as his *pièce de résistance*, his chance to show what he could do on true linksland, and on a spectacular stretch at that.

"When I first saw the piece of land chosen for the new course at Ballybunion I was thrilled beyond words," Trent Jones later wrote. "It was the finest piece of linksland that I had ever seen, and perhaps the finest piece of linksland in the world."

Trent Jones's design made few concessions to the difficulty of building a golf course on such steeply contoured terrain, and construction was something of a nightmare. But when the course finally opened, there were many instant admirers. The well-known golf writer Peter Dobereiner, for one, called it "the greatest links course in the world." Others were considerably more cautious with their praise, though they had to admit that there was no links like it. Whereas an architect like Hackett would have been content to tap the fantastic natural contours of the land, Trent Jones went a step further. The course is very much in the links tradition, but the hand of the architect is everywhere in sight. It is obvious that Trent Jones felt that each hole had to have some element of high drama.

The result includes some of the most wondrous links holes in the world, especially the par 4s and 5s that tumble in, around and over the steepest of the sandhills. Whereas the Old Course has a natural charm, Ballybunion New has a surreal kind of beauty. The par-5 fifteenth, for example, requires a second shot played downhill through a narrow chute into a hollow that is almost encircled by gigantic dunes. There is an arresting hush even on the windiest of days as the dunes cut off the wind and all outside sound. The wild terrain and almost unearthly sense of solitude would make a good set for a science-fiction movie.

The par-4 fourth is an utterly different experience, marked by a drive from an elevated tee that seems to take in the whole world. Though only 350 yards, the hole uses up acres and acres of ground, as Trent Jones succeeds in creating an impression of almost unlimited space. The stunning panorama, which includes a river on the left and the ocean on the right, makes it difficult to find the correct line on the ill-defined fairway far below.

In between these extremes of seclusion and exposure are many arresting holes. What Ballybunion New lacks in elegance it makes up for in variety. Each hole seems to have a different theme, and the changes of pace are frequent and always dramatic.

It is also notoriously difficult to walk—a complaint Trent Jones dismisses, but which is a real constraint in Ireland, where electric carts are considered sacrilegious and are banned on all but a handful of courses. Not only are there steep climbs on many holes, but the trek between green and tee is often an exercise in mountain climbing. As interesting as many of the holes are, a round at Ballybunion New is always something of an ordeal. Some members flatly refuse to play it.

A few of the holes just haven't worked that well. The club has already eliminated one of the most spectacular—a right-angled par 4 in which the drive was taken from the top of one sand dune to a narrow strip of fairway and green on the top of another sand ridge, like hitting between the roofs of two skyscrapers. It has been replaced by a straight-forward par 3 (the twelfth) that no one would confuse with a Trent Jones original. Another par 4 (the fifth) that runs tight along the seawall has been cut to a ridiculously short length because no one has figured out how to grow grass on the first part of the fairway.

"When they were building the new course I walked it and met Trent Jones and he told me that he could grow grass on those areas by the sea," recalls John Moriarty, a long-time trustee of the club. "I told him 'if you can, you should be out on the Sahara' because we had tried everything possible. We'd grow weeds if we could. He didn't listen but he learned the hard way."

Less severe modifications have been made elsewhere to reduce the penal aspect of some of the holes, and the word around the clubhouse is that Tom Watson—a great friend of Ballybunion's—may be asked to make further changes at some time in the future.

It is to be hoped that the members don't go too far. For while Ballybunion New (also called the Cashen Course) may have some flaws, it is ambitious and imaginative, an example of a great architect at the height of his creative powers.

Location:	On Sandhill Road, just south of Ballybunion; sixty-five miles from Shannon Airport and forty miles from Killarney.
Green Fee:	£25 (one round); £50 for both New and Old Course
Restrictions:	None
Manager:	Jim McKenna
Address:	Ballybunion, Co. Kerry
	phone: (068) 27146 fax: (068) 27387

WATERVILLE.

Founded: 1973
Designed by: Eddie Hackett

I have never seen a more consistent succession of really strong and beautiful golf holes than I have seen here.

SIR HENRY COTTON, *three-time British Open champion*

Likely the best links built anywhere in the last fifty years, Waterville is a stern and stunning test of championship golf set in the kind of rugged linksland for which Ireland is famous. The "Magnificent Monster" (as the course was dubbed by Sam Snead) begins on relatively flat land and builds steadily to a crescendo of great finishing holes that rumble through the dunes and along the Atlantic shore. Set along the picturesque Ring of Kerry, Waterville is the one place where the Irish architect Eddie Hackett had the money to do exactly as he pleased, and the result is extraordinary.

THE WATERVILLE GOLF LINKS HAS SOMEHOW MANAGED TO combine the attraction of a resort golf destination with the charm and personality of a local club. Despite its out-of-the-way location, Waterville attracts over ten thousand foreign golfers each summer, more than half of them Americans. Visitors are pampered with electric carts (a rarity in Ireland), a modern, well-appointed clubhouse and, if they wish, first-class accommodation in Waterville House, where they have access to fabulous salmon fishing.

Not surprisingly, the village of Waterville (population 500) is given over to the tourist trade in the summer, but by October everything begins to change. The tourists have left and the locals have more time on their hands. Quite suddenly, the accents in the club's lovely bar are more likely to have a Kerry lilt than a Texas drawl.

"In the last five years, golf has really taken off with the locals," says Secretary-Manager Noel Cronin, who has been associated with the club in various capacities since that day in the late 1960s when millionaire Jack Mulcahy arrived from America to build his dream.

"Today every family in town would have at least one golfer, though when I grew up it wasn't like that," says Cronin. "There was a little bit of hoity-toity in golf then. It was a school teacher or a priest or someone up the ladder that was playing. That has changed, and changed for the good."

It is ironic that a first-class golf resort that charges £60 a night (though you do not need to stay at Waterville House to play the course) should have heralded such equality on the links, but that does seem to be what happened. As with everything at Waterville, part of the credit must go to Mulcahy, the Irish-born millionaire with a working man's touch (see p. 22). But the new owners appear determined to maintain the unique flavor of the place.

"We thought to ourselves—how often do you get a chance to buy a championship links?" says Jay Connolly, one of nine Wall Street executives, all of them of Irish descent, who bought the property from Mulcahy in 1987. By all accounts, the transition has gone smoothly.

Sitting in the bar in the Waterville clubhouse it is hard not to think of Connolly and his colleagues (and Mulcahy before them) as walking billboards for the American Dream—the kind of living, breathing evidence of American opportunity that has inspired generations of Irish emigrants. In 1925 almost half of all people born in Ireland lived outside the country, and though the pace of emigration has slowed considerably in recent years we're hardly surprised to learn that Cronin's son—a four handicap—is off to New York the following week to caddie and do some odd jobs at a golf course.

Connolly, who splits his time between Waterville and Connecticut (he is also a member of Winged Foot) is obviously comfortable in the land of his ancestors, and enjoys the camaraderie of the townspeople who, by any definition, are of a different economic class.

"My life revolves around the things I like to do—golf, fishing, a few pints and meeting people," he says. "And this is a great place to do all of that."

The local members we met at Waterville were often protective of the owners of the resort that has brought so many economic benefits to the community. Vincent, a local *ghillie* (fishing guide), expressed genuine concern that the consortium were "digging into their own pockets" too much in an effort to maintain the course in the kind of condition that appeals to American visitors.

The ties between Waterville and America are more than metaphorical. Over the fireplace in the bar is a piece of transatlantic cable—a relic of the period, beginning in the 1880s, when Waterville was one of only a handful of transatlantic cable stations. It was the employees of the Commercial Cable Company who created an earlier version of the Waterville Golf Club on the same site in 1889.

The cable industry didn't last forever. By the end of the Second World War emigration from the parish of Waterville was endemic. Noel Cronin remembers that the most popular form of entertainment was crossroad dancing.

"You'd have the village of Cahirciveen meeting with the village of Waterville, and vice versa. But then ballroom dancing came up and mushroomed all over the country and took it over."

When it comes to sport, golf is enjoying a similar boom in popularity today. County Kerry is famous in Ireland for its athletes, and you don't need to be in the area long to hear a reference to the county's phenomenal success at Gaelic football in national competitions. For the longest time golf was considered a sissy sport, but times have changed.

"All through Kerry golf has been taken up completely," says Cronin. "You are proud of the juniors when they get on the bus [to go to a match], and they are all dressed up like Nick Faldo.

"But we encourage all our juniors to play Gaelic football as well as golf, and it has made a lot of difference in them. A golfer that hasn't played any other sport, he finds it difficult to accept defeat, he's not a genuine sportsman. It's a lot easier for young lads who have played another sport."

THE COURSE

Connolly and the other owners have a multi-year development plan to improve further the conditioning of the links at Waterville, and have engaged the American architect Thomas Doak to make some revisions necessitated by erosion. It is to be hoped that they don't get carried away, for Waterville in its present form is already a classic.

"I walked the place for five days, until I got the feel, and the inspiration as to where to start it, how it would flow," remembers architect Eddie Hackett. "It sort of came to me then. I put the first design on an envelope, and it departed very little from that routing.

"It was a lovely site, and it's compact, though there's no cramping. The last twelve holes, they cost us a fortune."

The opening holes were cheaper because they skirted Waterville's most mountainous terrain, but they are by no means weak. The first two holes flirt with the boundary fence, and the second was chosen by Christy O'Connor Sr. as one of the best eighteen holes in Ireland. The third is a dangerous par 4 with a green that leans into the River Inny, and the fourth is a picturesque and unsettling par 3 to a green partly hidden in a circle of shaggy dunes. On another course the fifth and sixth, elegant holes through low-lying hills, would be among the best, but on Waterville they are merely a prelude.

There is, admittedly, a hiccup at the seventh—a par 3 over a clumsy man-made moat that is being redesigned—but after that Waterville is flawless, with one arresting and challenging hole after another. For all its severity, Waterville has a lovely rhythm. There are no debilitating walks between holes, no overly theatrical moments. Instead, the course progresses with a persuasive logic, the relatively exposed opening holes gradually giving way to the more muscular and dramatic sections of the course.

There is a kind of aesthetic climax at the eleventh—the oh-so-aptly named "Tranquillity"—an exquisitely natural par 5 in which the golfer finds himself suddenly secluded from the rest of the course by a row of dunes on a twisting and tumbling fairway. On a lovely day its beauty sends shivers up your spine, a hole you just don't want to end.

The twelfth—the Mass—is a long par 3 over a natural chasm that was used as a place of worship in the days when Irish Catholics had to practice their religion in secret or risk persecution.

"It's one of my favorite par 3s," says Eddie Hackett, a devout Catholic who attends church daily. "There's not a bunker on it, either. It doesn't need one and that's the best tribute you can pay a hole."

The course ends with six more absorbing holes of great variety. They begin with a reachable par 5 from a spectacular elevated tee, followed by a tough uphill dogleg par 4 called "The Judge" (at Waterville the names given holes are unusually evocative and precise), and a devilish two-tiered par 4 offering an exciting downhill approach shot. The sixteenth is a 330-yard par 4 shaped like a quarter moon, and the par-3 seventeenth is the famous Mulcahy's Peak (the founder's ashes are buried underneath the tee box) with its riveting views and heroic shot over a vast wasteland. The final hole is an appropriately dramatic par 5 that hugs the ocean. The challenge is multiplied by the fact that no two holes in this stretch are parallel. The ever-present breeze has a different effect on almost every shot.

It is one of the great back nines in the world. And after playing it you will appreciate why Waterville has been ranked so highly by those who have gone before you. Raymond Floyd, for one, has written that it is one of his five favorite courses in the world.

The clubhouse at Waterville is a nice surprise, a low-lying modern building that isn't garish. It's pleasantly low-key inside, the focus on the exceedingly comfortable bar (on a cold day, the hot whiskeys are indescribable) that contains interesting memorabilia, a dignified bust of Jack Mulcahy, and some rather impressive golf art.

After less than twenty-five years, there is already a palpable sense of tradition at Waterville that is worthy of its founder, and of its magnificent and timeless links.

Location:	At western end of Ring of Kerry; one mile west of town on the coastal road
Restrictions:	None
Green Fee:	£30-40
Secretary:	Noel Cronin
Address:	Waterville, Co. Kerry
	phone: (066) 74102 fax: (066) 74482

KILLARNEY

(Killeen & Mahony's Point Courses)

Founded: 1893
New Course Built: 1939   **Expanded:** 1972
Designed by: Lord Castlerosse, Sir Guy Campbell, Dr. William
O'Sullivan, Fred Hawtree

When anyone sees Killarney, even if he is the basest heretic, he must believe in God.

LORD CASTLEROSSE

Set on the edge of one of the planet's most enchanting lakes, Killarney is the one inland golf experience in Ireland that you won't want to miss. The serene and luscious beauty of its thirty-six holes is a complete departure from the exposed, rugged links that are Ireland's principal legacy to the sport. Each hole is deliberately charming at Killarney—greens and fairways are thoughtfully framed by woods, lake and the marvelous Macgillycuddy's Reeks, Ireland's highest and most pleasing mountains. On a calm day, this is the mistily tranquil Irish landscape of Hollywood fantasies. Indeed, visiting celebrities such as Bob Hope and Bing Crosby (who crooned "How Can You Buy Killarney") helped to make Killarney synonymous with Irish golf in foreign eyes.

IF IRELAND HAS A "TOURIST TRAP" IT IS KILLARNEY, BUT then some say that an Irish tourist trap has a charm all its own. Certainly it cannot be argued that each year tens of thousands of people thoroughly enjoy their quaint tours—in horse and carriage or jaunting cars—of the lakes, woodlands and mountains that surround the town. It has all been going on in one fashion or another since Killarney was first "discovered" by holidaying gentry in the eighteenth century.

Not surprisingly, the history of golf at Killarney has been tightly tied to the tourist trade. In March 1894 the club captain wrote to the *Irish Times* to inform its readers that "in addition to the enchanting scenery of Killarney the visitor who has the good fortune to be a golfer can now have all the delights of 'Ye Royal and Ancient Game' on capital links—the Earl of Kenmare has given the use of his Deer Park and has become President of the local club."

It was the next, and final, Earl of Kenmare—known for most of his life as Lord Castlerosse—who would make the most lasting contribution to golf at Killarney (his unlikely achievements are described on p. 22). Although some of the more outlandish parts of Lord Castlerosse's vision (such as lining each fairway with flowers of a different color) didn't come to pass, his prediction that the course would become a "bait" for foreign tourists proved to be accurate. By the 1960s, more than 13,000 visiting golfers payed homage to Killarney's beauty each year, and the course received worldwide attention on *Shell's Wonderful World of Golf.*

"Never in forty-two years of golf have I seen such a beautiful course," gushed host Gene Sarazen. "And I've seen them all."

None of this was lost on Bord Fáilte, the government tourism agency, which proposed to underwrite the construction of a second eighteen holes on land partly purchased from the owners of the old Kenmare estate—if the club would manage it for them.

Once again the driving force was a colorful and domineering figure with a passionate love for Killarney. Dr. Billy O'Sullivan, a local golfing hero who won the Irish Amateur in 1949, was determined that the new holes would surpass Castlerosse's efforts. Taking all but complete control over the building process, he proposed that two new courses be created, each combining a mixture of original and new holes. And, like Castlerosse before him, he made great use of other people's money, serenely confident in his own vision. Expanding on the original plans of British architect Fred Hawtree, O'Sullivan insisted that several new holes be laid out along a stretch of wild and swampy shoreline just west of the clubhouse. A generation before, Lord Castlerosse had tramped over his estate in pink plus-fours searching for good golf holes; now "Dr. Billy" could be seen splashing about in his waders doing the same thing. Parts of Lough Leane were reclaimed, huge expanses of bog were cut out, and an elaborate drainage system was installed, all at enormous cost. Work literally came to a standstill on the seventeenth hole when the grant provided by Bord Fáilte was used up.

Eventually the work was completed. The two new composite

courses— Killeen and Mahony's Point—were unveiled in 1972 to wide-spread acclaim. For a while some obstinate members kept playing the "old course" (now split over two courses); others wondered wistfully about what could be had if the best holes on both courses were combined. But with the passage of time, the wisdom of O'Sullivan's approach became widely accepted. Killeen was chosen to host the Irish Open in 1991 and 1992, and it proved a formidable test. Nick Faldo won on both occasions with 72-hole scores of 5 under and 14 under par.

Today, more than forty thousand visiting golfers sample Killarney's charms each year, about half of them foreigners. Though the courses are essentially owned by the Irish government, they continue to be very much managed by the club, which is once again bursting at the seams. Plans to build a third course on adjacent lands have been blocked, at least for the time being, by environmentalists who object to the idea of leasing part of the National Park for a golf course. Now the goal is to build on some privately owned lands nearby.

THE COURSES

In common with great golf courses everywhere, Mahony's Point and Killeen are very much a product of their natural surroundings. There is an aesthetic quality to Killarney, and a self-conscious reverence for nature. Modern architectural gimmicks are noticeably absent. It is perhaps not entirely irrelevant to point out that during the nineteenth century Killarney had a special appeal for the English Romantics who were so fond of lakes and woods. One suspects that Castlerosse, in his own mind at least, had a Romantic sensibility.

The courses are utterly different, of course, from the great Irish links courses. Instead of stark sand dunes, there are gently rolling hills, trees and flowering shrubs. Instead of a roiling ocean there is a glittering lake. Instead of devastating pot bunkers there are sand traps of the more graceful and shallower kind.

The two courses have different personalities. In general, the best of the new holes are on Killeen, and the best of the old are on Mahony's Point.

Killeen is the sterner test. The penal quality of its lakeside holes—all built by Hawtree and O'Sullivan—is immediately evident. The first hole is a kneeknocking dogleg around a lagoon to a green half-surrounded by water, requiring more confidence and precision than just about anyone has on the first shots of the day. And it doesn't get easier. During the 1991 tournament, the best of Europe's professionals complained that the greens on the sixth, seventh, eighth and tenth were unfair—balls were too likely to roll off the green and into a water hazard, even after a good approach. When it was built, the par-5 seventh also had the dubious distinction of being Ireland's most expensive hole. Built entirely over a former bog, the builders had to dig out and remove the peat (eight feet deep) over the entire length and breadth of the hole, replacing it with properly draining soil. However difficult, Killeen is certainly an exciting course to play, a modern test of golf that is still splendidly natural, still pure Killarney.

Mahony's Point is more old-fashioned, and its memorable holes are the ones fashioned by Castlerosse and Sir Guy Campbell. The latter's contribution consists of what may still be the most exquisite three finishing holes in golf. After a drive over a hill, the par-5 sixteenth descends in gorgeous fashion to a green at the edge of the water, Macgillycuddy's Reeks providing a perfect backdrop. The seventeenth is a terrific par 4 that hugs the outrageously picturesque lake for its entire length, and the famous par-3 eighteenth, over a natural inlet, is a hole so flawlessly beautiful that it almost seems a violation to play it.

Prior to this memorable finish, the best hole is the thirteenth, a singular, rolling par 5 designed by Castlerosse that leads ultimately to a charming, elevated green that is well trapped and frustratingly difficult to breach. Slightly misjudged chip shots will be rejected down the steep hills that surround the green. But the views are ample compensation. Elevated greens—favored by Castlerosse—remain a feature of Killarney on both courses.

On the whole, less attention seems to have been paid to updating Mahony's Point (David Jones made further changes to the Killeen course in preparation for the 1991 Irish Open), and there are more places to relax and enjoy the scenery. The fairways are more generous, and the hazards less onerous. But if it is less consistently challenging than Killeen, it is one heck of a great walk in the park.

Location:	Three miles west of town on R562
Restrictions:	None
Green Fee:	£28 per round
Manager:	Tom Prendergast
Address:	Killarney, Co. Kerry
	phone: (064) 31034 fax: (064) 33065

LAHINCH

Founded: 1892
Designed by: Alister Mackenzie (with Old Tom Morris, James McKenna, Charles Gibson, John Burke and Donald Steel)

I think that if my suggestions are carried out the course should not only compare favourably, as a test of golf, with any of the British Championship courses, but will become so interesting, exciting and popular that it will attract hundreds of visitors from overseas.

DR. ALISTER MACKENZIE, 1927

Known widely, if somewhat misleadingly, as the St. Andrews of Ireland, Lahinch is a marvelous place. There is no community in Ireland with a stronger sense of connection to the sport, and the club's evolution has in many ways paralleled the history of Ireland itself. The championship quality and classic feel of the links is the work of Alister Mackenzie (of Augusta and Cypress Point fame) but there is a charm and a quirkiness that belongs only to Lahinch. And you get a glorious whiff of Old Tom Morris at two of golf's most famous and exquisite anachronisms—the holes they call the Dell and Klondyke. Lahinch is an entirely successful blend of old and new, and when the greens and fairways are firm and fast there are few places that are more delightful to play.

SYMBOLICALLY AT LEAST, THE TURNING POINT IN THE STORY of the Lahinch Golf Club came during the final of an important match-play tournament in September, 1920. As the finalists teed off, a large crowd of spectators were startled by the sight of a band of Irish Volunteers marching into the clubhouse. The revolutionaries removed the club flag, and raised the Irish tricolor. While the match progressed, British soldiers arrived from nearby Ennistymon with orders to remove and burn the nationalist flag and raise the club flag once again. Before the contest was over, the Volunteers had returned and put up another tri-color.

The game of musical flags seems amusing in retrospect, but the back-drop was the deadly serious confrontation known in much of Ireland as the War of Independence. Only a few months earlier, the giant sand ridges on the Lahinch links had been a place of refuge after a British Army unit (the infamous "Black and Tans") set fire to most of the town in revenge for the ambush killing of four soldiers by the IRA.

That the golf club should find itself embroiled in the independence struggle is no surprise given its early associations with the privileged class. Founded in 1892 by a group of wealthy Limerick merchants with close ties to the army, the club's first quarter-century was dominated by the Protestant elite. There were no members from the Catholic village that lent its name to the links. However, it seems that most residents wel-comed the golf course as a much-needed tourist attraction to complement the swimming that could be had on the fine Atlantic beaches. The impact of the golf club on the village's fortunes is evident from this excerpt from the *Clare Journal* in 1907:

> The interesting and rising little seaside resort of Lahinch is bête en fête this week as several golf championships are being played off. The Lahinch Links are regarded by golfers as not second to any other in the Kingdom. The otherwise quiet seaside place is, for the time being, transformed into a centre of passion and gai-ety. Among those who arrived on Saturday was the Right Honourable Lord Chancellor of England with a distinguished Party.

With the building of a railway link from Dublin, Lahinch became Ireland's foremost golfing destination. Aristocrats in London could board the train at 6:00 p.m., and even with the ferry crossing be at Lahinch at noon the next day. They could then check-in to any one of a number of fine and newly-built hotels and lodges.

The atmosphere at Lahinch changed quickly after the establishment of the Irish Free State in 1921. The First World War greatly depleted the ranks of the aristocracy, and the club finally began to admit local mem-bers. One of the first was John Burke, whose brother had been part of the volunteer brigade that burned the club flag. Burke became Ireland's best player after teaching himself the game through some lessons printed in an English newspaper.

It took time, but eventually the golf club became a genuinely local affair. There is a nice symmetry to the fact that in 1976 the club which was once a target of Irish nationalists had the honor of seeing one of its members (Dr. P. J. Hillery) elected as President of an independent Ireland. Dr. Hillery served as President for fourteen years, and it was with genuine pride that the members of Lahinch used to claim that he was the best golfer among all of the heads of state in the world!

The Course

Lahinch's early fame must be credited to Old Tom Morris, who laid out the original course for one pound plus travel expenses and made no secret of the fact that he thought the links to be one of the best in the world. But the course was largely overhauled in 1907 by Charles Gibson, a professional from Westward Ho!, and then again, and in a more profound fashion, by Alister Mackenzie in 1927.

Mackenzie's influence on golf architecture continues to the present day, through the example of his work and the persuasiveness of his writings, which established many of the principles of modern design. In this context, it is interesting to note that in the same year he designed Cypress Point in California, Mackenzie decided to keep intact two of Lahinch's most famous holes—Klondyke and the Dell—which feature blind shots unthinkable today. The passage of time has only confirmed Mackenzie's wisdom. The charm of Lahinch remains its sense of timelessness, and these two holes remind the golfer of the very roots of the sport.

Mackenzie's work at Lahinch has also been revised over the years, partly due to the erosion that swallowed up two seaside greens. The most notable addition may be the third—a stiff par 3 designed by John Burke.

The front nine at Lahinch is a history lesson. For more than a century its highlight has been the Dell—a blind par 3 over a large dune to a precious rectangle of green set between sandhills. The line is provided by a white stone that is shifted depending on the pin position, and the best shots often bounce off the hill behind the green. The Dell has been controversial since its inception, and has perhaps been saved by the childlike charm of its hidden putting surface. If you don't take the Dell too seriously, it is pure fun to play. It will be the shot you remember best after the round.

Klondyke, built in 1897 after Morris's design, is a better hole and just as delightful. "The Klondyke is one of the prettiest holes in Ireland," reported *Irish Field* magazine in 1909. "The drive [is] down a narrow valley where a perfect lie can be had. The second shot should be a good iron over the Klondyke, a formidable sandhill, to the green."

Today the hole has been lengthened to a par 5, meaning that the approach is only blind for long hitters going for the green in two. But the sense of entrapment after the first shot (the valley is surrounded by steep hills) and the feeling of escape in hitting the second over the wild, fescue-covered ridge, is perhaps unique in golf. After playing Klondyke and the Dell back-to-back (they are the fifth and sixth holes at Lahinch) you will appreciate what an adventure early golf must have been. Half game, half exploration—one can't help but wonder whether Old Tom might have found the modern version rather boring.

Following the Dell are a series of classically designed holes more imbued with the imagination of Mackenzie than Morris, with elevated tees, multi-tiered greens and wide, sweeping fairways. The variety of holes is remarkable. Some follow narrow passages between sandhills; others convey an exhilarating sense of space, at least on the drive; while still others, such as the singular fourteenth, do both. The back nine includes a combination of punishing long par 4s in excess of 400 yards, two very short holes (the par-4 thirteenth is a tantalizing 268 yards in length, but the green is raised and wickedly undulating) and a couple of reachable par 5s. To use a well worn, but apt phrase—at Lahinch there is something for everyone.

We sometimes think that Lahinch's famous goats call attention away from the merits of a remarkable course, but they can hardly go unmentioned. In the clubhouse there is a broken barometer accompanied by a small notice that reads, "See goats." If the animals are huddled next to the clubhouse it apparently means that poor weather is approaching.

It is an original bit of local lore to be sure, but if you have only one day at Lahinch, it will take more than a little weather to keep you off its fairways for a second round.

Location:	In town of Lahinch, thirty-five miles west of Shannon Airport
Restrictions:	None
Green Fee:	£30
Manager:	Alan Reardon
Address:	Lahinch, Co. Clare
	phone: (065) 81003 fax: (065) 81592

TRALEE

Founded: 1896
Present Course Built: 1984
Designed by: Arnold Palmer and Ed Seay

Robert Louis Stevenson was wrong, and by a long chalk, when he described the Monterey Peninsula of California as the finest conjunction of land and sea that this earth has to offer. As a spectacle Tralee is in a different class.

PETER DOBEREINER

If Tralee doesn't quite live up to its setting, that's hardly a criticism. The views of cliffs and beaches are mind-blowing, and constantly draw your attention away from the admirable efforts of Palmer and Seay. Although there are lots of contenders, Tralee is certainly in the running for the most stunning seaside golf course in all the world, and film buffs will perhaps recognize the landscape for David Lean's Ryan's Daughter. *There are also some tremendous golf holes at Tralee, and its true character won't really be known until the course fully matures. There are places where the American architects seem to be trying too hard, and Tralee doesn't have the consistent style that marks the greatest courses. But like a charging Arnold Palmer, it will sure get your adrenaline going.*

IN ED SEAY'S OPINION, IT WAS NO KIND OF WEATHER IN WHICH to be laying out a golf course. He felt as if he was wearing every piece of clothing he owned, yet it was no defense against the ice-cold rain whipping off Tralee Bay. He had to admit, however, that Michael O'Brien didn't seem to be bothered. The two of them were choosing the final tee location for the sixteenth hole of the new course at the Tralee Golf

Club—O'Brien was a member of the greens committee. The future six-teenth green was set up in the dunes next to a cliff, requiring a long carry over wasteland. There would be no place at all to bail out.

It is a moment Seay can remember as if it were yesterday.

"I turned to Michael and told him, 'If we put the tee here you'd need a driver on a day like this,'" says Seay in his Florida drawl. "And if you were short of the green you'd get a 12.

"I remember Michael O'Brien looking at me straight on and saying, 'What's wrong with that Ed? It beats a 13.'"

For Ed Seay, the design partner of Arnold Palmer, it was another sign that this was no ordinary assignment. It was an introduction to an entirely different way of looking at golf, and at life.

"They taught me a great deal about what the true essence of golf is," he says. "We've lost it completely in the United States."

Ed Seay was not the first architect to have adventures at the Tralee Golf Club. "When I laid out the new course [at Tralee] times were diffi-cult in this country," wrote Lionel Hewson in *Irish Golf* about his expe-rience in 1922. "Laying out the course . . . was a little upsetting as men sat around on the demesne walls watching me measuring, and bullets used to fly in those days on little provocation."

Hewson was, after all, laying out a golf course during a civil war. Just a year earlier, a government soldier was shot and killed while play-ing golf at the club, the only on-course fatality in Ireland that can be attributed to political violence.

Sixty years later, the members of Tralee were on the move again. Their nine-hole course near the town of Tralee was getting awfully crowded on weekends, and they had just purchased a much larger and spectacular property near the village of Barrow, eight miles away.

Though the club had precious little money in the bank, the members continued to think big. Only a famous architect would do, and that is how Ed Seay—ex-U. S. Marine, noted golf course designer and partner to the most recognizable name in golf—found himself along the edge of a precipice, in the west of Ireland, in 1982.

"It was my first real observation of a European linksland," Seay remembers, the excitement of that day still evident in his voice. "It was magnificent! Set out on the cliffs and with these tremendous dunes—it was as pretty as any site I'd ever seen in the world.

"I called Arnold on the phone and said, 'this place is dynamite. You don't get an opportunity like this every day.'"

Unbeknownst to Seay, the club had also asked four other architectural firms to bid on the project, and the greens committee was meeting that day to hear Seay's proposal.

The meeting took ten hours.

"I don't know if you have had any experience in a meeting at an Irish golf club," Seay says. "There is a lot of talking and drinking, I'll tell you that.

"They were as tough as ninepenny nails to begin with. And rightfully so, they had absolutely no money. They hoped to sell the land from the tiny nine hole course—but I mean my back yard is bigger.

"So we offered them a deal. If they would put the money they would have paid us into the course then we'd do it [at a reduced rate]."

Eventually Seay and Palmer landed the contract. Seay did most of the day-to-day work, though his celebrated partner did fly in for a day, hold a press conference, and charm the pants off everyone. ("We were very impressed with Mr. Palmer," Michael O'Brien told us. "He is very down-to-earth and he answered all our questions.")

The culture shock that Seay experienced continued during the building process. The club couldn't afford to hire an outside contractor to construct the course, so Seay and Palmer agreed to fly in a supervisor from the United States. The club somehow came up with a bulldozer. Much to Seay's amazement, the club also decided not to install an irrigation system.

"They were sure that the Good Lord would provide the water. And I guess they were right."

The Good Lord also provided plenty of wind, however, and the grass seed the club planted was blown away time and time again. O'Brien now thinks that it might have been better to use a different mix of soil, but the club didn't help matters by insisting that Seay create the most dramatic holes possible.

"On number three they wanted to move the green as far out [on the edge of a cliff] as they could," he says. "Because of the salt and the wind I told them they were going to have to rebuild it every year. They didn't care."

The twelfth is Tralee's most famous and controversial hole, a vicious par 4 of 440 yards that requires a perfect approach shot to a green set high on a shallow plateau, surrounded by fierce links rough. "They [the members] wanted no mercy. I told them that with the wind in your face it's going to take a one or a two iron. But they wouldn't hear of any changes."

When Seay inquired who the superintendent was going to be, he was in for another surprise. There wasn't going to be one.

"They hired a landscaper to cut the fairways once a week and the greens every three days," says Seay. "It was the damndest thing I've ever seen."

The course opened in 1984. Though it was immediately proclaimed to be one of the most breathtaking in the world, the cash-strapped club had to allow more traffic than was healthy for the fragile soil. The condition of the links left much to be desired, and revenues were not keeping up with expenditures. Eventually, a national raffle was organized to raise money for the club, and in the late 1980s the tide finally began to turn. The grass had finally taken properly, a new clubhouse opened, and golf was booming in Ireland.

Both Seay and club officials seem perfectly pleased with the way things have turned out, despite the trials and tribulations. The club is looking forward to the day when Arnold Palmer finally plays the course he is so closely associated with, and one gets the feeling that the golfers of Tralee have left an indelible impression on Ed Seay.

"Their idea of par comes from another era," he says, "and they suckered me into doing a couple of things I wouldn't do normally. They're match play guys all the way. Their attitude is that it's always the same for the other guy."

THE COURSE

We don't pretend to have enough words in our vocabulary to describe the scenery at Tralee. We suggest you rent *Ryan's Daughter* from the video store instead. Suffice to say that the power of the views is magnified by the fact that they hit you suddenly, after a painfully slow, claustrophobic drive from town.

The first hole is really just an excuse to get to the cliffs, and the spectacular view of the Barrow Strand from the second tee eloquently explains what Tralee is all about. One of the best par 5s in the country swings around the cliffs in a kind of Irish tribute to Pebble Beach. If the wind doesn't knock you over, the panorama will. The complexities of the hole, which include a difficult approach to a tiny green backed by an enormous U-shaped trap, seem almost too much to take in so early in the round. If only this could have been the eighteenth.

The third is a short par 3 on a little point with the whole world behind it. There's even a picturesque stone turret in the picture frame, as if the natural wonders weren't enough.

The rest of the front nine cannot live up to the expectations raised by the second and third, and the next few holes offer a rather jarring change of pace which may be inevitable at Tralee. The land is rather prosaic and the holes somewhat ill-defined. The first-time visitor will keep wondering when the course will head back to the cliffs. The eighth hole does so rather gloriously but then you have to wait until well into the back nine.

It would be fun to watch the professionals tackle the eleventh and twelfth, but we don't enjoy playing them ourselves. The extremely long eleventh (560 yards from the regular tees) features a steep climb following the drive, and offers precious little charm in compensation.

The twelfth is considered by some to be one of the greatest holes in Ireland (it is certainly among the most difficult). We find it rather irritating. Unless the wind is right at your back, there's no way for an average golfer to get anywhere near the green in two, and you have to lay up almost one hundred yards away at the bottom of a hill.

Fortunately, the thirteenth hole, a lovely par 3 set deep in the dunes, puts everyone back in a good mood. And up ahead is the exciting cliffside stretch that you've been waiting so patiently for. On a windy day the sixteenth is almost as uncompromising as Ed Seay said it would be, while the fifteenth and seventeenth are short par 4s with fiercely sloping fairways that threaten to send your ball into the ocean. When the wind is up, these are among the most dangerous holes in Ireland, requiring precision, patience and a rock-steady golf swing. Should you waver, you won't be the first to wreck on the rocks below—countless drowned ships lie at the bottom of the sea.

The inland holes at Tralee would benefit from some imaginative bunkering, but the relentless winds have made it almost impossible to keep the sand in the bunkers. If, in the final analysis, Tralee feels more fragmented than a great course should, it is nevertheless a worthy achievement and an appropriate legacy for the daring golfers of Tralee, for Ed Seay, and for golf's most exciting player.

Location:	Eight miles west of Tralee, through villages of Spa and Churchill on very narrow roads
Restrictions:	None
Green Fee:	£25-30
Supervisor:	Michael O'Brien
Address:	West Barrow, Ardfert, Co. Kerry
	phone: (066) 36379 fax: (066) 36008

CEANN SIBÉAL

Founded: 1971; Extended: 1992
Designed by: Eddie Hackett and Christy O'Connor Jr.

There is a strong cultural orientation here. We're the only club that is Irish speaking. Everyone that works here is Irish speaking and we try to create an atmosphere and an occasion for speaking it.

BERNARD O'SULLIVAN, *former captain of Ceann Sibéal*

Set out like an afterthought on the western extremity of the Dingle Peninsula, Golf Chumann Ceann Sibéal is a little-known but friendly enclave of Gaelic. The links by the stunning cliffs of Sybil Head are in one of the last remaining Gaeltacht—everything at Ceann Sibéal is in Irish, from the scorecard to the signs on the washrooms. The most westerly course in Europe, the links itself is eloquent in any language, one of Eddie Hackett's most bewitching creations. The setting is mesmerizing, too—with the Three Sisters rock towering behind the course, and the sea crashing against the cliffs just below. If the legendary giants of Irish lore played golf, this might be where they'd play.

❧

FOR OUR MONEY, JUST DRIVING TO CEANN SIBÉAL IS ONE OF golf's great experiences. Forget the drive into Augusta's Magnolia Lane (you'll need an invitation anyway). Try instead the three-hour spin from Killarney to the Irish-speaking village of Ballyferriter along the coast of Dingle Bay. It is an astonishing drive, as colossal cliffs push the road almost into the sea at times, and Macgillycuddy's Reeks look glorious in the distance across the bay. As the terrain becomes starker and more spectacular it becomes harder to believe that there is a golf course at the end of it. Eventually, you arrive in Dingle, a remote fishing port that is also a base for sightseers and hikers. But the golf course is several miles farther west, past Ballyferriter, to a craggy spot called Sybil Head (or

Ceann Sibéal in Irish). It is all cliffs and surf and haunting desolation. On a stormy day it feels like you are at the end of the earth.

Of course this *was* the end of the earth for many centuries, at least as far as Europeans were concerned. The remains of ring forts of Irish kings dot the surrounding landscape. There are also several impressive Christian ruins dating back a millennium or so, a reminder that Irish monasteries were the last refuge of Christian learning during Europe's Dark Ages. Just off shore are the Blasket Islands. Though unpopulated today, these islands once produced some of the best writers of Gaelic literature.

On our first visit to Ceann Sibéal, we found that some people still consider the area a kind of refuge—a place apart from the pressures of modern life.

"The only things I miss really are baseball and hockey—especially the Red Sox," says Danny Mitchell, a thirty-year-old fisherman with a Boston accent. It turns out that Mitchell spent a year here with some relatives following college in 1984, and decided to stay. Now he's one of five crew members on an eighty-five-foot fishing boat, and he has completed a course for aspiring skippers in Donegal.

"My family visit me *here*," says Mitchell, clearly implying that he doesn't travel to Boston. "My father can't believe there's a golf course of this quality in the middle of nowhere. And that we have it to ourselves for most of the year."

Our other playing partner is Mitchell's friend Paul Duffy, an artisan who moved his family here from Dublin in the late 1980s because of his concern about crime. He purchased a piece of land near Ballyferriter and put up a trailer on the site. His wife and two young children love it, and his pottery business is working out just fine.

Although they have adapted well, Mitchell and Duffy are still outsiders in this tightly knit, ancient community. And in some ways, that's not so bad.

"People around here would call us *blow-ins*," says Mitchell. "So they don't expect so much of us—you can push the boundaries a bit as far as behavior is concerned. You have to get used to the quiet, but people look after you. And it's quite cosmopolitan in the summertime."

Today, however, it is late October, and the hurly-burly of the tourist trade has long subsided. Only a trickle of golfers are trying their luck on a gloriously sunny and windy day.

A good number of Dingle's members are blow-ins, including some of the Germans who are snapping up coastal properties on the peninsula.

There are also several hundred "country" members from Dublin and other cities, who travel to Dingle to play golf during their holidays.

This influx of golf-related tourism is what the founders of Ceann Sibéal had in mind when they asked Eddie Hackett to lay out an eighteen-hole course in 1969 (he was also designing Waterville at the time). The thirty original members found, however, that they had only enough money to build nine of the holes, with precious little left over for maintenance, let alone for building a clubhouse.

The club lay almost dormant for a decade, but the success of other community golf developments along the west coast of Ireland encouraged the members to organize a fundraising drive to finish the project and build a clubhouse. Fortunately, the stakes that Hackett had used to lay out the back nine were still lying in the ground—almost twenty years later!

THE COURSE

It is to the credit of Eddie Hackett and Christy O'Connor Jr. (who finalized the design of the second nine using Hackett's basic layout) that the spell cast by Dingle's beautiful, elemental surroundings is not broken by the golf course itself. Ceann Sibéal is built on the side of a hill that slopes down to the sea, with the clubhouse at the top. You can see most of the course from the first tee, and at first it doesn't look like much. The fairways don't seem well-defined, and the huge sand ridges of Ballybunion or Waterville are conspicuously absent.

But what you can't appreciate without teeing off are the undulations that, in combination with the natural slope of the land, will severely test anyone's short game. Hackett has made use of every swale and hollow, and of a creek that winds through ten holes, without resorting to gimmicks (not that the club could have afforded them). As intriguing as the course is, it does not try to compete with the drama of the natural surroundings.

Faced with land that generally slopes only in one direction, Hackett has mixed difficult uphill holes with thrilling downhill tee shots. Ceann Sibéal is particularly exposed to the wind, and when the fairways and greens are hard and fast, there is really no place to relax. If anything, its course rating of 71 from back tees of 6,700 yards is too low.

There's something to rattle the nerves on just about every hole, even though few look difficult at first glance. The third, for example, is only 359 yards, but there is a small pot bunker smack in the middle of the fairway that causes alarm far in excess of its size. There is thick rough on the right to catch those who compensate too much, and an elevated and sloping green that makes pitch shots difficult.

The par-4 fourteenth, 342 yards straight downhill, is another illusion. It looks easy, but Hackett has left intact a strange mound just in front of the green that knocks pitch-and-run shots off course, and provides precious little room to stop the ball with a high pitch.

On other holes the natural undulations are used to provide the severest test of shotmaking. The tenth, at just under 200 yards, is one of the toughest par 3s in Ireland. Slightly uphill, the hole is visually intimidating, since you can't see the putting surface over the rugged expanse of rough. And the green slopes severely from front to back, making it extremely difficult to hold a long iron. (When asked if the hole is perhaps a bit unfair, Hackett looked perplexed. "It is what was *there*, you see," he said.)

At Ceann Sibéal, what is *there* is a heck of a lot of fun. The three excellent and utterly different par 5s on the back nine (which made up the original course) are good examples. The eleventh starts from an exhilarating, elevated tee and then snakes over the creek to a well-guarded green. The thirteenth doglegs at right angles around the tiny village of Ballyloughtra (the brave will try to cut the corner by flying across the stone wall that marks the village's border). And the eighteenth is straight uphill to the clubhouse, which sits rather forlornly against the barren mountainside. After a tough round, the eighteenth looks menacing (and exhausting), but those who bear down and concentrate can end the round on a high note, and drink in the marvelous views with added enjoyment.

Location:	Sybil Head, west of Ballyferriter, western end of Dingle Peninsula
Restrictions:	None
Green Fee:	£18-20
Secretary:	Garry Partington
Address:	Ballyferriter, Co. Kerry
	phone: (066) 56255 fax: (066) 56409

DOOKS

Founded: 1889
Designed by: The Members

Lying on a promontory jutting out into Dingle Bay, the Dooks course commands as fine views of sea and blending mountains as one could desire. On a fine sunny day the vista is magnificent, and a yellow strip of sandhills stretching across the blue waters of Dingle Bay form a contrast to sea and purple mountain that is charming to the eye.

IRISH GOLF MAGAZINE, 1909

You will have a marvelous time at Dooks, a lovely little club with famous views that has been thoroughly overshadowed by its more famous neighbors of Ballybunion, Killarney and Waterville. The course is unpretentious, but full of variety, challenge and amusement (wait until you try to find the eighteenth green). And to top it off, the clubhouse bar is well-nigh perfect.

～

IF YOU THINK THE ADAGE "TOO MANY CHEFS SPOIL THE broth" applies unfailingly to golf course design, then you haven't been to Dooks. The club has always prided itself on its self-sufficiency (its motto is *Per ardua ad astra*, "through hard work to the stars") but the members took the principle to an extreme in the early 1970s when they decided to expand their nine-hole course. Strapped for cash, the members decided to do it themselves. A committee of nine was struck, and each committee member was given the responsibility for designing one hole!

In any other place, this would surely be a recipe for disaster, but at Dooks, believe it or not, it has been a great success. The new holes are, for the most part, terrific. The members did all of the construction work themselves as well—from shaping greens to digging bunkers, to finding sod from construction sites. They even managed the difficult task of building a couple of lovely seaside holes on what had been pure beach sand.

It took a few years, but they saved a few pounds all right. The total cost of the nine-hole expansion, including design and construction, was about £2,500.

It is only one of the many curious developments that pepper Dooks's colorful history. The club, one of the oldest in Ireland, was founded in 1889 along the usual lines—a group of upper-class Protestants, bewitched with the new fad of golf then sweeping high society, were attracted to the beautiful setting on a somewhat protected piece of shoreline on Dingle Bay. Since then, however, life at Dooks has been decidedly unconventional. For example:

- Unusual for golf clubs of the time, Dooks attracted fervent Irish nationalists as members as early as 1908. However, club officials crossed out the names of signatures made in the Irish language from club records. The course was seriously damaged and temporarily closed during the political unrest of the early 1920s.
- In 1921 the captain of the club was a woman (Lady Gordon), a situation all but unheard of in Ireland, before or since. Another woman (Lina Hickson) held the important post of Honorary Secretary for sixteen years.
- In 1942, club members from the local area craftily held a meeting during a petrol shortage, and wrested control of the club from the monied vacationers who had run the club since its inception.
- In the 1960s the club faced eviction at the end of its lease. The members launched a national media campaign, comparing the situation to the famine of the nineteenth century when some absentee landlords let their tenants starve. A "Fighting Fund" was established, the landlord succumbed to rhetoric and public pressure, and the members bought the property outright for £7,000.
- The tables were turned in 1981 when environmentalists complained to the media that the club planned to drain a vital breeding ground for the Natterjack Toad. Turning the situation to their advantage, the members became the toad's great advocate, building new breeding sites for the amphibian and adopting it as their club logo.

The strange happenings seem set to continue. During our last visit to Dooks, members alerted us to the fact that the "yellow strip of sandhills" that *Irish Golf* described in 1909 was a favorite wooing spot of the former Bishop of Galway, whose reported affair with an American woman scandalized Ireland in 1992.

THE COURSE

The many challenges faced by the Dooks Golf Club have given it a strong identity, and cemented its far-flung membership (though the gentry has vanished, even today many members are vacationers from Dublin or Cork). It is matched by the strong personality of the links itself.

The first three holes and the last six are remnants of the original nine, but the middle holes are the result of the bizarre, design-by-committee process. At least one of the committee members—Dr. William O'Sullivan, the genius behind Killarney's expansion—had design experience, and *his* hole, the seventh, is where the course really comes alive. From a stunningly elevated tee the hole descends majestically down to the shore, with the gentle hills across the bay forming a graceful backdrop. The strong visual quality is, not surprisingly, reminiscent of Killarney.

After the seventh, there is a stretch of satisfying and difficult holes that weave in and out of the dunes and, in the case of the eleventh, run parallel to the beach. Though the course is not long (just over 6,000 yards) the greens are often elevated and undulating, a good test of one's short game.

Because the additions were made on the cheap there are no artificial touches. The course has a natural, traditional feel about it. The last six holes include two memorable par 3s—one has a saucer-shaped green and the other is played over the Natterjack Toad's breeding ground—and two par 4s rimmed with gorse that remind you a bit of Royal County Down.

Then there is the eighteenth, a thoroughly charming, if archaic par 5 with an invisible green. After hitting two good shots, first-time visitors to Dooks will find themselves on a fairway leading to nowhere. Some additional hunting will reveal the goal, set like some secret encampment in a depression just over a ridge. Yes, the approach shot will be blind, but anyone with a sense of humor will be charmed by the eighteenth, and will also have a great time in the wonderfully intimate bar.

Dooks is, in short, a great member's course. There are real and varied tests of judgment and skill at every turn, but prodigious length is not a requirement. The course remains a work in progress (after the success of the do-it-yourself expansion everyone at Dooks considers himself an architect!) and each successive captain seems compelled to leave his own mark on the links. What remains constant is the genuine Irish hospitality and the peaceful, seaside setting that makes a detour to Dooks so satisfying.

Location:	Eight miles southwest of Killorglin off N70 (Ring of Kerry)
Restrictions:	Guests may play weekdays, weekends by arrangement
Green Fee:	£16
Manager:	Michael Shanahan
Address:	Glenbeigh, Co. Kerry phone: (066) 68205 fax: (066) 68476

DIVERSIONS
The Southwest

COUNTY KERRY BOASTS WHAT MAY BE THE MOST BEAUTIFUL
scenery in all of Ireland. It includes the majestic Macgillycuddy's Reeks
mountain range and two breathtaking peninsulas, the Iveragh (better
known for the name of its principal roadway, the Ring of Kerry) and the
Dingle. It is also blessed with the golfing shrines of Ballybunion,
Waterville and Killarney, as well as fine links at Tralee, Dooks and Ceann
Sibéal. Indeed, an extraordinary golf journey may be had without leaving the confines of County Kerry.

Some may wish to base themselves in **Killarney** while they play
Kerry's golf courses. We think that would be a mistake, but the over-
touristed town is nevertheless the beginning point of the Ring of Kerry
and full of bed and breakfasts, currency exchanges and other tourist services. Stretching south and west from Killarney is Killarney National
Park, which is dominated by beautiful Lough Leane. For those who do
not get enough of the Lough when playing golf at Killarney, boat trips
and horseback excursions are easily arranged.

Macgillycuddy's Reeks form the spine of the Iveragh peninsula. The
tallest peak, Carrantuohill, is also the highest point in Ireland at 3,400
feet. The peninsula is encircled by the 100-mile **Ring of Kerry**. The
scenery, with deep lakes and mountains on the inside of the Ring and
cliffs and crashing surf to the outside, is simply spectacular. Most tour
buses circumnavigate the peninsula with few if any stops, in about four
hours. You will undoubtedly be stopping, however, at Waterville, which
lies almost exactly halfway around the Ring from Killarney, and perhaps
also at Dooks. Other interesting detours are Staigue Fort, which dates
from 1000 B.C., and Skellig Michael, a monastery which was established
around 600 A.D. Skellig Michael is located on Great Skellig island and
may be reached by boat most days from Ballinskelligs or Portmagee. The
trip takes just over an hour and can be thrilling in its own right on a blustery day. Skellig Michael is an eerie and austere site, with its ancient
buildings devoid of windows, and populated now by nothing but sea birds.

The otherwise unremarkable town of **Killorglin** is home to Puck Fair each year in August. This is the annual national gathering of the "tinkers," the nomads who have roamed the country for centuries. It is also a pagan fertility rite, having at its center a live male goat which is hoisted onto a fifty-foot-high platform. The pubs do not close for the duration of the fair's seventy-two hours, and musicians and dancers seem to be everywhere. It is not for the faint of heart.

Immediately north of the Ring of Kerry, across Dingle Bay, is the **Dingle Peninsula**. At its end is a fine links course, Ceann Sibéal, and the scenery one passes in getting there is awe-inspiring. Dingle is one of the few authentic *Gaeltacht* regions where the Irish language is widely spoken. It is covered in ruins, many from early Christian times. One of the best-preserved is the Gallarus Oratory, just east of Ballyferriter, which has been remarkably waterproof for over a thousand years. The ruins, the barren landscape and the often misty weather combine to create a haunting, mystical atmosphere on Dingle. Its roads can seem impossibly narrow at times, so slow down and take your time. The main center on the peninsula, Dingle Town, has only about 1,500 permanent residents, but there are well in excess of fifty pubs! This is an excellent place to search out traditional Irish music.

From a tourist's point of view, northern Kerry has little to match Dingle or the famous Ring. This can pose a problem for non-golfers if their companions have settled in at Ballybunion. The limited sightseeing options include Ardfert Cathedral, a Romanesque church about twenty miles to the south (most of the way back to Tralee); and the town of Listowel (ten miles away), which has the ruins of a castle in its main square. If you are driving between Ballybunion and Lahinch take advantage of the car ferry across the River Shannon between Tarbert and Killimer. It will take fifty miles off your journey.

If you decide to take the long way around the River Shannon, or you are using Shannon airport, **Limerick** will be close at hand. The Republic's third-largest city is rather drab and has a reputation for violence (the Limerick Leader newspaper and the American guidebook Let's Go Ireland became embroiled in something of a controversy when the latter referred to Limerick as "stab city"). The most important sight is St. Mary's Cathedral, which dates from 1300.

For those whose first order of business upon arriving in Ireland is to get to a pub, the famous (and tourist-packed) Durty Nellie's is just seven miles from Shannon Airport, on the main road to Limerick. Despite the crowds, the pub can be attractive on an evening when the weather is good—walk outside to the bridge and enjoy the fine view of the floodlit Bunratty Castle.

County Clare has two of Ireland's most important natural attractions—the Cliffs of Moher and the Burren. Even in a nation known for some dramatic coastal headlands, the **Cliffs of Moher** stand out. They stretch north for five miles from Liscannor, which is just a mile or so north of Lahinch. In fact, part of the cliffs are visible from several points on the Lahinch links, but they are much more dramatic when viewed from close range (just how close to the edge you wish to venture is a test of bravery or foolhardiness—the cliff edge is unstable in many places). The cliffs grow progressively higher from south to north, reaching about 700 feet. Perhaps the best vantage point of all to view the cliffs is from O'Brien's tower, at the north end. If the weather is clear you can see the Irish coast from Kerry to Connemara.

The **Burren** is a vast area of northern County Clare that is often compared to the moon. Burren literally means "rock," and that is about all you need to know. It is the home of many rare species of flowers which manage to sprout up between the limestone outcroppings in the spring. It also has literally hundreds of ancient stone forts. All of this is explained nicely at the Burren Display Centre located in Kilfenora. If by chance you are a cave explorer, the area is also for you. But for most, it is an eerie, barren desert.

Two villages in County Clare also merit a mention, if for very different reasons. **Doolin**, a tiny coastal village about ten miles north of Lahinch, is famous for its traditional Irish music. Try O'Connor's, McGann's or McDermott's pubs (or better yet, try them all—each is renowned throughout the country). Do not be confused if your map calls the village Fisherstreet—this is one and the same place. **Lisdoonvarna** is five miles to the east of Doolin. It is known as a spa town, but has achieved international fame for its annual matchmaking festival in September. This is not a joke; it is far from unheard of for tourists in attendance (especially young women) to receive serious offers of marriage.

It may be wishful thinking to call the southwestern coast of Ireland the Irish Riviera, but don't be surprised if you find palm trees and other sub-tropical plants in parts of County Cork. This is due to the influence of the Gulf Stream, which keeps the temperature between forty-five and sixty degrees Fahrenheit throughout the year. Indeed, there are many examples of trees and flowers that are otherwise found only in the Mediterranean countries. It is also extremely wet and, it almost goes without saying, very green. "There isn't much climate," a local saying goes, "but there's a lot of weather." The area around Cork City is also home to several new high-end golf clubs.

Cork is the largest city in the southwest by a wide margin and is Ireland's second city. Like any second city, it exhibits a fierce independence mixed with a touch of an inferiority complex. In the pub, for example, this is the only part of the Republic where Guinness does not hold utter superiority. The local Murphy's stout (and even the newcomer Beamish) are very popular here. Also, it is perhaps more Euro-centric than Dublin, with both English and French expatriate communities and respected film and jazz festivals.

Cork does not have an abundance of historic sites—much of the city was destroyed in the Civil War. The main attraction may be simply strolling through the compact downtown, sampling from the abundant pubs and cafes. The main shopping area is Patrick Street. The most important tourist attraction is the rather fanciful St. Finbarr's Cathedral, built in the 1870s in neo-Gothic style, whose spires are visible from much of the city. Also worthwhile is the Crawford Art Gallery, which has a strong collection of Irish art, particularly from the nineteenth century.

Some of Ireland's most famous tourist attractions may be easily reached from Cork. The **Blarney Stone** is located at Blarney, just five miles away. The stone is set high on a hill in Blarney Castle and, as most everyone knows, kissing it is said to confer "the gift of the gab." More likely, you will be the victim of the tourist trap, as Blarney is frightfully busy with tour buses and souvenir stands much of the year.

About forty-five miles to the north is **Cashel**, with the magnificent castle and cathedral on the Rock of Cashel. Much of the current structure dates from the eleventh through fifteenth centuries, though the site was the seat of the King of Munster in the first millennium and is said to have been visited by St. Patrick. It is most impressive when viewed from a distance, as it rises up from the flat plains known as the Golden Vale, and is reminiscent of Mont St. Michel in France or Assisi in Italy.

Kinsale, just to the west of Cork, is fast acquiring a reputation as the country's culinary capital. It was at one time a true fishing village, but has been considerably gentrified. It is now charming and quaint. The gourmet reputation was built chiefly on the establishment of the "good food circle," a group of upscale restaurants which focus primarily on the plentiful seafood available in Kinsale. The town was also the site of the Battle of Kinsale in 1601, in which the Irish aristocracy and their Spanish allies were defeated by the English. This was a decisive battle in the

English occupation of Ireland which would follow for the next 300 years.

The Irish Distillers Ltd. complex at Midleton is where all of the major Irish whiskies, with the exception of Bushmills, are produced. Recently, the Jameson Whiskey Heritage Centre has opened here, with a tour, various audio-visual presentations and tastings all available. Anyone interested in whiskey should take either this tour or the one offered by Bushmills in Northern Ireland.

THE GREAT ADVENTURE

ALTHOUGH FAMOUS IN THE VICTORIAN AGE, THE fascinating links in this thinly populated region have until recently been largely forgotten. Once a mecca for aristocratic holiday-makers from Britain, the counties in the Northwest were particularly affected by the Troubles, which sharply reduced traffic from Northern Ireland. The lingering sense of isolation in Sligo, Donegal and Mayo makes it our favorite part of Ireland. It is here where the sense of golfing adventure is most keen, where you will travel hours on narrow country roads to encounter excellent courses all but unknown outside Ireland. Some of these links are simply astonishing, while others offer an intoxicating mixture of seclusion, great golf, and matchless rural hospitality. And it is a pleasant surprise to learn that in many cases your green fee is supporting community development enterprises. Be it the magnificent light at Rosses Point, the pretzel-like drive to Rosapenna, or the cows you encounter on the fairway at Narin and Portnoo, there is lots to remember in the Northwest.

Of Princes and Peasants: Donegal's Rediscovered Golf Treasures

THERE IS PERHAPS NO MORE romantic adventure in all the golf world than a journey to Rosapenna and Portsalon, the obscure, almost forgotten links on the rugged Donegal coast.

Not long ago these nineteenth-century jewels were overgrown and neglected, in grave danger of fading into the fescue-covered sand dunes. But now they have been patiently and lovingly restored, the golfing equivalent of a rediscovered art treasure. To play them today is a unique thrill—one that combines intense nostalgia, an exquisite slice of golf history and some of the most enchanting and challenging links golf anywhere.

Rosapenna and Portsalon are not well-known names even in Ireland, but in the twilight of the Victorian era these were golf destinations of the highest order. Situated only a few miles apart, they were among the very first golf resorts—the Pinehursts and Pebble Beaches of their day.

Rosapenna was built in 1890 by the Earl of Leitrim, one of Ireland's biggest landowners, after a design by Old Tom Morris, golf's first great professional. The Earl built a splendid hotel out of Norwegian pine next to the links on picturesque Sheephaven Bay, and promoted it as a wilderness retreat for the English nobility.

Not that the guests were roughing it. The Rosapenna had its own orchestra, a first class wine cellar, and formal evening dress was expected at dinner. Recreation included lawn tennis, croquet, hunting, fishing (on a private lake) and the new art of photography (the hotel boasted its own dark room).

"Nothing is wanting to promote the comfort of visitors or enhance their pleasure or sport while staying at this liberally conducted establishment," raved an 1896 guidebook to Ireland.

At almost exactly the same time, a similarly luxurious resort was taking shape a few miles to the east on Lough Swilly, a fjord-like finger of the Atlantic. The Portsalon Hotel and Golf Links had its own well-connected founder—one Colonel B. J. Barton, High Sheriff of Donegal and later aide-de-camp to Edward VII and George V. The resort even ran its own steamer to ferry guests from the train terminus farther south. In 1896 Portsalon was called "one of the best, if not the best course in Ireland" by *Golfing*, a prestigious British golf magazine of the time.

Photographs and postcards from the era show gentlemen golfers in waistcoats and bow ties (and often a pipe) and lady golfers in corsets, long dresses and long sleeves. Only the caddies—in bare feet—strike a discordant note, a reminder that the resorts were only for the few. In the late nineteenth century, Donegal was as impoverished as the Third World countries where many golf resorts are built today. The local Irish peasantry lived in thatched huts and the terrible famines of the 1840s, when fully a third of the Irish people died or emigrated, were a living memory.

Irish independence did not immediately change the class system, and Rosapenna and Portsalon flourished until after the Second World War. In 1962 a fire broke out in one of the Rosapenna's guest wings. As the smoke seeped into the dining room, it is said that the Duke of St. Albans ordered another bowl of soup, explaining to the waiter that he wanted to be "the last person to eat in the Old Rosapenna."

And so he was. The building was destroyed, and a newer, less majestic hotel gradually took shape. The golf course deteriorated rapidly under a succession of indifferent owners. By the late 1970s it was difficult to distinguish it from the surrounding grazing land.

A similar fate befell Portsalon. As the stream of aristocrats from war-weary England dwindled, the hotel declined rapidly and the once great links became a ghost of its former self. The few travellers who came upon it paid their green fee in Rita's Bar, a local watering hole. Records show that in 1975, a mere £174 was spent on golf course maintenance.

As the 1980s began, Rosapenna and Portsalon teetered on the edge of extinction. But then the story takes one more, happily ironic turn. These splendid courses, designed as playgrounds for English aristocrats, were to be rescued by the descendants of their barefoot Irish caddies.

In the case of Rosapenna, the savior was one Frank Casey, who bought the rundown hotel complex for £500,000 in 1981. Casey's father had been the Old Rosapenna's head waiter, and had served the Duke of St. Albans his famous bowl of soup.

"When I was a boy, no local would dare think of going into the front door of the Rosapenna Hotel," remembers Casey, who left Donegal as a young man to seek his fortune. "It was full of Bentleys and Rolls Royces."

Casey is a thoroughly practical man and can't quite see the romance in his own story—the son of the head waiter returning as owner. He insists the decision to purchase and revive the golf course was strictly business.

"Everyone who comes here has a set of clubs in the boot," he says. "The golf course puts heads on beds and makes the money."

The course today is more likely to be played by a middle-class German tourist than an English peer, but the unspoiled and haunting beauty of the rugged Atlantic coastline remains a chief attraction. Though few reliable records survive, we do know that Harry Vardon lengthened and revised Morris's course in 1906 with the new and longer rubber-core ball in mind. He promptly declared that "Rosapenna Links can now take rank with the best championship courses in the United Kingdom." It is thought that James Braid assisted Vardon and that H. S. Colt (designer of Royal Portrush and Rosses Point) made slight revisions some time in the 1930s.

If so, the Rosapenna that Frank Casey restored was an amalgam of the efforts of four of the greatest names in golf history, and this may explain the very different quality of the two nines. The front side is surprisingly flat (given the large dunes all around) and subtle, while the back curves around a steep and windswept hill between Sheephaven Bay on one hand, and Mulroy Bay on the other.

The change of pace begins in earnest on the uphill eleventh—an adaptation of an Old Tom Morris original—where a decent drive is needed just to clear the busy road that heads into Rosapenna village.

The short par-4 twelfth is also vintage Old Tom. The choice is to lay up 220 yards out in front of another road (as Old Tom surely intended) or let it all hang out and try for the green. There is more than a bit of anticipation for the big hitter as he crosses the road and slips through the cattle gate—will he have an eagle putt, a blast from a pot bunker, or an impossible shot from the fierce rough?

These two holes are, alas, also on death row. Insurance coverage on the four road-crossing holes is prohibitive, says Casey, and the old course will soon be merged with a new eighteen designed by the outstanding

Irish architect, Eddie Hackett. There will be an Old Tom Morris Nine, but some of the Scot's most intriguing work will disappear forever.

After years of decline, the Portsalon Hotel also went up in smoke. The adjacent land, including the golf course, was put up for sale in 1984. A clutch of local golf enthusiasts discussed buying the course, but their semi-formal "club" had exactly £67 in the bank. The asking price was sixty-eight *thousand* pounds—a pittance, in retrospect, but a fortune for a handful of rural families in a small village in one of the most depressed areas of a relatively poor country. No bank would loan them the money, so the club members organized a lottery of a thousand tickets at £100 apiece. Much to their own astonishment, the scheme worked. On November 28, 1986 the deed of the land was solemnly transferred in a ceremony in Rita's Bar.

"I remember Portsalon golf club long ago when it was the exclusive domain of a chosen few and locals earned one shilling and six pence [15 cents] a day for caddying if they were lucky," said club president Neil Blaney in a speech. "It is appropriate that Portsalon is now owned and run by local people for the benefit of this community."

As enjoyable as Rosapenna is, it is difficult to compete with Portsalon for sheer golfing pleasure. A century after an obscure Portrush pro named Thompson laid out the original course, its seaside setting can be spoken of in the same breath as Pebble Beach. Situated on the curve of a perfectly arched and deserted beach, with the Knockalla mountains all around, Portsalon offers a series of unsurpassed views from its many elevated tees. You won't find your ball in cattle hoof prints at Pebble Beach (a free drop at Portsalon), but you won't find a day's worth of exhilarating golf for the equivalent of twenty dollars, either.

The excitement begins at once—there are few courses in the world where salt water comes into play so quickly and dramatically. The first is an uphill dogleg around a high cliff next to the bay that just dares you to cheat too much. The tee box for the par-3 second is found *under* the same seawall you just played over—you shoot entirely over water to a green that juts into the bay. The third, unchanged from 1891, is an outstanding downhill par 4 played across and along the beach, with a green guarded by two ancient rock formations. It is perhaps the best opening three holes in Ireland.

The rest of the course is in no way a letdown. The glorious beach is a constant visual companion, and often a threat. On a couple of occasions you tread, Robinson Crusoe style, through drifts of sand to the tee. The fairways are often narrow and extraordinarily undulating, harkening back to a pre-bulldozer age.

Like Rosapenna, Portsalon has been lengthened and modified to respond to twentieth-century equipment, but at least seven holes are more than a century old. They include the eighth, a delightful par 3 that features a tiny green set inside a horseshoe of high mounds. The mounds are so close to the green that anyone who hits a wayward drive must try a zany bankshot on their second.

Another par 3, the twelfth, is uphill and completely blind, and crosses the eleventh green for good measure. It is followed by the Matterhorn, a singular double-dogleg par 4 that looks about 800 yards long from the elevated tee. The views of the beach are stunning.

Portsalon is no less challenging for being quirky, and the par of 69 (over 5,900 yards) is a daunting target. The members are considering changes to do away with the criss-crosses, so it's worth playing before too many old-fashioned wrinkles are ironed out.

In the new clubhouse after the round you just might meet Cathal Toland, an unemployed mill worker who is also the extremely accommodating honorary secretary. Memberships at Portsalon cost only £150 a year, and the club has grown by leaps and bounds. Greatly improved conditioning has also drawn a lucrative influx of Irish visitors. Since the members took over in 1986, annual revenue from green fees has swelled from £2,000 to over £100,000.

While spending more time is highly recommended, it is certainly possible to play Rosapenna and Portsalon in a day. If so, start with Rosapenna; even if you don't stay overnight at the new hotel (as modern and forthright as Frank Casey himself) it's worth having a breakfast of fresh kippers in the comfortable dining room.

"From Rosapenna it's a 16 mile drive to Portsalon—weird in the extreme." This description from a 1912 travel guide is not entirely outdated—the road winds madly around Mulroy Bay and you are as likely as not to encounter a flock of sheep blocking your way. Count on forty-five minutes.

The upside of this remoteness is that on a weekday these extraordinary, old-fashioned links are apt to be all but deserted. It is easy to feel transported back in time, to an era of waistcoats, steamships, brassies and gutta-percha balls. But as lovely as the nostalgia is, it is satisfying to know that these wonderful golfing destinations are no longer oases of privilege, but are, at last, as Irish as a glass of stout around a peat fire.

King of the Links

IT IS A NUMBINGLY cold November morning, and we are stumbling our way through a rough field along the seawall near the tiny village of Ballyconneely on the west coast of Ireland. I cannot recall when I have ventured out of doors on a nastier day. It is no more than forty-five degrees and I am being thrashed by rain whipping off the ocean. The wind is deafening and the raindrops feel like ice pellets on my cheek.

We have reached a sturdy barbed-wire fence, and my companion, a frail eighty-five-year-old man in rubber boots and a heap of black rain gear, has taken it into his head that we need to roll *underneath* it. The bottom wire can't be more than a foot from the ground. But Eddie Hackett is already on his hands and knees before I have a chance to suggest an alternative course of action.

"Jack Nicklaus wouldn't do this, would he?" shouts the dean of Irish golf architects, as he lays flat on his back and begins to squirm his way under the dangerous-looking wire. There is a gleam in his eye and just a hint of mischief in his lilting Irish voice. "Maybe he would design the course from an aer-o-plane."

Frankly, at that moment the inside of an airplane sounded pretty good to me. So did a hot whiskey in front of a blazing fire. I didn't fancy rolling under that fence. Or three others like it. I didn't feel like wading through a creek, or stomping through heaps of seaweed. I have never been so wet, or so cold. But it was a once-in-a-lifetime chance to see the greatest links designer of our generation in action.

Don't be embarrassed if you've never heard of Eddie Hackett. Almost nobody has outside his native Ireland. And you could be forgiven for finding it hard to believe that he has never even *seen* a course designed by an American architect, except on television. Or that his fee for creating some of the best seaside courses in the world was £200. Or that he goes to Mass every day and reads the *Imitation of Christ* every night. Or that he's still going strong at the age of eighty-five.

But it is, if I may say so, no blarney.

"I find that nature is the best architect!" shouts Hackett as he trudges through knee-high grass, pacing the width of a fairway that at this point exists only in his mind. "I just try to dress up what the Good Lord provides. Of course He gave us a lot in this place."

On this most miserable of mornings, Hackett is designing an additional nine holes for the Connemara Golf Club. He laid out the original course in 1970 for a local community group that thought a golf course might spur economic development in a region devastated by unemployment and emigration. The golf course weaves through a stark landscape of exposed slabs of rock, and on a fair day it is hauntingly beautiful, swallowed up by the natural elements.

"They had no money, you know," Hackett continues. "I told them if you're that keen on golf, I'll go down and I'll put a stone in for a tee and a pin in for a green, and you can pay me when you can."

Connemara is only one of a string of magnificent seaside courses along Ireland's rugged western coastline that have earned Hackett a permanent and unique place in golf history. They are not only beautiful and challenging tests of golf, they will be among the last links courses ever built.

There is, alas, no linksland to speak of in the United States, though courses such as Shinnecock Hills and Pebble Beach imitate some of the features of links golf. It is the famous links of Scotland—St. Andrews, Muirfield, Troon and Turnberry—that are best known to golfers (and even non-golfers) in North America, thanks in large part to the television exposure of the British Open.

But the fantastic linksland found in Ireland is in a class of its own. It is not only the historic and world-famous links of Ballybunion, Lahinch, Portmarnock, Royal County Down and Royal Portrush that set the Emerald Isle apart. It is that Ireland also has *new* links. Until recently, the west coast of Ireland was the last place on earth with large stretches of undeveloped linksland. Much of this potentially priceless golfing ground was found on commonages—grazing land owned jointly by local farmers. While better known designers jetted around the world, producing luxury resorts from Morocco to Bali, Eddie Hackett worked patiently with communities that wanted to turn these largely unproductive lands into golf courses.

"Eddie is the unsung hero of Irish golf," says Pat Ruddy, Ireland's leading golf journalist and an architect himself. "At a time when there was no money, Eddie Hackett travelled the highways and byways of Ireland. Half the people playing golf in Ireland are doing so because of Eddie Hackett. And I don't know anyone who has said the slightest bad word about him."

Father Peter Waldron, an avid golfer who spearheaded the development of Connemara, goes further.

"Oh Eddie Hackett is a saint, you know. He is totally self-effacing, and he has more integrity than almost anybody I have ever come across. And he works for pennies."

Hackett's best-known creation is probably **Waterville,** a severe but breathtaking test of golf on the picturesque Ring of Kerry that is now ranked (by *Golf World* magazine) as the best golf course built in Britain and Ireland in the last fifty years.

But if you travel north up the thinly populated coast from Waterville, you will encounter a string of hauntingly beautiful links with lyrical names that are every bit as memorable. All were designed by Eddie Hackett, often on shoestring budgets, and all are accessible and inexpensive for the visiting golfer.

The first stop is **Ceann Sibéal**—an undiscovered gem thrust out on the farthest extremities of the Dingle Peninsula. **Connemara** is next, followed by **Carne,** a new course built as a non-profit community project on the remote and economically depressed Belmullet Peninsula. Whereas Connemara is relatively flat, Carne is a breathtaking ride through some of golf's most imposing sand dunes, a kind of Ballybunion on steroids.

Although tamer and less exposed to the Atlantic winds, **Enniscrone,** in County Sligo, is one of the most popular links among Irish golfers, with thrilling elevated tees, superb par 3s, and a series of exquisite short par 4s through wonderfully contorted terrain. Further up the coast Nick Faldo warms up for the British Open at **Donegal,** a sweeping, stately layout that many consider Hackett's finest achievement. Finally, at the northern tip of Ireland, you can put your feet up at the historic **Rosapenna Hotel,** where Hackett has expanded the existing course by Old Tom Morris and Harry Vardon.

Hackett's graceful and natural designs are the perfect complement to the much older west-coast links of Ballybunion, Lahinch and County Sligo. Together they make up what is arguably the most stunning stretch of seaside golf in the world.

So why is Eddie Hackett not better known? The remoteness of his best courses has certainly played a part, as has the fact that Hackett has stayed so close to home. In the last thirty years he has designed or remodelled all or part of eighty-five courses—a remarkable total for a man with no partner and no employees—but *every last one of them* has been in Ireland (Robert Trent Jones, in contrast, has built courses in at least twenty-three countries).

But the main reason for Hackett's relative obscurity is surely his striking reluctance to blow his own horn. I asked him about it when I met him again in the relative calm of his cluttered Dublin house (a widower, he lives alone, though his children live nearby).

"We Irish had a terrible inferiority complex, with the English occupation and the way we were terrorized and savaged," he explained. "It's only starting to go with the new generation."

Hackett's gentlemanly manners were very much in evidence during my visit. A teetotaller, he kept lifting himself out of his ancient easy chair to fill up my glass of Jameson's. He wore a cardigan over a shirt and tie, and as he told his life story, with the aid of yellowed newspaper clippings and faded photographs, it struck me that Hackett is one of golf's most important connections to an earlier, golden age. He must surely be the last man alive who can say that he had lunch with James Braid, Harry Vardon, and J. H. Taylor—the Great Triumvirate that dominated golf at the turn of century. It happened at the British Open at Hoylake in 1936 and is one of Hackett's most cherished memories.

Born in a Dublin pub in 1910, twelve years before Irish independence, Hackett survived a Dickensian childhood of periodic penury and grave illness (he spent long stretches in hospital with tuberculosis). One of the brighter moments of his youth came the day his father announced proudly that he had become one of the first Catholic tradesmen to be allowed into a golf club in Ireland. Young Eddie took to the game too, the one sport his doctors would allow him to play.

His father went bankrupt while Eddie was still a teenager, so Hackett was thankful to get a job as a clubmaker at the Royal Dublin Golf Club. He worked on his game, became an assistant professional, and in 1939 landed the job as the head professional at the exclusive Portmarnock links for the princely sum of £10 a week.

"As the professional I was never allowed into the clubhouse," Hackett remembers. "I'm an honorary member now, and I still don't go into the clubhouse. It's just the way I am."

Hackett left Portmarnock in 1950 to take part in an ill-advised business venture. The next few years turned out to be the worst of his life, and he spent another nine months in bed in a near-fatal battle with meningitis. Hackett returned to golf almost by chance in the early 1960s when the Golfing Union of Ireland asked him to give teaching clinics across the country. One of the clubs was looking for someone to design a golf course (one of the first full-length courses to be built in thirty years) and Hackett's name was recommended. He stumbled his way through the job and suddenly he was an expert. For all intents and purposes he was Ireland's only golf architect.

"In those years, there was no one else to go to," says Hackett, "unless you went to an English architect, but they were expensive. All my life I've been charging too little, but at that time, you see, I wouldn't have the confidence in my abilities."

On occasion, Hackett even tried to convince clubs *not* to hire him.

"I told them that if I was in your position, and I wanted to make some money, I wouldn't use Hackett, I'd use a Nicklaus or a Palmer or a Trent Jones."

In two notable cases, clubs followed his advice, and hired Arnold Palmer (Tralee) and Robert Trent Jones (Ballybunion New). Both are worthy efforts, built on spectacular terrain, but they have a theatricality out of sync with the great Irish and British links. The consensus in Ireland is that they don't rank with Hackett's best, which have an air of maturity and grace rare in young courses of any kind.

Hackett's courses tend to be long from the back tees, with clearly visible landing areas, large greens and spectacular elevated tees. Despite his great love for the classic links of Ireland and Scotland (which he played as a young professional), Hackett eschews two of their most common features—blind tee shots and hidden hazards—and prefers to make a hole's challenges clearly visible in the modern style. Every one of his links courses is enormously enjoyable, even thrilling to play, with at least a half-dozen holes that will stop you dead in your tracks in admiration.

The admiration is always as much for Mother Nature as for the architect, however. Hackett never draws attention to himself. There are no bizarre sandtraps, ostentatious ledges, artificial mounds or strangely shaped greens so common in modern design. One of his most beautiful holes in Ireland is the eleventh at Waterville, which tumbles entirely naturally through a long channel of majestic dunes. The very next hole, called the Mass, plays over a valley that sheltered Catholics as they worshipped in secret during periods of religious repression at the hands of the English.

"When I made that hole the contractors, local men, came to me and they said, 'Eddie, we're not going to dig up or touch this ground for you. Because Mass was celebrated in the hollow.' I said 'You needn't be worried.'

"And we never touched it. It's a plateau green, it's natural. And there's not a bunker on it either. It doesn't need one and that's the best tribute you can pay a hole."

Because Hackett's layouts are so sensitive to the natural terrain, there is always a consistent style and rhythm to his links that takes its theme from the specific natural surroundings. Nothing seems artificial or imposed. Hackett would be horrified to think his courses looked like one another—he doesn't want to leave his signature about. He doesn't talk so much about designing golf holes as *finding* them, and he is proudest when he can point to a hole and say "it's just as nature."

"I could never break up the earth the way they tell me Jack [Nicklaus] and Arnold [Palmer] do," he says. "You disrupt the soil profile and anyway, it's unnatural. I use what's there within reason. You're only as good as what the Lord gives you in features. And you can never do with trees what you can do with sand dunes."

Hackett has also made a virtue of necessity. Many of his clients couldn't afford bulldozers. But in the process he has touched the lives of ordinary people in a way that few architects have.

"Looking back it was a growing and achievement point, and a self-believing point for the community," says Father Peter Waldron of the original golf development at Connemara in 1970. "And economically it turned the key to a whole new area of opportunities."

Built for perhaps £50,000 with huge amounts of volunteer labor ("we never had to move a rock," Hackett says proudly), the golf course is now responsible for pumping more than £1 million a year into the local community from overseas and Irish visitors.

Waldron, who is still on the board of Connemara, told me that Hackett was seriously ill before embarking on the expansion. It's not something that Hackett raises during my visit with him, but near the end of my talk I ask him about his faith. Religion can be a delicate subject in Ireland, and at first Hackett seems reluctant to talk about it, as if he could be misinterpreted.

"You could say I would be religious, yes, but that doesn't mean I can't be friendly with others," he replies. "I'm not narrow.

"But my own faith is very strong. There's one prayer from the *Imitation of Christ* that I read every night: 'Dear Lord, give me grace to be meek and humble of heart, to be glad when people think little of me.'

"I've been very lucky in my life. Most people never get to design a links. I've done ten. When I'm out [on the course] I pray to the Lord to give me the light to do what's right."

A Miracle at Connemara

(The following story is based on actual recollections. It is a true story, although a few artistic licenses have been taken.)

IT WAS DURING THE friendly chatter and tea-cup clatter of an Irish baptism that Peter Waldron's dream began to take shape. It was 1968 and he had just been transferred to Clifden, a remote seaside town of one thousand souls on the perimeter of fabled Connemara. Between biscuits and cucumber sandwiches, the twenty-eight-year-old priest said hello to Eddie Foley, a respected local businessman and father of the child he had just baptized.

"I heard about your golf course idea," Eddie Foley said with a good-natured smile. Some of Father Waldron's tea spilled onto the floor. "You're mad, you know that. But whatever chance you have, you are best off keeping a low profile and keeping your cards close to your chest."

A day later, Father Waldron heard a knock on his door. It was Paul Hughes, a local hotelier, a man he had not met properly before. Like himself, Hughes was new to Clifden, something of a *blow-in* in the tightly knit and economically depressed community. After a minimum of pleasantries Hughes came to the point.

"Padre, I've just bought the Abbeyglen and I want to build the place up," he said. "The way I see it, this town needs things. Most of all, it seems to me, it needs what you are after."

After a few seconds it dawned on Father Waldron what the man might be getting at.

"You're talking about the golf course?" he suggested, a bit hopefully.

"Yes."

"Are you interested?"

"Definitely."

The two men shook hands. What it all meant, however, Father

85

Waldron wasn't at all sure.

In his spare time, Father Waldron had taken to stalking a beautiful stretch of shoreline about five miles from the edge of town. The rocky terrain had been used for centuries as grazing land by a group of local families. With the exception of the occasional herd of sheep, it was usually deserted and Waldron could visualize his dream in splendid solitude. But one day his reverie was interrupted by a man wearing a pair of football boots and swinging an ancient golf club.

"I'm Paid Kennelly, the local teacher," the man said, shaking hands. Once the introductions were over, he said:

"I hear you're interested in building a golf course."

"Actually I am," the young priest replied, not a little surprised. "Are you interested?"

"Well, I couldn't do much for you, but I could tell you who owns what."

The teacher went on to explain that there were three parcels of land. The first was a commonage of 176 acres, with twenty-two owners. That wouldn't be easy, in fact impossible to buy. But the second parcel was a commonage with 110 acres and only eleven owners.

"I think you may well be able to buy that," the teacher said.

"But aren't commonages notoriously difficult to buy?" asked Father Waldron, knowing full well that any sale would require the agreement of each and every farmer.

"That they are," replied Kennelly. "But particularly with yourself being who you are, I think you might be able to do it. If you go about it right! The third parcel is owned individually by the McDonough family, a chap named Mickey McDonough. Mickey is positive about things, one of nature's gentlemen. I think you'd find Mickey very nice and easy to deal with."

Building a golf course had not exactly been part of Peter Waldron's future plans when he accepted a place in the venerable seminary college at Maynooth, not far from Dublin. The heart of Catholic learning in Ireland, Maynooth sent wave after wave of young priests across Ireland to take up positions of intellectual, educational and moral authority that had been the lot of the priesthood for a millennium. As far back as the eighth century Irish monks had been renowned throughout Europe for their erudition and wisdom, and Ireland had been a lonely beacon of Christian learning during the Dark Ages. If the idea of an Irish state had been battered by subsequent invasions and the barbarities of English conquest, the authority of the Church had survived and even been strengthened. During religious oppression, Irish Catholics turned to their Church to express their nationalism, attending Mass in secret. After independence in 1922 the first leaders of the Free State gladly ceded control over much of Ireland's social policy to Church leaders.

Priests did more than preach and attend to their pastoral duties—they were expected to lead all local institutions. There was one thing that the parish priest, the school principal and the president of the local Gaelic Games club had in common—he was almost always the same man!

In the 1960s Ireland was an oasis of faith in an increasingly secular Europe, but Maynooth was not inured to the social change occurring elsewhere. Civil rights and anti-war movements in America, student activism in France, the emergence of new nations in Africa and Asia—it was an exciting and potent backdrop for the impassioned debates taking place inside the stone walls of the seminary.

Peter Waldron and his classmates were weaned on the doctrine that they should make a positive contribution to the communities they would serve. If you were a priest you were a community leader. And you must exercise that responsibility for the benefit of the people, in whatever way you saw fit.

Waldron's graduation also coincided with a resurgent "Save the West" movement. The coastal communities in the west of Ireland were in catastrophic shape. Much of the land was agriculturally poor, the fishing industry had no future and tourism was still in its infancy. Young people were leaving in droves for the streets of London and New York. Peter Waldron embraced the broad definition of a priest's responsibilities, and was pleased to be posted to Clifden in July, 1968 (he would assist Father Dan Corcoran, who had just turned eighty-five).

The idea of building a golf course as a form of community development struck Father Waldron very early on. For one thing, he had played golf since the age of ten. For another, he knew the Irish Tourist Board was subsidizing a course in Westport in neighboring County Mayo.

Clifden was different, however—much poorer, smaller and more remote. Most people in Connemara had never even seen a golf course, and the only club they had swung was a hurling stick. The lads also played Gaelic football, and the girls a bit of camogie (a form of hurling), but mostly life was an effort to put food on the table.

In Clifden, and indeed in the whole of Connemara, there was no place at all to play, unless you counted the pitch-and-putt course that the lighthouse keepers had built on Slyne Head to relieve the boredom. The nearest proper course was in Galway, fifty miles away over twisting, narrow roads.

But if not a golf course, what? The idea got stuck in the young cleric's mind, and either he couldn't or wouldn't dislodge it. It was hard to look at a vacant piece of land without imagining a flagstick on it, and on more than one occasion he found himself lamenting that the most promising holes always seemed to be on bogs.

All this he kept to himself as he threw himself into his duties. Life in any new parish was an endless cycle of house calls, baptisms, weddings, funerals, Masses and meetings, with visits to the hospital, orphanges and the convent thrown in. And since Old Dan was ailing, the young lad was expected to pick up the slack.

He loved it, of course. He felt privileged to have the opportunity to serve, and he genuinely loved the straightforward integrity of the inhabitants of this rugged and starkly beautiful land. If any people were the salt of the earth, these people were. Father Waldron wanted to explore every corner of his parish, meet every family, and learn about the lives they led. And the more he learned, the more he wanted to make a difference here. The idea of a golf course percolated in the back of his mind. Until that fateful day in May, that is, when he decided to take a drive down the Ballyconneely road.

It was a beautiful morning, and Waldron was full of anticipation. In five months he had developed a keen sense of responsibility for his new parish, even a sense of proprietorship, and he enjoyed getting to know his new "territory." Navigating his way down the pretzel-like road past Ballyconneely village and further past the primary school, he turned right into a narrow lane bounded by stone walls.

After a hundred yards or so the road suddenly opened up into a wide stretch of grassland. Father Waldron stopped the car in amazement, and found himself walking knee deep through this unexpected "prairie." To his left it extended to the edge of the headland, some fifty feet above the crashing surf. To his right it rose gradually into a wild tumble of Connemara rock. In the distance the Twelve Bens provided a stunning backdrop. But it was the sudden expanse of grass and sea and sky that overwhelmed him.

Although he was very much alone, Father Waldron let out an audible sigh, followed by a self-mocking chuckle. "Here then, Peter, is your golf course!"

As always, it was all a person could do to keep up with Eddie Hackett, as he strode up through the fields that still belonged to Mickey McDonough. On this early July morning he was going over the layout one last time with Father Waldron, showing him where he had put the stakes for each tee and green. There was such a vivid sense of purpose when Eddie was out on the linksland, at such odds with the reserved sixty-year-old gentleman that Father Waldron had first met in the Abbeyglen Hotel just a few months earlier. Father Waldron was amazed (and initially alarmed if the truth be told) that Eddie—as he was known to everyone—had done the work so quickly and so confidently. The course seemed to just fall together before his eyes. Even before the land had been secured, Father Waldron had spent hours and hours debating with himself and others the merits of this and that routing. The possibilities seemed to be endless. But for Eddie there was only one.

A man from the tourist board had introduced the Connemara golf course committee to Eddie Hackett. The committee had hoped to secure a development grant, but so far the board had agreed only to pay Hackett's expenses for an appraisal of the golfing potential of the land. Hackett had been well known in golf circles as a club professional at Portmarnock in the 1940s, but had turned to golf architecture rather late in life. He had only a couple of courses to his credit, though he was designing the grand new course down the coast at Waterville—the dream project of Jack Mulcahy, an Irish-born American industrialist with (the word was) bottomless pockets.

On the day of that first visit—a fine October day in 1970—Peter Waldron had been unaccountably nervous. What if Eddie Hackett didn't see what was so obvious to him, that this was a place blessed by God and by nature—a perfect place for a golf course?

The doubts were vanquished by the gleam in Eddie Hackett's eye as he emerged from Paul Hughes's car to shake his hand, not far from where the young padre had first met the local school teacher. Eddie didn't say much—preferring to listen to the explanations and theories that came tumbling out from Hughes, Waldron and Graeme Allen, another member of the committee.

"Do you have any ideas yourself about how the course should be laid out?" Eddie asked them, and indeed they did. He heard them out, all the while taking in the land with an intensity of a general examining a battle plan.

"You have a marvelous piece of land here," he told them at last. "And it will make a fine golf course indeed." Then he inquired about where he could go for evening Mass.

In the intervening months Hackett had returned to the course to finalize the design—undeterred by the growing worries of Paul Hughes and the committee. Not for the last time they had run out of money, and despaired about building the course. They simply couldn't pay Mr. Hackett for another trip to Connemara.

"Eddie, there's no use coming down," Paul Hughes said over the phone to Eddie's home in Dublin. "We have no money to build the golf course. I don't think we go ahead just now."

"Listen Paul," Eddie told him. "Let me go down there. I'll design the course for you and you can pay me when you can. We'll put pins in the virgin soil. You just have to promise me one thing—even if you can't mow the grass at first, you'll stick to the right design."

So Eddie had come, and spent two more days scouring the landscape from every possible angle, considering each swale and rock. He was intent on disturbing as little ground as possible, on weaving the course through dark Connemara rock which protruded through the ground in many spots. This was fine with the committee, which had precious little money for bulldozers, but for Hackett there seemed to be a principle at stake.

"Mother nature is the best architect," he told them. "I just try to work with what the Good Lord provides."

Now it was the following summer, and Eddie and Father Waldron had reached the fifteenth hole. It was a long par 4, in the heart of Mickey McDonough's old property. Eddie pointed out the stake for the men's and women's tees and trudged through the knee-high fescue to the site of the green. Father Waldron was confused.

"So that's the stake for the fifteenth green, Eddie," he said, gesturing to a stake at the foot of two massive outcrops of rock.

"That's right," said Eddie Hackett.

"But what's that stake up there, then, *behind* the rocks. It can't be the next tee can it?"

Eddie Hackett looked up at where Father Waldron was pointing and assumed his most thoughtful countenance.

"Well now, let me explain. Sometimes I put down a stake for an alternative green. I like to put down the idea." He paused, as if this new level of abstraction required time to sink in.

"I know in your circumstances you will be going in the short term for this stake here. But certainly the *idea* would be the other one. It would, of course, be very difficult in your circumstances and I know that you really can't afford that now. But I wanted to put down the idea for you to consider. For the future, you understand."

It was funny how a simple stake in the ground could put one into such turmoil. Father Waldron's brain was saying one thing, his heart another. The last thing the project needed was another financial surprise. But elevating the green behind the rocks would make for an incredible hole. Out here, today, in the bracing morning air, in the heady company of Ireland's foremost architect, that green seemed to make all the difference. It seemed to make it all worthwhile—the meetings, the negotiations, the haggles with the bank and the tourist board. He could literally feel himself rise to the bait.

"Don't be so sure, Eddie, I think we can afford it. It looks right to me. Sure we'll find the money. Somehow."

"Are you *sure*?" asked Eddie Hackett gravely, as if the young priest was making the most important decision of his life. "Because it's going to be expensive. You are going to have to knock about six feet off a huge sheet of rock—an awful lot of rock. But I must say it will make such a lovely hole. Are you sure, now?"

"I'm sure, Eddie."

A huge smile spread over Eddie Hackett's face, his back straightened and he seemed almost to rise from the ground. It reminded Father Waldron of a bird puffing up its feathers.

"Father, that decision changes everything. It puts this project on a whole new plane." Eddie reached over and shook the priest's hand. "Now I know we're going for the best."

"Eddie, don't get my hopes up. It must be difficult for you working here after doing that course in Waterville with all of Uncle Jack's money."

"Oh no, no," Eddie Hackett said, turning his gaze to the austere beauty of the rocky terrain. "Mr. Mulcahy may have the money, but you've got the place. There's no place like here."

Now it was Father Waldron's turn to be puffed up. He knew he had been had, of course. In that completely disingenuous way of his, Eddie Hackett had engineered the whole thing. But Father Waldron didn't care one whit.

~

Although the McDonough property was critical to the project, Father Waldron knew instinctively that he should not rush Mickey. He had met with him many times, updating him on the plans and the progress, but never mentioning money. Father Waldron would tell others on the committee that Mickey was the most reasonable, fair, positive, intelligent, humorous man you could talk to—but he had no idea what he would ask for the land. If we trusted Mickey, he would do the right thing.

That was a fine position to take, but time was beginning to run out. Most of the owners of the commonages had by now agreed to sell. Eddie Hackett had laid out the course. No one was going to contribute funds to the project without an agreement in place with Mickey McDonough. After all, he owned the back nine!

But just then, during another of Father Waldron's visits, Mickey took him by surprise. After the obligatory pleasantries, Father Waldron had shown Mickey the fifteenth green and how it had been transformed from an idea to a reality.

It was as if Mickey was reading his mind.

"Father, you know we haven't mentioned money at all," Mickey said out of the blue.

"I know that Mickey."

"You know it's time for us to mention money."

"I know Mickey," Father Waldron said with a mixture of anticipation and dread. "So you're talking about it now."

"What do you think it's worth?" Mickey asked, gesturing to the tumultuous landscape that was all but useless for farming, but perfect, they both knew, for golf. The young priest was quiet for a moment, and then said carefully:

"Well, what were you thinking of asking, Mickey?"

Mickey looked the other way, back towards the crashing surf and said: "Well, I know what you gave the tenants, fifty pounds an acre. But I'd want eighty pounds."

"Geez, Mickey," Father Waldron whistled involuntarily under his breath. "That's eight-and-a-half-thousand pounds altogether. That's an awful lot of money."

"It's an awful lot of money if you don't have it," said Mickey McDonough. "It's nothing at all if you have." The witticism was so perfectly placed, and so wise, that Father Waldron had to work hard to suppress a smile.

"It's an awful lot of money to us, Mickey."

"Well, I'd be glad to sell it for that."

"Then you've got a deal."

~

Father Waldron couldn't believe what he was reading, and he couldn't believe he was reading about it in the *Boston Globe* instead of the *Irish Times*. Yesterday, on January 30, 1972, British police had shot dead thirteen protesters in Derry. The tabloid press were already calling it "Bloody Sunday."

Though he knew he had solid reasons, Father Waldron couldn't help feeling a bit silly—as his homeland seethed here he was in America trying to buy a bit of land for a golf course.

His host in Boston was Rose Flanagan, an Irish-American women in her seventies. Father Waldron was a cousin of Rose and her two distinguished sons—one a professor of psychology at Boston College, the other a district attorney. Father Waldron was staying with the Flanagans while he negotiated with the last holdout from the commonage—a farmer who had left Connemara and sought work in America.

Only the day before Rose had engaged her guest in a discussion about Bernadette Devlin, the mini-skirted, twenty-year-old member of the British Parliament who had galvanized protests against the unfair treatment of Catholic workers in Northern Ireland.

"What do you think of Bernie Devlin?" she had asked over tea.

From the tone of Rose's voice, Father Waldron knew he was on dangerous ground. "I'm surprised you asked me that question."

"Well I'm interested in your answer," said Rose pointedly.

"Well, she's really an articulate young lady, and bold as brass you know, and some people like her and some don't. Why do you ask?"

Rose could hold it in no longer—the words came out in a torrent. "Well I want to know where she gets the idea that she can come over here and tell our president how to run our country, with her skirt up to her ash-can!"

Father Waldron had howled at that, but there was nothing to laugh at this morning in the news reports. What made it worse was that things were not going all that well in Boston. The last negotiation was a difficult one. Every Irishman abroad wants to come home—and have something to come home to. The young emigrant from Ballyconneely was no different. He had resisted all the arguments, pleading and psychology that Waldron and the Flanagans could bring to bear. They could only sit and wait.

∾

"You can't bring people here just for the scenery," said Paul Hughes passionately. "Golf is the kind of destination activity we must have to turn this community around economically, and to compete with the others."

Two hundred people were packed into the small meeting room at the Clifden Hotel, and most were nodding their heads. "Now that Father Waldron has secured the last part of the commonage it's time to move ahead while we still have the momentum."

Father Waldron had returned triumphant after all, closing the deal at the last possible moment at the Boston airport. An offer to guarantee the emigrant's son employment for five years should he ever return to Connemara had been the clincher.

Few in the room had laid eyes on a golf course, but optimism was in the air. There were hard questions, the usual suspicions, but you could tell people wanted the project to succeed. After years of seeing their community emptied, bit by bit, of its youngest and brightest, here at least was some hope to grasp onto. The combination of skills on the committee had proven to be effective. While Paul had the business skill, and an innate sense of when to pull back, the young priest was the committee's ace in the hole. Everyone knew that his presence meant that no one was going to line their pockets with this project. Hadn't he gone all the way to America to make it happen?

A corporation had been set up and supporters could buy shares at £500 apiece. They could pay £175 now and the rest later. Five thousand pounds had been raised at the first meeting. Not enough, but a fantastic start. Until this point the committee had operated on faith alone, drawing up agreements in principle without a penny in the bank. The budget for the trip to America had been £87!

Whether it was from the jet lag or the flu bug he had picked up in Boston he wasn't sure, but Father Waldron felt lightheaded as he sat in the room and watched things fall miraculously into place. More from relief than exhilaration, he allowed himself a smile. Not only was the idea becoming a reality, but it was happening in just the way he had hoped and prayed it would. It was truly a community project now.

❧

"What do you mean we don't own the land!" Father Waldron all but shouted into the phone. Never in his life had he felt such a mixture of surprise and dejection. He simply could not believe what he was hearing. It only happened in the movies.

But it was true. Four years earlier a group of businessmen from Galway had secretly bought a small wedge of land, also from Mickey McDonough, near the shore. The maps hadn't been all that clear; even Mickey McDonough hadn't realized that the property encroached on ground being used for the clubhouse.

"How much do they want?" Father Waldron couldn't believe his ears. The amount seemed astronomical—many times per acre what the farmers on the commonage had received. The entire project was in jeopardy. Just as it had gotten off the ground.

Since the exultant meeting at the Clifden Hotel, the community had rallied solidly around the project. Joe Clark, a local builder, had agreed to do the first landscaping for a mere £365. He already had the first tee in and had hired local lads to carry out the job. Suddenly there was a little work out there. The clubhouse was being put up, with more enthusiasm than sense, around a rock that stuck up through the floor of the bar. It was daft—the rock would have to be burned out—but the point was to keep moving on. Someone had borrowed a book on clubhouse development from England. Everything was being done on a shoestring, but no one cared. There was even some crazy talk about the course being open in June—just weeks away.

Now this—a community project threatened by land speculators. It couldn't be allowed to happen.

❧

This time Father Waldron was reading the *Irish Times*, and this time he was thoroughly enjoying himself. Paul McWeeney, bless his soul, had written a magnificent piece in praise of the new Connemara links. It couldn't have come at a better moment. Though the course had opened the month before (Father Waldron had played in the first fourball with

Eddie Hackett) the club was far from out of the woods. The debts were piling up (the machinery was so expensive!) and there was no money yet from the tourist board. The clubhouse, fashioned so enthusiastically, already needed to be changed.

The last-ditch negotiations with the men from Galway hadn't helped things, of course. After months of often tense negotiations, they had gradually lowered their price. Still, it had been an agonizing decision to fork over £8,500 for such a small parcel of land.

McWeeney's article would tell the world what Father Waldron, in his heart, already knew—that the blood, sweat and tears had paid off, that the dream had been worth pursuing.

He knew what even Paul McWeeney couldn't—that the golf course had turned the community around. Not the course, but the project. Looking back, Father Waldron could see that it had become a self-believing point for the community. By working together, by supporting the committee, and by applying their own individual gifts they had shown what they could do. The golfing visitors had not yet material-ized—they could expect only a handful of paid green fees this year. *But it was there.* The community had made it happen without the help of any big developer or big government grant. What had been done elsewhere for millions of pounds had been done here for a hundred thousand. And when the money did start rolling in it would go to the local bed-and-breakfast owner, the lad who worked with Joe Clark on the greenkeep-ing crew, the waitress in the Abbeyglen.

Peter Waldron put on his jacket and headed for the door. Tea at the Joyce's—a post-baptism party for Patrick junior. He was a tiny mite now. But would he grow up to be Connemara's first amateur champion?

ROSAPENNA

Founded: 1892
Designed by: Old Tom Morris, Harry Vardon,
Eddie Hackett, et al.

It would be difficult, if not impossible, to find country better suited for golf than that around Rosapenna. There are fine natural hazards, the turf is good and the scenery is delightful. . . . There is rare cliff scenery, and the air is bracing and exhilarating.

1908 TRAVEL GUIDE TO DONEGAL

The ghosts of Old Tom Morris, James Braid and Harry Vardon still whisper at Rosapenna, though the links has been rearranged any number of times, most recently as part of an expansion to twenty-seven holes overseen by Eddie Hackett. In an odd way, Rosapenna is perhaps more out of the way than it was when construction began on the grand Rosapenna Hotel in 1890. This seclusion is just one reason why it is well worth a visit, particularly in conjunction with a trip to nearby Portsalon.

~

"I WAS OUT THERE THIS MORNING ON THE ELEVENTH HOLE," shouted Frank Casey over the phone. "We've got a bulldozer working there, and I found a golf ball that must be at least one hundred years old. I was pretty happy to find that I can tell you."

It made us feel good, too—to think that Rosapenna's rich golfing heritage was something you could still touch as well as feel. In a moment of fancy, we imagined someone carrying out an archeological dig on the site of the old Rosapenna Hotel (destroyed by fire), using toothbrushes to lovingly brush the soil away from mashies, niblicks, gutta-percha golf balls and perhaps a bottle of 1884 Château Latour. They were all there, once, at Rosapenna.

We imagined the shiver that Frank Casey must have felt when he found that golf ball. It must have been like reaching back through time, like shaking hands with Old Tom Morris. "At Rosapenna," the local wags would surely be saying, "the rough is so thick it takes you one hundred years to find your golf ball!"

We had called the owner and manager of the new Rosapenna Hotel and Golf Course for an update on his expansion. As usual, Frank Casey's matter-of-fact voice was full of plans and optimism and hard work. Casey is the kind of honest, straightforward fellow who gives entrepreneurs a good name—he's determined to turn dreams into reality, but he's not going to harm anyone along the way.

"The peace in Northern Ireland is going to make a tremendous difference to Donegal," he said. "We've had more English tourists in the last six months than in the last fifteen years. And Donegal is the natural place for people from Northern Ireland who may have been going to Scotland [during the Troubles]."

The recent boom in golf in Ireland has spawned any number of fancy new golf hotels with luxurious appointments and spanking new American-style courses. But Frank Casey has been there for the long haul. His remarkable rise from waiter's son to owner of the hotel is chronicled on p. 73. Now his focus is very much on the future, on the new twenty-seven-hole complex that he will open as soon as he possibly can.

The opening of the revised course will be a bittersweet moment for anyone who has played Rosapenna and is aware of its remarkable pedigree. It will be painful to see the demise of several fascinating holes on the back nine, including at least two laid out by Old Tom Morris in 1890. On the other hand, there is the anticipation associated with the birth of ten new holes designed by Eddie Hackett. They will be among his last links creations, and among the last true links holes built anywhere. The doomed, road-crossing holes by Morris are described more fully elsewhere, but we will also be extremely sad to see the changes proposed to the thirteenth. Apparently laid out by either Harry Vardon or James Braid (the records aren't very clear) the 455-yard par four sweeps majestically downhill towards picturesque Mulroy Bay. It is one of the most natural and prettiest holes in Ireland.

Given his need to eliminate holes that endanger passing cars, Casey hasn't had much choice in making these changes. In expanding to twenty-seven holes, Casey has built a new nine on untouched linksland that was too rugged for anyone in Morris or Vardon's time to work with. To his credit, Casey chose the perfect architect to do the job. There is something sweet, sane and just in the idea of there being a golf course that begins with a Tom Morris original, swings through a series of classic links holes laid out by Vardon and Braid in 1908, and then ends with a crescendo of holes through undulating terrain by the modern architect who best understands and respects the traditions of links design. If anyone deserves this kind of company, it is Eddie Hackett.

The new Rosapenna, though not as grand as the old hotel (which burned to the ground in 1962) is a popular holiday destination for golfers from Northern Ireland, and Casey has built an unusual but successful niche with Dutch and Scandinavian golfers. There is a busy golf school during the summer, but the main attractions are the beauty of the fjord-like coastline and the opportunity to get to know one of golf's most historic golfing grounds.

Location:	Rosapenna, two miles north of Carrigart off R245, twenty-five miles north of Letterkenny
Restrictions:	None
Green Fee:	£15
Manager:	Frank Casey
Address:	Rosapenna, Downings, Co. Donegal
	phone: (074) 55301 fax: (074) 55128

PORTSALON

Founded: 1890
Designed by: Unknown

Portsalon golf course [is] one of the best, if not the best course in Ireland.
GOLFING MAGAZINE, *August 1896*

A rediscovered and rehabilitated gem, the links at Portsalon are situated in a remote, seaside setting that can be spoken of in the same breath as Pebble Beach. The course is no less challenging and satisfying for being quirky, and while not quite of championship caliber, there are many tremendous golf holes among the criss-crossing fairways. Find your way to Portsalon before they iron out all of the old-fashioned wrinkles.

∾

IF NOTHING THRILLS YOU MORE THAN COMING ACROSS AN unexpected and out-of-the-way wonder in your travels, then include Portsalon on your itinerary. Keep your expectations low, and let yourself be seduced.

We think that Portsalon is one of the twenty best courses in Ireland. With a greenkeeping staff of two, it isn't Augusta, but the course is in very acceptable condition since its purchase by club members in 1986 (for the remarkable story of how Portsalon was saved from extinction, and for more details on the course itself, see p. 73). It helps that the fine fairway turf only needs to be cut a couple of times a month during the summer.

The locals insist that a foreign magazine rated Portsalon's beach (which comes very much into play) as the second-most-perfect in all the world. It could be true. On a fine day, with the heather in bloom, and the Knockalla mountains in clear view, the setting is magical. We played it once after a light shower, and when a rainbow appeared the view from the twelfth tee was so beautiful it seemed *exaggerated*—like a fanciful drawing in a children's book.

It would be worth a detour just to hit a golf ball in such surroundings. What a delightful surprise it is, then, to discover that the links itself is outstanding, an unpredictable roller-coaster ride that is not quite like anything you have experienced before. After putting out on the eighteenth you will be eager to head straight to the bar and talk the round over. Very few foreigners visit Portsalon, and you can expect a friendly and inquisitive welcome from the clubhouse staff. The building, by the way, is patterned after the gate lodge of the nineteenth-century resort that brought golf to the village.

The days when Portsalon was the haunt of the British nobility may be long gone, but the golf has never been better.

Location:	At end of R246 on Fanad Peninsula
Restrictions:	Anyone who can find the course is invited to play
Green Fee:	£10-12
Secretary:	Cathal Toland
Address:	Portsalon, Fanad, Co. Donegal
	phone: (074) 59459

DONEGAL

Founded: 1973
Designed by: Eddie Hackett

You don't have to wear your plus-fours or your bow tie to come in here.
PATTY McLAUGHLIN, *member of Donegal*

A big, bold, beautiful links, Donegal is a masterpiece of the out-standing Irish architect Eddie Hackett. Most everything is writ large at Donegal—the 7,200-yard course with its expansive fairways and greens, the panoramic views of the Atlantic Ocean and the Donegal Hills, and the hospitality of the members. Still not well known, it may emerge as one of the great links courses in Britain and Ireland.

DONEGAL'S HISTORY IS A FORTUNATE ONE, MADE POSSIBLE BY an aristocratic fire sale and difficult soil. For generations, the linksland on the Murvagh Peninsula in Donegal Bay belonged to the family of Captain Hamilton of Brownhall. He had a country home—Murvagh House—not far from the present-day course. In a pattern familiar all over Ireland, death duties played a part in forcing Captain Hamilton's estate to cede much of the land to the state in the 1960s. The Forestry Department planned to reforest much of the area.

Any golfer could have foretold what was going to happen next. The sandy linksland on the Murvagh Peninsula proved to be stubbornly uncooperative, refusing to retain enough water even for the hardy species of trees the department had in mind. This was just the opening that a group of local golfing enthusiasts, then playing on a modest nine-hole course, was looking for. With the help of a couple of sympathetic local politicians, the group managed to lease the land from the Forestry Department for a nominal sum.

What was a forester's nightmare became a golf architect's delight.

Irish designer Eddie Hackett was engaged for his usual modest fee (about £200 at the time) to design a championship links that could be built without a lot of expensive earth-moving machines.

"We just used one old fellow from the area who had a bucket and one bulldozer," remembers Hackett. "Some of the greens were just as we found them. We just rolled back the sod, levelled the ground a bit, and laid the sod back on."

The club had eighty members when the full eighteen holes were unveiled in 1976. Since then membership has grown steadily, and today there are about 700 full members, several hundred country members from Northern Ireland, and a fair number of overseas members as well. There is a waiting list for anyone living beyond a seven-mile radius of the course, which despite its remote location is now ranked among the top 100 courses in Great Britain and Ireland.

Club members are proud of the fact that class and religious distinctions are left at the door of the club, and that annual membership fees are still only £190. The utilitarian clubhouse, with its large second-floor bar, is as neighborly a place as you'll come across, and after a pint or two it is always possible to retire to one of the lovely pubs in Donegal Town only nine miles away. If you go to McGroarty's in the town square, be prepared for the same sense of *déjà vu* we experienced—we were served by the same bartender who was patrolling the golf club's bar just a couple of hours before!

THE COURSE

There is an infectious enthusiasm to the efforts at self-promotion of many small Irish clubs and Donegal is no exception. The club's brochure proclaims that the links "offers the greatest golf challenges, unsurpassed beauty and tranquillity that is almost impossible to find in the modern world."

It is a tribute to Donegal's quality that while the brochure may exaggerate, you wouldn't want to accuse anyone of false advertising. The challenges are great enough that Nick Faldo has taken to visiting Donegal by helicopter in order to tune up for the British Open. And the calm, stately beauty of the links is stirring indeed.

As far as tranquillity is concerned, the club can thank the zealous foresters, as the drive into the club from the main road passes through a dense wall of national forest. The club just about has the Murvagh peninsula to itself. The sense of being away from it all is reinforced by Eddie

Hackett's sensible use of the generous quantities of land he was afforded. One result is length—Donegal was once the longest course in Europe. More important, the holes are widely spaced from each other, and even on busy days one is secluded in a way that is unusual on a natural links. While sand ridges define Donegal's holes, they are less vertical than, say, Ballybunion's; they echo instead the gentle Donegal hills that serve as a visual backdrop for many of the greens. The sweeping fairways and large putting surfaces perfectly match the sprawling quality of the linksland.

Hackett may have worked largely without bulldozers, but he was clearly at the height of his powers as an architect. He has composed a steady rhythm of excellent golf holes that inject new energy into a tired cliché: Donegal does indeed test every club in the bag.

The first few holes are elegant and gently rolling. Then the golfer is confronted with the Valley of Tears, an aptly named par 3 with a fiercely sloping green set in wild-looking dunes. There is no place to bail out, and many find themselves in a voracious bunker near the bottom of a steep hill in front of the green. It's the hardest sand save in Ireland.

"We didn't have to touch that green, it's just as nature put it there," remembers Hackett fondly.

"A lot of people said you couldn't play that hole, and I said that's one of the best holes and I hope you never change it. Of course, then they got to love it and now won't let anybody touch it."

There is an attractive unity to the holes at Donegal. The holes are cut from the same cloth, and the changes of pace are logical and welcome. The many sweeping, generous fairways on the front nine, for example, are punctuated by the penal fifth hole and the deliciously tight and curvy par-5 eighth. And the two short doglegs at nine and ten are well deserved respites after several extremely long par 4s. The back nine is equally forceful and absorbing, if lacking the seaside thrills of a Ballybunion or Tralee.

The challenges at Donegal are usually plain to see from the tee. The landing areas are generous when they should be, the greens make good if well-guarded targets, and the hazards justly punish shots that are more than slightly wayward. It is, in short, a splendidly balanced course, one that effectively uses the double circular routing that Old Tom Morris invented at Muirfield. Donegal is not Muirfield yet, but there are the same classic lines, and the same combination of proportion, understated beauty and demanding golf. Like a fine wine, the passage of time will do Donegal good. It will be interesting to see how future generations compare it to the world's best.

Location:	Murvagh, about nine miles south and west of Donegal Town off N15—the turn off of N15 is not well marked
Restrictions:	Visitors may play Monday to Saturday, and Sunday from 11:00 a.m. to 1:00 p.m.
Green Fee:	£15-18
Administrator:	John McBride
Address:	Murvagh, Laghey, Co. Donegal phone: (073) 34054 fax: (073) 34377

NARIN AND PORTNOO

Founded: 1930
Designed by: Unknown

*A ball may be cleaned and dropped without penalty if manure interferes
with stroke or stance.*

SCORECARD AT NARIN AND PORTNOO

*Known affectionately to some as Narin and Portmoo, this would
be just another of Ireland's striking and formidable seaside links
were it not for the four-legged bystanders you meet on the fairways. Set in a working-class resort area that is a favorite holiday
retreat of Catholics from Northern Ireland, the course has the
usual ocean views and a series of extremely difficult holes. But its
charm comes from the echoes of the past that resonate every time
you hop a cattle fence. This is Irish golf at its most splendidly
unpretentious.*

⌁

"WILL WE MISS THEM WHEN THEY'RE GONE?" ASKS TONY
Boner, repeating the question in a startled voice. "You mean the cattle?"

When it dawned on the former secretary of the Narin and Portnoo
Golf Club that he was probably dealing with a city slicker, he chuckled
ruefully. "I don't think that we will. When you step in the produce a couple of times you'll know what I mean."

Not so very long ago livestock were as familiar to Irish golfers as a
stiff breeze. Typically, courses were leased on land from farmers who
retained grazing rights. Even the members of Portmarnock had to contend with the cow of Maggie Leonard, who lived behind the first green.
The cow allegedly ate some of the stray balls, while the sharp-tongued
Maggie kept the rest, secretly passing them on to an enterprising member in exchange for a half-ton of the best coal.

Other clubs actually *encouraged* grazing as an inexpensive way to improve course conditioning in the absence of expensive grass-cutting equipment. Members at Portstewart voted to open up many of its holes to flocks of sheep, while Lahinch offered its lush rough to the village donkeys. Of course, Lahinch has always been way out in front in the use of animals—their famous goats have been used to forecast the weather for years.

After the Second World War, golfers became fussier, and the amiable coexistence with livestock began to fray. The official history of The Island Golf Club notes rather irritably that cattle could still be found on the course in the 1970s, and that they "trampled greens, used the flag-poles as scratching posts and generally caused nuisance and damage. The dung they left on the course was more often than not in the wrong place and of no immediate benefit for the course."

It's a problem Tony Boner can relate to.

"They cause terrible damage," he says of young calves who some-times ignore the electric fences that the club has erected around the greens. "It's terrible for the workers—they get the greens in pristine condition and then they get trampled on."

There are other courses in Ireland on which cows and sheep are still free to roam, but Narin and Portnoo is by far the best. Built in 1930 in the traditional out-and-back fashion, Narin and Portnoo boasts a series of strategically exciting outward holes and an inward half that can be downright beastly into the wind.

Until recently, the links also boasted about seventy head of cattle; golfers were forced to enter each green through a gate in a high fence. The number of cows has since dwindled to twenty, and the club has installed the much lower electric wire.

Although they can undermine concentration, the cows of Narin and Portnoo are really no threat to golfers. Vigilance is nevertheless recom-mended. Boner remembers a day when his playing partner left his golf bag too close to a cow while putting. What happened next will go unde-scribed, but Boner recalls that "it was a frosty morning and you could see the steam rising off his bag all the way up the next fairway."

Cohabitation does not seem to have prevented Narin and Portnoo from enjoying something of a renaissance in recent years. Although the club receives only a handful of overseas visitors, the links have become a magnet for the golf-crazed folk of Donegal and Northern Ireland.

"Golf is spreading like wildfire—during August the course is chock-a-block every day," says Boner, a local school principal. If the visitors see anything unusual about sharing the course with cows, "they're too polite to say anything."

Since the Troubles began in 1969, most of the out-of-county visitors have been from Northern Ireland. They are attracted by the area's tranquillity and by the beaches, which are considered to be among the cleanest in Europe.

While cows remain on the property nearest to the clubhouse, the club recently managed to purchase the grazing rights to most of the rest of the course. As the grass in the rough has been allowed to grow, the fairways have become more pleasingly defined and the true links pedigree of Narin and Portnoo has emerged more forcefully.

"She's now very striking to look at," says Boner proudly.

THE COURSE

If you have a bovine phobia of any kind and the cows are out to pasture, then you may not enjoy the first two holes at Narin and Portnoo. The difficulties are substantial even on a cow-less day, with out-of-bounds to contend with all along the right side. The second hole, a par 5 of only 500 yards, is particularly dangerous. You can go for the electric fence (green) in two but you'll have to fly your approach across the corner of a pond in order to make it.

The front nine at Narin and Portnoo is a slicer's nightmare. The prevailing ocean winds whip across from the left (and slightly from behind) and more often than not there is out-of-bounds on the right. The one occasion when the wind is directly behind you—at the short par 4 ninth—there is a rock-hard green backed by the Atlantic Ocean.

The tenth is an excellent ocean-side par 4 requiring all the faith at your disposal to tackle the blind, uphill, upwind tee shot, while the eleventh is a colossal and endangered par 3 along the water's edge. There used to be one hundred yards between the tee and the cliff. Now there's about ten feet and club members will soon have to choose between a new configuration or expensive erosion control.

If the wind is up, the finishing holes wear you down, and you will wonder how such a little-known and modestly long (5,900 yards) course could do so much damage to your handicap. The fourteenth and fifteenth, back-to-back par 5s, are particularly tough slogs, requiring lots of patience and one wind-cheating shot after another. The course gives some of the yardage back on the sixteenth, called High Altar, but it's no bargain. Considered the signature hole by many, it's only 120 yards from the tee to an exposed and elevated green that drops off on all sides. Three irons into a gale are not uncommon.

The drive on the narrow seventeenth should be aimed at a fence that marks the return to cattle country, and from that point on the most important obstacles will be living and breathing ones. City slickers will find the temptation to take photographs irresistible. Just watch where you leave your golf bag.

Location:	Near village of Narin, about six miles north of Ardara
Restrictions:	Weekdays are best, and it's a good idea to make a reservation in the summer.
Green Fee:	£10-14
Manager:	Sean Murphy
Address:	Narin, Co. Donegal
	phone: (075) 45107

COUNTY SLIGO *(Rosses Point)*

Founded: 1894
Designed by: H. S. Colt and Captain Willie Campbell

Where the wave of moonlight glosses
The dim grey sands with light
Far off by furthest Rosses
We foot it all the night.

WILLIAM BUTLER YEATS, *"The Stolen Child"*

In a country chock full of spectacular golfing scenery there is nothing quite like the exhilaration one feels teeing it up on the fifth hole at County Sligo. It is a gorgeous, thrilling drop to a wide and welcoming fairway. There are mountains on three sides—including Benbulben, made famous by W. B. Yeats—and up ahead, beyond Rosses Point, the harbor stretches out into the endless sea. Go ahead, "grip it and rip it"—even a weak shot here will seem to soar—and savor the sense of anticipation and privilege as you bound down the hill towards one of the greatest stretches of links holes to be found anywhere. While Drumcliff Bay never actually comes into play at Rosses Point, it is a constant and magnificent presence, and seems to infuse the links with a special glow and tranquillity.

DUST OFF THE COLLEGE POETRY ANTHOLOGY BEFORE YOU arrive in County Sligo, because there is no escaping William Butler Yeats here. Winner of the 1923 Nobel Prize for literature, Yeats was often in dire financial straits when alive. But today his name alone appears to enhance the prospects of just about any enterprise—including shops, pubs, museums, hotels, a summer school and, of course, organized literary pilgrimages.

The commercializing of Yeats's name is tame by American standards, however, and in no way diminishes the attractions of Sligo Town. Although devastated by the famine of the 1840s (at the height of the catastrophe as many as thirteen boats, filled with desperate human cargo, left the harbor each day) Sligo recovered to become an important port and commercial center. Today it is a bustling and charming little city with old narrow streets and exquisite pubs. The surrounding countryside is full of important archeological sites and contains the scenery that so moved the great poet.

Rosses Point is about five miles from Sligo. William Yeats and his brother Jack, an accomplished painter, spent some twenty summers there at the home of their uncle, George Pollexfen. The beauty of the surrounding landscape and the rich variety of local legends, which Yeats heard first-hand, are incorporated into some of his best writing. In his later years Yeats spent more time in Dublin, but he asked to be buried within sight of Benbulben mountain. The famous epitaph on his gravestone has not, however, been heeded:

Cast a cold eye
On life, on death.
Horseman, pass by!

Though a Protestant, Yeats believed in Irish independence, and it is difficult to believe he would have shared political beliefs with those who started the County Sligo Golf Club in 1894. A cousin of Yeats was one of the founders, but the club was dominated by Freemasons. In any event, Yeats was no golfer. As described in his autobiography, his personal connection to the club seems to be limited to the fact that he had his first sexual experience on the beach beside the course.

The club's first captain was Lieutenant Colonel James Campbell. A leading Freemason in the region, Campbell managed to persuade the local branch of the Masonic Lodge to join the fledgling club *en masse* in 1894 as a show of support. Campbell much preferred polo to golf, but he apparently believed the links was an important enhancement to the community. In any event, he and a couple of like-minded business associates ran the club with commendable efficiency in its first quarter-century, and there is a certain no-nonsense tone to Rosses Point that survives even today.

The first nine holes were laid out by George Combe, the guiding force behind Royal County Down, and nine more holes were added in 1907 by the Colonel's younger step-brother Willie. Only the present day twelfth and thirteenth (both the work of the younger Campbell) remain in anything like their original form.

County Sligo is in most respects the work of H. S. Colt. At the height of his career—with Sunningdale, Wentworth, and the Eden Course at St. Andrews behind him—Colt remodelled the course during a week in June of 1927 for a fee of £50. In fairness to Colt, it should be pointed out that the club rejected his design for the second hole, a dull uphill slog which is everyone's least favorite hole on an otherwise masterful layout.

If you are poking around Sligo's clubhouse you will come across the name Cecil Ewing at every turn. A world-class amateur player in the 1930s and 1940s, Ewing brought much glory to the then little-known club by winning the key match in the 1938 Walker Cup at St. Andrews. A large, heavy-set man, he swung with his feet remarkably close together and relied on his forearms to hit the ball lower and straighter than perhaps any golfer of his era. It was the perfect game for Rosses Point where, in Ewing's words, "when the winds blow, the only hiding place is to be found back at the clubhouse."

Until recently, Sligo was something of a well-kept secret, but visits by that roving ambassador of Irish golf—Tom Watson—and tributes by Bernhard Langer and others have helped to establish its reputation outside Ireland. It remains one of our favorite places to play.

THE COURSE

The links of County Sligo run out and back in the manner of St. Andrews. You start on high ground near the clubhouse, descend into a kind of plain that is almost level with the beach, and then rise again onto some turbulent linksland on the extremities of the course. On the back nine you retrace the journey, only closer to the sea.

The five holes on the high land near the clubhouse are comparatively ordinary, with the exception of the fourth—a lovely par 3 which Henry Cotton considered one of the best examples of a bunkerless short hole.

The fifth, called the Jump, is a transition hole, and surely one of the best dead-easy par 5s anywhere. It is a glorious tease—the fantastic elevated drive makes you feel you can take on the world.

The course exacts a toll for its early favors, however, building slowly but surely in difficulty and interest. The outgoing holes in the plain are fairly flat, though made more intriguing by the threat of a winding creek, and the front nine ends with a lovely par 3 that features a heavily bunkered green in front of a picturesque stone fence.

The second nine is a much stiffer test, beginning with three tight and rugged holes that loop around the cliffs at the end of the narrow arm of land that is Rosses Point. These holes are wonderfully scenic and seem to be in a world of their own. The tilting fairways and undulating greens demand a new level of precision, especially if the wind is up. But they are only a prelude to a heroic sequence of holes which define County Sligo as a championship golf course. The fourteenth and fifteenth are very different par 4s, but both require length and accuracy off the tee and precise long irons (or fairway woods) to difficult greens. At well over 200 yards, there is no respite at the par-3 sixteenth either.

It all culminates in the seventeenth, the Gallery, a favorite of Tom Watson and every other professional who has played County Sligo. One of the most difficult holes in Ireland, it doglegs back up towards the clubhouse, stopping at a green perched half-way up the hill. There is a turbulent sort of no man's land at the corner of the dogleg that must be respected as if it were a hazard, and the second shot requires a courageous, uphill carry to a partly hidden target. At 455 yards, the Gallery is punishing yet fascinating, qualities it shares with another famous seventeenth—the Road Hole at St. Andrews.

Like its counterpart at St. Andrews, the seventeenth at County Sligo gives way to a rather anti-climactic par 4 that at least allows you one chance to calm your nerves before heading into the attractive, Tudor-style clubhouse with its fine bar. Unless it is raining, however, you won't want to stay inside for long.

Location:	Rosses Point, five miles west of Sligo Town on R291
Restrictions:	Weekdays are unrestricted, though Tuesday may be difficult; play is possible on weekends by arrangement.
Green Fee:	£18-25
Manager:	(Mr.) Enda Lonergan
Address:	Rosses Point, Co. Sligo
	phone: (071) 77134 fax: (071) 77460

CARNE

Founded: 1995
Designed by: Eddie Hackett

If ever the Lord intended land for a golf course, Carne has it.

EDDIE HACKETT

Carne is a startling new links in the most unpromising of places—the remote and thinly populated Belmullet Peninsula. Carne is a wild ride through Ireland's most rugged linksland, but Eddie Hackett has kept the roller coaster just tame enough to make the trip enjoyable, and to make it a true test of golfing skill. Carne is not only a thrilling golf course, it is a remarkable example of community development in an area of few economic prospects. You will have to go out of your way to get to Carne, through miles and miles of tawny bog, but you will be richly rewarded.

⌒

"IT ALL STARTED IN THIS PLACE, RIGHT IN THIS ROOM," SAID Michael Mangan. He was seated in an easy chair in front of a fireplace in a sitting room of Belmullet's Western Sands Hotel. "This is where we held our first meeting in 1984."

It was ten o'clock on a Tuesday night, and I had just arrived after five exhausting hours on narrow, unlit roads. Despite the late hour, Mangan and Liam McAndrew, the Honorary Secretary of the Carne Golf Course, had donned ties for the occasion. It is not every day that a golf writer makes it all the way to Belmullet Town.

Belmullet is one of those places that looks alarmingly isolated even on a map. The town is stuck out on a talon-shaped peninsula of the same name that looks as if it could break off and float away into the Atlantic Ocean at any moment. The last half of my drive, through empty bogland, was dark and lonely, the light of a passing car something of an event. On the outskirts of the town I passed an experimental power plant which a sign indicated was built with aid money from the European Community. The plant was powered by windmills, using the unrelenting Atlantic wind. Drained from the drive, and a bit disoriented, my first impression of the dimly lit square of Belmullet Town was that it was as bleak and raw as any I had seen in Ireland—it reminded me both of the market towns I had seen in the Third World, and of the muddy frontier towns you see in old Westerns (I learned later the mud comes from the peat, which stretches in all directions).

But inside the Western Sands Hotel, with a hot whiskey in my hand and a cheese sandwich to cut my long-drive hunger, I listened to Michael Mangan put an entirely different and optimistic spin on what I had seen.

"I've always said that you can market isolation today," he said with conviction. "Look what happened to Connemara after they built the golf course. Property values have gone way up."

Two gulps into my Jameson's and I could already detect an energy and determination in Michael Mangan that would not seem easily contained in this stark place. As the remarkable tale of the development of the Carne golf course unfolded, I was not surprised to find that the first chapter begins with Mangan himself.

In the early 1980s, Mangan returned to County Mayo to set up a retail business after spending several years in London. He also bought a small farm near Belmullet that had a one-seventeenth share in a commonage—agriculturally poor land where farmers traditionally share grazing rights. Not being a farmer, the land had no value to Mangan, so he didn't give it another thought.

A couple of years later he heard that the Irish government was using development money from the European Community to persuade farmers to divide up the commonages. The theory was that farmers would be more likely to develop the land if they had control over their own little plot (and didn't need the consent of a dozen or more other families). Each farmer was to get £1,100 towards putting up concrete stakes to mark his property, and five rows of barbed wire to put around the perimeter. Mangan had still not even seen the commonage he had a share in, but he went to a special meeting, picked a number out of a hat, and was awarded a plot.

"The next day I took a walk with my next-door neighbor who showed me where it was," said Mangan. "Half of it was what I would call good grazing land, and the other half was just sand dunes. I saw it would be an ideal site for a golf course and that it would be a pity to see it divided up. It was the eleventh hour, but there were no wire fences yet!"

Until this point in the story Liam McAndrew—a much younger man than Michael Mangan—had kept a respectful silence. But now he burst in.

"We used to have fantastic common areas adjacent to the sea," McAndrew explained with obvious feeling. "There were thousands of acres of magnificent land with beautiful beaches. In the summer just about every community would have their sports day and they'd run it on these commonages near the beach, hundreds of people. Imagine what that was like and what it meant to the community.

"Well that's all wired in now. You can't even get on to it, you know. One massive stretch of wire. You can't let kids on to it because they'll get tied up with wire fences. We saw the golf course development as securing one last open area."

The richness of the tale caught me by surprise and took the edge off my fatigue. Though I had heard through the grapevine that Carne was a special place to visit (its official opening was still a few months away but the course was open for play), I knew nothing of its origins. I ordered a second whiskey and waited for Michael Mangan to take up the story again.

"As I said, five of us met in this very room, and we put five pounds each into a kitty to pay for phone calls. The first thing we did was stall the land commission from proceeding any further."

The group envisioned developing the commonage as a community project rather than seeing it cut up into economically unviable plots. According to Mangan, the idea quickly gained support in Belmullet—where there was precious little economic activity of any kind. But there were two giant obstacles: all seventeen owners had to agree to sell, and money needed to be found to buy. Even at a modest offer of £500 an acre, a total of £130,000 would be needed—a fantastic sum in Belmullet. Undaunted, Mangan and a few others set up a non-profit company and started lobbying for government support.

But first the farmers had to agree, in principle at least, to sell.

"We conducted seven or eight meetings in this same hotel room," Mangan said in a tone of voice that I thought still contained a hint of amazement, these many years later. "The first night eleven out of seventeen agreed, and every other meeting there was one or two who threw in their hats. Eventually it boiled down to one individual, who had land right in the middle of what would be the tenth fairway. He didn't want to know about money. He wanted to get another seventeen acres somewhere else instead.

"Finally, we went into the dining room there and said, 'We can't give you anything that we don't give the others, so the whole deal is off.'"

Mangan isn't sure exactly what happened after he went home, the project seemingly off the rails before it had got started. He did know that a lot of the other farmers were angry at the lone hold-out.

"The following morning he came into the shop and said, 'I have to live in this village and I canna be the odd bod out.' So he was going to throw in his hat as well."

Getting the land turned out to be the easy part. The all-volunteer organizing committee didn't realize what it was in for—years of painstaking effort to piece together financing, of navigating through bureaucratic red tape, and then of managing what turned out to be a £2 million project. In order to be eligible for the necessary money, the plans called for the golf course to be only one part of a larger recreational complex.

"It was trojan work," said Mangan. "We kept fairly tight rein and ran it as efficiently as possible. But quite frankly the size of the work we are doing is too big for a voluntary organization."

Eighty-four families eventually became shareholders in the project (Belmullet has a population of about 1,000) and hundreds more contributed to local lotteries that raised the money necessary to leverage matching money from government. Eventually, financing was secured through a complicated mix of grants and interest-free loans. But the money didn't always arrive on time, and it is at this point that the savior of so many golf projects in Ireland—architect Eddie Hackett—makes his inevitable appearance in the story.

"An exceptional gentleman," says Mangan in a low reverential voice. "It was never a question of money with Eddie Hackett, it was a question of good results and getting the best out of what we had.

"He was almost eighty years old, but he walked the course for three days, making drawings each night in his B&B. And he was enthusiastic from the very word go. 'If ever the Lord intended land for a golf course Carne has it,' he told us.

"Eddie wanted to disturb as little as possible the natural territory but there were places we went into where there were just massive sand dunes and we had to create fairways somehow. A few fairways cost twenty or thirty thousand pounds and others cost us nothing."

At this point I asked Mangan and McAndrew if they could spell out, as best they could remember, the financial details of the project. Even though much of the work had been done years before, the facts and figures jumped off their tongues. They knew the cost of every bulldozer and water sprinkler, the size of every loan, and the amount received each week now that green fees were starting to come in. The only people who made any money out of the development, they said, were the construction workers—under the terms of the government welfare grant they had to be local people who were unemployed. Only now was a paid project manager being hired.

"It was never our intention to take a big bank loan," said McAndrew, explaining why the course was built in phases. The prudence had paid off. Cash from paying visitors was already ahead of projections, and with the completion of a new clubhouse, the future looked rosy. They had just learned that *Golf World* magazine was going to name Carne one of the ten best new courses in Britain and Ireland.

I was surprised to find that it was already last call. Mangan and McAndrew had become more animated in the telling of their story, their voices containing a mixture of pride in what they had done and excitement about what the future would hold.

Granted, I had not yet played the golf course, had not even left my seat in this unfamiliar hotel in this town I had yet to see in the light of day. But it sure seemed like a textbook example of successful community development to me. I wished that someone from an MBA school somewhere was taking down the details for a case study.

It seemed all the more remarkable when Michael Mangan described the fate of the government scheme to encourage private production.

"The whole thing is reversed now," he said with a tone of sorrow rather than vindication. "They're paying farmers fifty pounds an acre not to fertilize and to leave it idle for the next five years. And if you wire it in and put no cattle in it they'll give another ninety pounds an acre per year. Just let the bushes grow on it. Overproduction you see. The whole thing is reversed."

THE COURSE

The story McAndrew and Mangan told me took on larger dimensions the next day when I finally saw the golf course. The brand new bed and breakfast I stayed in, just out of town, had an optimistic air about it, and I was decidedly more upbeat about Belmullet as I headed down towards the beach. It was a windy and cold morning, however, and McAndrew had warned me that there might not be anyone at the two caravans which served as the office and the changing room while the clubhouse was being built. He was right. But the door to the changing room was open, and there was a box in which visiting golfers could deposit their £15 green fee. It was about nine o'clock and there wasn't a soul anywhere.

I was nearing the end of a long trip, and I had seen and revisited some of the greatest links in the world. But Carne was still a revelation. I'd like to think my astonishment shared a little of the quality felt by the early "discoverers" of Ballybunion, although modern communications and travel being what they are, Carne won't stay undiscovered for nearly as long.

The round began with a bang—a short, careening par 4 with a fairway that disappeared from sight between fantastic sand ridges, like some kind of pathway to another world. The magic continued on the second, a secluded par 3 featuring a green set in front of a perfect, pyramid-shaped hill. It is the kind of place you would imagine Druids—Ireland's pagan holy men—performing strange rituals.

On the third tee everything suddenly changed. I found myself looking inland from a high tee. I soaked in superb views of farms and bog and a body of water called Blacksod Bay.

The third hole descended into more low-lying terrain, and I soon discovered that the rest of the front nine was laid out on the bay side of the first hole. I realized later that the linksland was relatively sedate compared to what lay ahead, though it sure seemed rambunctious enough at the time. The par 4s were particularly fine, requiring well-positioned drives and precise irons to some of the loveliest green sites in Ireland—each one tucked into a natural theater of mounds. None of the holes were overpoweringly long. The front nine was an engaging battle of wits rather than brawn, over dramatic golfing terrain.

I had yet to see other forms of life, but that changed when I stopped by the trailers after nine holes. The little office was buzzing, and a group of perhaps sixteen juniors were getting ready for an inter-club match. In the office a woman named Eileen, whose son was playing, told me that there had been no juniors at the old nine-hole course at Belmullet and that "people just didn't have the same interest in golf as they do now." Although one of the conditions of the tourism development grants was that tourists always receive priority at Carne, the club already had 278 members.

On the back nine I found everything turned up a notch. The tenth hole was played parallel to number one, on similarly undulating terrain, and was an outstanding, rollicking par 5 of exceptional beauty. The eleventh and twelfth, although perhaps just a bit too similar a golf challenge, were short dogleg par 4s played between steep sandhills of astonishing size. Then the mood changed again, as I emerged from the fantasy of dunes to a long, dangerous par 5 with panoramic views of the Atlantic and endless stretches of deserted cliffs and beaches. When I focused on the shoreline I could see that Liam McAndrew, alas, was right. This beautiful seaside land was being "wired" in neat rectangles.

After a pretty, if uneventful, par 3, the links climbed back into the hilliest terrain of all. The fifteenth was an arresting par 4, with a valley between tee and green that featured a fairway with the severest of undulations. They reminded me of the moguls created for freestyle skiing events at the Olympics, only these were natural. The sixteenth was a wonderful steep-drop par 3 to a green encircled by shaggy yellow dunes.

But it was the seventeenth that turned out to be Carne's *pièce de résistance*. The tee had grand views of the ocean behind, but the challenge in front of me was just as stunning. The drive had to find a narrow plateau of a fairway—only twenty-five yards wide in places—set along the edge of a chasm, to be followed by a long approach to a green perched just as precariously. To top it off, the hole was played through a surreal, heaving landscape right out of a science fiction novel. Being surrounded by dunes is nothing unusual on Irish courses, but these were gigantic and raw, with gaping wounds of white sand.

Then I got lost. There was no arrow to the next tee and I wandered disoriented through a maze of virgin sandhills that towered on all sides. It was a good ten minutes before I stumbled out onto the eighteenth fairway.

Feeling rather foolish, I retraced my steps to the tee box, which topped all that had gone before. I was so high up I could see the Atlantic behind me as well as Blacksod Bay in the distance. And all of the incredible, heaving linksland in between.

Needless to say, the hole itself was spectacular, not to mention provocative. The huge swales where the drives are supposed to land made the fifteenth fairway seem like an airport runway, and Hackett had left intact an incredibly deep valley just before the green. ("It creates a conundrum, all right," Hackett told me later at his home in Dublin. "But I always say you are entitled to stiffen the exam at the end of a round. Maybe in years to come, people will fill in that valley on eighteen and take away the mounds on the fifteenth, but I won't do it. That goes against the grain for me, because it's all natural.")

I should mention that Carne is not yet a polished links, and the condition of the fairways and greens on the back nine left something to be desired. Back at the caravan, the head greenkeeper told me that it would take a few years for the grass on the back nine to mature, and that Eddie Hackett had promised to add more bunkers when he found out where the most divots were!

I left Belmullet less than eighteen hours after I had arrived. Driving past the windmill station just out of town I felt a bit dazed by the experience. I wondered if I was right in thinking that Carne might be the best natural golf links ever, or if I had been swept away by my own thrill of discovery—and of learning, so unexpectedly, of the community effort that had produced such a gem. Michael Mangan had found the land, and Eddie Hackett had given it form, but the entire community of Belmullet could take pride for making it possible. It was, and is, their masterpiece.

Location:	On Belmullet Peninsula, one-and-a-half miles west of Belmullet, a long way from anywhere
Restrictions:	None
Green Fee:	£15
Secretary:	Liam McAndrew
Address:	Carne, Belmullet, Co. Mayo
	phone: (097) 82292 fax: (097) 81477

ENNISCRONE

Founded: 1922 Redesigned: 1974
Designed by: Eddie Hackett

Enniscrone is . . . the sort of course that brings out the best in you by challenging at every turn with a shot you want to make. I was concentrating on golf now, but somehow it felt more like a game than it does at home. I was playing golf and the key word was playing.

STEPHEN GOODWIN, *in the Washington Post*

Another of Eddie Hackett's low-budget miracles, the links close by the tiny village of Enniscrone in County Sligo may offer Ireland's most enjoyable game of golf. Although a championship test from the back tees, Enniscrone is also pure delight for the middle handicapper—with a series of thrilling elevated tee shots, four marvelous par 3s, and some truly sublime linksland.

～✎

THERE MAY BE NO GROUP OF GOLFERS WHICH HAS SHOWN more patience, and been more deservedly rewarded for it, than the cluster of determined men and women who decided to expand the golf course in Enniscrone in the late 1960s. Until then, Enniscrone had been a flat, uninspiring nine-hole course which hardly made use of the muscular linksland that rose beside the Bay of Killala just south of the village.

"There were only about twenty or twenty-five members at the time," remembers Jim O'Regan, now the co-treasurer of the club. An earnest and obviously sincere man, O'Regan turns deadly serious when discussing the club's frustrating history.

"There was a determination to achieve the goal, to develop a product of high quality against the odds," he says. "That was very much in people's minds."

Although fundraising in the local community was successful enough, the area only has a few hundred families, and the club was understandably short of cash. Just as understandably, it turned to Eddie Hackett, Ireland's national architect. As he had done in so many other cases, Eddie charged a modest fee, and worked with local volunteers and contractors to somehow build a championship course on the cheap (the budget was about £4,000). Hackett revamped several of the holes on the front nine as best he could, and designed an entirely new back nine deep in the dunes. Many of the new holes remain among Hackett's finest creations, and from the beginning the members knew they had a jewel.

The project was plagued by the lack of proper financing, however, and the links took five years to build. Even then, it was too raw and ill-maintained to attract visitors. The club teetered on the brink of financial calamity.

It must have been dispiriting for the members to see their new golf course—truly a diamond in the rough—sit unnoticed. Until the course was in better condition, nobody would visit. But until people started visiting there would be no money for improvements. It was a Catch-22 that lasted almost a decade.

When we first visited Enniscrone in 1988, things had improved somewhat. The course had grown in and was in excellent shape. After a thrilling round of golf we had a whiskey in the ramshackle clubhouse and were astonished to learn that only a handful of visitors were making their way to what we felt was an extraordinary golf course. Sean Connery had played it (a photograph of the actor had pride of place on the wall) but the members seemed resigned to it being always the "undiscovered gem."

"It was frustrating," says O'Regan. "But by getting there the hard way you're more aware of the achievement, and you appreciate its value."

The very next year, however, the corner was turned. Taking what must have been a huge financial risk, the members built a new clubhouse. Irish golfers were travelling within Ireland as never before, but they were looking for clubs with decent facilities.

"At first we didn't put a lot of stock in a clubhouse because we were more determined to have a fine course," says O'Regan. "But from the point of view of attracting visitors the decision to build a new clubhouse has been a major boost to us."

Indeed, no club in Ireland has benefitted more from the boom in golf travel in recent years. The number of visiting rounds each year at Enniscrone has risen *twenty-fold* in the last decade.

"We never thought we would be the *in* place, but that seems to be what has happened," says O'Regan, finally allowing himself a smile.

"People like to be part of a success story."

The golf course has also had an economic impact. With fourteen local employees, the club is one of the village's largest employers. The benefits spill over to restaurants, hotels, bed and breakfasts and other local businesses. Although Enniscrone's fine beaches attract some summer holiday traffic, the golf course is the only attraction for the rest of the year—even its oddly timed Open Week between St. Stephen's Day (December 26) and New Year's Day receives an overflow entry.

Enniscrone is now firmly on the golfing map, and is a favorite of American tours through the Northwest. But the success doesn't seem to have gone to anyone's head.

"The quality of life is important here," says O'Regan. "No matter who you are, no matter if you are low-waged, or middle income, or a millionaire, once you turn the avenue into the club here every fellow is the same. That's the policy of the club."

THE COURSE

With the possible exception of Ballycastle, no course in Ireland starts as misleadingly as Enniscrone. Taken together, the first two holes are perhaps the dullest thousand yards in Irish links golf, though the authors of the course guide point out that having two par fives to begin the round "helps to speed up play!" Though sedate, the third and fourth holes are at least of strategic interest, and the fifth, a pretty par 3 set in sandhills, provides a pleasing taste of what is to come.

But not just yet. The sixth and seventh are anomalies at Enniscrone, running on low land alongside Scurmore beach. The sixth is gorgeous, a dogleg quite close to the water that narrows at the green. But the seventh, which used to feature an eccentric, humpback fairway, is now a travesty. Since our first visit it has been utterly flattened by the members, and is now as interesting as yesterday's newspaper.

No such havoc has been visited on the rest of the course, fortunately, and Enniscrone begins to sing when you start to look for the next tee, up high in the sandhills. The eighth is a wonderful par 3 to a green set in unruly duneland, and it is followed by the best back-to-back par 4s in Ireland. This is not because they are overly difficult, but because they are so beautiful, so natural, and so thoroughly delightful to play.

The drive on the ninth is hit over a dangerous valley and between huge hills. When you reach your ball you notice that the second shot is just as dramatic—the target is a lovely yet devilish green on a natural plateau set in the side of a hill. Though the hole measures only 345 yards from the back tees, there is no bunker of any kind. It only gets better as you climb even higher to the tenth tee, where there is a sudden and marvelous view of the ocean. The drive, however, is unnerving—an off-kilter and very downhill affair to what appears to be a small island of fairway in a sea of dunes. It's not quite as difficult as it looks and, as on the ninth, a straight drive of even modest length will have you clicking your heels with joy. The reward is a very short iron to a picturesque green set perfectly in natural swales.

Due to their shortish length, the ninth and tenth are perhaps most exhilarating to the average player. At the long par-4 eleventh, however, Hackett stiffens the challenge with another great driving hole. This time length as well as accuracy is demanded.

The routing for the final seven holes consists of two more journeys into the high linksland, and majestic descents out of them. There are two very fine par 3s—the uphill and bunkerless thirteenth, where the natural, tilting terrain creates illusions and difficulty, and the seventeenth, a shorter hole set in high dunes overlooking the sea. The latter would be one of the world's most satisfying short holes if a caravan park behind the green did not blight the view.

We have rarely played a course where it is so much fun for the person of average length to drive the ball, and the eighteenth is no exception. The only truly blind shot on the course, a well-struck drive over a high ridge of wasteland will be rewarded with a free fall to the green.

By now the rather pedestrian opening holes are completely forgotten (perhaps they make the thrilling holes at the heart of the course that much more unexpected and magical) and it is time to sample the offerings of the clubhouse that has done so much to revive Enniscrone's fortunes.

Location:	Six miles north of Ballina, turn off R297 at sign
Restrictions:	Visitors may play weekdays, and weekends by prior arrangement
Green Fee:	£15-18 (there are also special "husband and wife" rates)
Secretary:	John Fleming
Address:	Enniscrone, Co. Sligo phone: (096) 36297 fax: (096) 36657

CONNEMARA

Founded: 1973
Designed by: Eddie Hackett

*Looking back it was a growing and achievement point and self-believing
point for the community. They had never done anything like this.*

PETER WALDRON, *founding member of Connemara*

*Connemara is profoundly unlike any other course in Ireland and
perhaps anywhere. Winding its way at times through great slabs
of rock, Connemara is a raw and exposed place, wide open to the
relentless Atlantic winds. It is also uncommonly beautiful, as
uncompromising and majestic as the region that gives it its name.
Built entirely by the local community, after a design by Eddie
Hackett, the links at Connemara is golf at its most elemental—a
striking example of a course dictated by nature, and all the better for it.*

THE REMARKABLE STORY OF CONNEMARA'S BIRTH IS COVERED
in some depth on p. 85. Since that great community project became a
reality, the club is thriving beyond the dreams of its founders. As many
as twenty thousand visitors—most from other parts of Ireland—visit the
club each year. They come for the same reason that Europeans are buying up coastal property in the area—the mix of remoteness and stern
beauty.

No one appreciates the peculiar appeal of the place more than Eddie
Hackett, who designed the course for next to nothing in the early 1970s.
At the age of eighty-five, he is now laying out an additional nine holes
even closer to the sea. One gets the feeling that Hackett, a deeply religious man, believes it is something of a miracle that a golf course took
shape at all in Connemara's distinctive rock-studded landscape.

"You'll notice that the rock doesn't interfere with your play at all," says Hackett with a mixture of pride and lingering amazement. "And we didn't move one rock."

Connemara has few of the high, wild dunes that characterize many of Ireland's links. The terrain, especially on the front side, is relatively flat, and completely exposed to the winds that whip off the sea. Above, ever-moving clouds orchestrate endless shifts in shadow and light. With the imposing Twelve Bens mountain range astride one horizon, the crashing sea stretching across the other, and a tumultuous sky overhead, it is easy to feel very small indeed.

With more money, and a different designer, the land on the front nine might have been torn up and reshaped to provide more "feature" to the holes. That could well have irreparably harmed the elemental quality of the place. Though straightforward, the front nine has enough subtle variations in bunkering and green sites to keep one's interest. But it is on the glorious back nine that Connemara comes into its own.

The excitement really begins at the twelfth—a terrific, undulating dogleg that pulls you right into the most rugged part of the course. But it is the astonishing par-3 thirteenth that is Connemara's show-stopper. After being so exposed to the elements, you suddenly find yourself secluded in a kind of rocky basin. Everywhere you look is wasteland, except for a green that is miraculously situated among a wild jumble of rocks, vegetation and marshland. The tee shot, obviously, is all carry. The full power and majesty of the hole is best taken in by moving back to the championship tees—take out a driver and an old ball, and go for it!

After the seclusion of the thirteenth you emerge with adrenaline flowing to an elevated tee, where there is a full view of the rest of the course and the ocean shore. From here to the clubhouse there is one excellent hole after another, featuring stunning downhill drives and dramatic greens set up in the rocks or on high, natural plateaus.

It is one of the very best inward nines in Ireland and at close to 3,600 yards from the *regular* tees (200 yards farther from the back sticks) it is a severe test even on a calm day, which is about as common as kangaroos at Connemara.

Location:	Ballyconneely, five miles south of Clifden
Restrictions:	None
Green Fee:	£12-18
Manager:	John McLaughlin
Address:	Ballyconneely, Clifden, Co. Galway
	phone: (095) 23502 fax: (095) 23662

DIVERSIONS
The Northwest

THE NORTHWEST OF IRELAND IS ONE OF THE MOST RUGGED and remote areas of Western Europe. There is uninhabited land on a scale much more familiar to an Australian or a Canadian than a European. It is not uncommon to find the road blocked by livestock. The scenery, particularly along the north Donegal coast, is often stunning.

Galway is a tourist and university center and a convenient base for exploration. It is a vibrant place, particularly in summer, and has become known as something of an artistic center—there is an Arts Festival each July. Galway overlooks the famed Galway Bay, notable both for its scenic beauty and its oysters.

Galway is a town of considerable historic interest. It was an Anglo-Norman colony for centuries, dominated by fourteen families who became known as the "fourteen tribes of Galway." They stubbornly kept the native Irish outside of the city and remained intensely loyal to the Crown. Galway grew in importance as it became a significant port for trade with Spain (particularly in wine), and architectural reminders of that period can be found throughout the old town. The best is probably the Spanish Arch, which now houses a small civic museum.

The town also contributed the word "lynch" to the English language. The Lynch family was pre-eminent among the fourteen tribes and in 1493 James Lynch was Lord Mayor of Galway. His son, Walter, stabbed a visiting Spanish merchant to death and was sentenced to be hanged, but because Walter was so popular (or the townspeople were so afraid of the Lynches) no one could be found to carry out the sentence. James Lynch, who as Lord Mayor was the judge in the case, executed his son personally, and lived the rest of his life as an unhappy recluse. The incident is commemorated on a plaque in the Church of St. Nicholas, formerly the Old Jail.

Western County Galway and County Mayo, though remote, contain some of traditional Ireland's most rewarding sites. The Irish language is spoken along the north shore of Galway Bay, and within that bay are the famous islands of Inishmore, Inishmaan and Inisheer—the **Aran Islands** that inspired the lyrical plays of J. M. Synge. Inishmore is the largest, and can be reached from Galway by air or ferry. It has lots of limestone, a few interesting pubs and no trees. The main tourist attraction is the impressive fort, Dun Aonghasa. There are also excellent views of both the Cliffs of Moher and the mountains of Connemara from this vantage point. The middle island, Inishmaan (Inis Meain in Irish) is the least visited, and did without electricity until 1978 and telephones until 1987. A large pier has now being built to allow access to Inishmaan, however, and ferries operate from Galway to Inishmaan in the hope that tourism can replace the dying fishing and farming economy.

Just northwest of Galway town is the island-dotted Lough Corrib, with its outstanding salmon fishing, and further west is the **Connemara** region, dominated by the mountain range called the Twelve Bens. This is a raw and other-worldly landscape. Even at the height of tourist season the dominant experience is likely to be solitude, unless you are fortunate enough to happen upon a herd of wild Connemara ponies. The area has been used in feature films dealing with rural Irish life, most notably *The Field*, starring Richard Harris, which was shot at Leenane, and the John Wayne classic *The Quiet Man*, filmed in and around the village of Cong. Connemara National Park, near Letterfrack, has a visitors' center which describes the region's landscape and natural history. But just about anywhere you go in Connemara will yield fine natural scenery.

In central County Mayo, about twenty miles east of Castlebar, is the village of Knock. The **Chapel of Knock** has been a place of pilgrimage since an apparition of the Virgin Mary, Saint Joseph and Saint John appeared in 1879. Even though it was raining that day, the area around the figures is said to have remained dry. In modern times, over 500,000 people make the journey to Knock annually, and the little village has, understandably, been rather overwhelmed. In 1976, a huge new church was built, and in 1986 an airport opened at Charlestown, just ten miles away. Despite predictions of failure, the airport has proved to be quite successful, and the influx of visitors (the vast majority from Britain, and by no means all religious pilgrims) has had a profound effect on County Mayo.

The region around Sligo Bay is known as Yeats Country and promoted as such. The literary tourist will want to visit Yeats's grave at Drumcliff, as well as Lough Gill (made famous in "The Lake Isle of Innisfree") and Lissadell House. The County Museum, in **Sligo,** has a section devoted to Yeats. Next door is the County Art Gallery with a good collection of Irish works, including a few by Yeats's brother Jack. Also extremely prominent (and very visible from the golf links at Rosses

Point) is the distinctive flat-topped Benbulben mountain, in sight of which Yeats asked to be buried. Even if you are not interested in Yeats, Sligo is a friendly and interesting town.

County Donegal is a region of thatched cottages, pine forests and superb coastal scenery. Donegal tweed is perhaps its most famous product, and is widely available in Donegal Town. At the center of town is a large square known as "the diamond," and most of the shops, pubs and hotels can be seen from this point. The coastal road from Donegal to Narin and Portnoo yields much worthy scenery, with the fishing village of Killybegs worth a brief look. At Portnoo, there are miles of beautiful sandy beaches, but the weather will rarely cooperate with any plans for an afternoon's sunbathing.

The northern part of Donegal is divided into four spectacular peninsulas—Horn Head, Rosguill, Fanad and Inishowen. The Rosapenna Hotel and golf course is on Rosguill, while Portsalon is situated in a commanding spot on Fanad overlooking Lough Swilly. The roads are winding and narrow. You are unlikely to travel more than thirty-five miles an hour no matter what your form of transportation. It would be a shame to go faster in any event, for an imposing cliff or secluded bay may be just around the corner.

FIVE GREAT LINKS

(and Dublin, too!)

GOLFING VISITORS TO IRELAND HAVE SOMETIMES overlooked the east coast in their rush to sample the undeniable charms of Ballybunion and the other famous links on the opposite side of the island. Culturally, the East is dominated by Dublin, and even the smaller communities are neither as rooted nor as distinct as they are on the west coast. But the eastern seaboard of the Republic now boasts a string of five world-class links. They are very different in character, ranging from the rollicking duneland of The Island and the European Club, to the subtle stateliness of Royal Dublin and Baltray. Green fees are a bit pricier, and starting times a bit more difficult to arrange, but there is a feast of golf to be had. One of the most ancient and convivial cities in Europe is also at your doorstep. A good strategy is to enjoy Dublin on weekends and golf during the week, when starting times are much easier to come by. The East also boasts a number of new, high-end parkland clubs—aimed at wealthy executives—which offer an undeniably high standard of conditioning and creature comforts for those who would rather be in Palm Springs. Sample these if you like, but not at the expense of the five great links.

Moondance with Portmarnock

THE IDEA WAS TO crash one of the most exclusive parties in Ireland, so dressing wasn't exactly a piece of cake. Not after two solid weeks of tracking down far-flung golf courses on winding back roads.

I had stuffed a sports jacket and tie into my suitcase for just such an emergency, but unravelling them a fortnight later I discovered creases in patterns worthy of Jackson Pollock.

Cursing, I flattened the tie under the heaviest book I could find in our Dublin B&B (a Bible, naturally) and hung my sports jacket outside the shower stall. Then I tried in vain to locate a pair of clean and matching pants.

Shoes were easier. There was only one cleat-less choice, a pair of brown dock shoes that I dusted off with some Kleenex.

Jerry, my travelling companion on this excursion, fared only slightly better. Fully if alarmingly dressed, we climbed into the rental and joined the rush-hour traffic heading north of the city.

The grand occasion was the 100th anniversary celebrations of the Portmarnock Golf Club—site of one of the most admired links in the world. A *Who's Who* of Irish society was sure to be out in force.

I had tried to use my writing credentials to wangle an invitation from a Mr. Buckley, the Honorary Secretary, but after some vague promises it had never arrived. Okay, so I wouldn't make the *Who's Who* of my street—I wasn't going to be discouraged so easily. Not on the centenary of my favorite golf course on the planet.

"The charms of Portmarnock are difficult to describe," was the imaginative 1902 assessment of Harold Hilton, the greatest amateur of his day, and a well-known writer to boot. He went on to say something lame like "the greens are keen and somewhat hard."

To be fair to Harold, that's the difficulty with Portmarnock. It doesn't have trademark features—nothing like the giant dunes of Ballybunion, or the flowering whins of County Down, or the dramatically shaped fairways of Royal Portrush.

Like the Old Course at St. Andrews, Portmarnock invites metaphors, not photographs. It is a mood as much as a place, its charm an accumulated effect of the variety, intelligence and grace of the layout. There is a wonderful sense of proportion at Portmarnock, a feeling that every piece is in the perfect place. If Mozart had been a golf architect, this would have been his masterpiece.

As it turns out, Portmarnock (like St. Andrews) just kind of evolved. A Scottish insurance broker had the first crack, but it has been tinkered with continuously by members who by some quirk of fate did all the right things.

And it's all reinforced by a strange and captivating seclusion, one that probably hasn't changed much since 1893, when a golfing nut named Pickeman rowed across the bay *on Christmas Eve* to check out the sand dunes. Today, Dublin's suburbs have encroached almost to the front gate, but Portmarnock remains insulated—sticking out on a tongue of land surrounded on three sides by salt water.

It was about six o'clock when Jerry wheeled into the drive that runs adjacent to Portmarnock's final two holes. The course lay empty and serene (it was a beautiful and calm summer night). But up ahead we could see that the parking lot was spilling over onto the practice fairway. What raised our anxiety level, however, was the *quality* of the automobiles. Ireland is by no means a rich country, but there were enough glistening luxury cars for a Beverly Hills nightclub.

We climbed out of our rental (which seemed to have shrunk), straightened our jackets and tried to compose ourselves as best we could. I was cramped over, brushing my hair in the side mirror, when an impeccably dressed couple in formal attire swept by. In my dishevelled state, they seemed like royalty from Monaco.

The function was obviously too big for Portmarnock's elegant but cozy clubhouse. A large tent, striped in green and white, had been erected beside the first fairway, just a short pitch from the Irish Sea. I stuffed my tape recorder into my pants pocket, made one last attempt to flatten the wrinkles out of my jacket, and tried to look as invited as possible. We walked, at a steadily decelerating pace, towards the elegant tent.

Jerry was more decently dressed than I, but given his Chinese heritage he was hardly going to pass for a former captain.

"Are you sure we want to go through with this?" Jerry asked, giving me one last out. I made a less than heartfelt attempt at "You only live once," and might well have turned back had I not felt the eyes of a security guard on me.

What was the worst that could happen? I asked myself, and too readily had an answer—in my mind's eye we were spread-eagled on a police cruiser. Turning around, I concluded, might cause more suspicion than carrying on.

But then something odd struck my ear . . . the sounds wafting out of the tent. I don't know what I was expecting, a string quartet playing Mozart perhaps, but this wasn't it. The noise was garish and brassy, surely as out of place as Jerry and I. And that song. . . . Nah, it couldn't be.

It was. Seconds later we were inside the tent (no questions asked) and suddenly it all became clear.

The song was "Knock Three Times" by Tony Orlando and Dawn. It was played by a police band in blue suits and thin black ties. The Guinness was flowing into plastic cups. The roar of the "crack" was as loud as the band. No one gave a damn whether we were invited or not.

A little voice inside me gave me the comforting news: *What did you expect, stupid? This is Ireland!*

Before the set of Tony Orlando and Dawn songs was over we were well into our second pint, and any lingering anxiety had been successfully treated by huge doses of Irish hospitality.

Through the crush of people, I managed to track down Mr. Buckley, who apologized rather abashedly for not sending us invitations. Apparently the police had taken one look at the invitation list and asked that journalists be kept away for security reasons. Perhaps as compensation, Mr. Buckley immediately introduced us to Joe Carr, captain of the Royal and Ancient, three-time British Amateur champion, and one of Ireland's most beloved golfing figures. Joe didn't say much—he seemed to be the only one present who saw the danger of mixing Guinness with a writer's tape recorder—but his exploits were recounted for him by a swarm of admirers. The fact that he putted with a 3 iron seemed to account for as much as his Amateur titles and ten Walker Cup appearances.

The conversation set off in all directions, and before I knew it we were half way into an Irish golf story that had begun I didn't know where.

"I heard a swish, so I set the cannon off, but he was only in his back-swing," said someone to general laughter.

"I was so startled I hit a high ball right into the water," replied another. "The first thing I did was cover up you know where!"

"We thought he hit it into the water to save a few pounds!" roared a third.

After the laughter settled down, I found out that the story referred to the annual "driving in" when the captain of the year hits a ceremonial drive followed by a one-gun salute. The caddie who retrieves the captain's drive gets a prize. In the explanation, the tale was told again, with even greater relish and embellishment, and I was able to laugh at the right spots.

I found it intriguing that almost everyone I talked to began, unprodded, by praising the golf course, and with a reverence that was no less genuine for being animated by a few pints. It was as if the links were some kind of pilgrimage site—golf's equivalent to Lourdes or Ireland's own Chapel of Knock—and the members were merely the temporary custodians.

It was much harder to get anyone to talk about the *club*. There just didn't seem much to say. After some prodding, the current club captain allowed that there had been "great atmosphere around the club this year," with the clear implication that being a member of Portmarnock was not normally a barrel of laughs.

It was something I had heard about Portmarnock. Impressive as its membership list was, and though the course itself kept gaining in reputation (hosting the Walker Cup in 1991), there wasn't the same camaraderie for which the rest of Ireland was famous. Even after a hundred years.

I heard several theories for this, the absence of women members being one. Others hypothesized that the members were too important to let their hair down, and that the course was used more for business than for pleasure. I also learned that it used to be common for members at Portmarnock to hold dual memberships—they played Portmarnock in the winter when the parkland courses nearer the city were too soggy.

I must confess, however, that my first-hand impressions were rather different. The members sure seemed to be having one hell of a good time on this, the 100th anniversary of the first driving in. Jerry and I joined the guests in a lusty verse of "Congratulations" to the band leader, who had recently, it seemed, been promoted to police superintendent.

We found it more difficult to digest the hors d'oeuvres. Passed around by formally dressed waiters on silver trays, they consisted of little fatty sausages and gray pieces of beef. There was a neon yellow sauce if you were so inclined. Everyone else seemed to think that the food and the music were terrific. A rather large member of the band started belting out "Sweet Caroline," much to the approval of the guests sitting at large round tables in the center of the tent. Others hovered around the edges, near the kegs of beer, and it was this group I was about to rejoin when someone—either Joe Carr, Mr. Buckley, or the guy who set off the cannon—suggested that Jerry and I go out and play a few holes.

We laughed, in unison, in that *you've got to be kidding* sort of way, but we also exchanged a tentative glance that meant *we couldn't really, could we?* We hadn't played Portmarnock on this trip (it had been off-limits to us during the centenary week events). And it was a clear, June evening—it would stay light until ten o'clock. But *still*.

"Off you go then, while there's still some light," someone else chimed in, with a few other heads nodding in agreement.

And the thing was, *they weren't kidding*. Dashing out to play a few holes in a dress shirt, several pints to the good, during the centenary bash of the world's most exquisite links, was clearly considered a perfectly sane proposition.

We had no proper clothes, but our clubs and golf shoes were in the boot. And once the idea was lodged in our heads there was no getting rid of it. To play Portmarnock tonight, on its 100th birthday, seemed suddenly, in my Guinness-soaked state, to have cosmic significance. To turn the opportunity down would be to thumb our noses at the gods.

So we did it. Downing our most recent pints, we galloped back to the rental like a pair of school boys, even letting out a hoot or two. Our initial anxiety had been supplanted by an exuberant cockiness. Citing the authority of the club secretary, and the Captain of the Royal and Ancient, we even sent someone inside the clubhouse scrambling for some scorecards. I remember teeing it up on number one, whistling the tune from "Tie a Yellow Ribbon," and thinking myself the luckiest man alive.

Do I need to say we had the course to ourselves? For two hours, in the red glow of the setting sun, we played with reckless abandon, glorying in the moment, crazed with the feeling of being in just the right place, at the best possible moment.

Call it a 1990s pagan ritual. In full view of the rising moon, we frolicked on this miraculous links. We *danced* with Portmarnock. And we didn't have to share her with anyone.

Unconcerned about our score or each other, we played speedily and well. We split the fairway on Portmarnock's glorious blind tee shots, clipped the ball cleanly off its famous springy turf, and drained putt after putt on its fast and oh-so-true summer greens.

Even the odd wild shot presented no problem. In the dwindling twilight, Portmarnock seemed to offer up our stray balls so as not to interrupt our reverie. I felt like a character in *Golf in the Kingdom*.

When we smacked two lovely drives on the par-5 sixteenth and couldn't see the green through the darkness, we reluctantly decided to pick up, though I insisted on walking the rest of the course to the eighteenth green. It was like walking the date of your dreams to her front door—you wanted everything to end just right.

We had little inclination to return to the party now, and with the slam of the trunk and the start of the engine the spell was broken. We roared back to Dublin, satiated, unsure if we had just enjoyed the silliest or most transcendent golf experience of our lives.

The Golf Theme Parks

OR SOMEONE FAMILIAR WITH the rugged, natural wonders of Irish links golf and the cozy informality of the typical Irish golf club, visiting the St. Margaret's Golf and Country Club, just a few miles from Dublin Airport, can be a disorienting experience.

The clubhouse is an enormous three-story structure of a style vaguely reminiscent of a nineteenth-century manor, but built with the clean, efficient lines of modern construction. The rather elaborate flower gardens in front of the building are splendidly tended, while the emblems of a variety of nations flutter smartly from flag poles.

Inside, there is the option of taking an elevator to the locker room, which is appointed in rich wood and gleaming brass. The fixtures in the washroom seem to be made of marble and, yes, that is a sauna.

The pro shop has the atmosphere of a chic men's clothing store. You half expect to be offered a Mont Blanc pencil with your scorecard. From the enormous, velvet practice green you can see shimmering, man-made lakes and glistening white sand traps in the distance. *Electric carts*, of all things, can be seen scurrying about.

But it is a large sign next to the first tee (immaculate and enormous, with four sets of markers) that really starts your head spinning.

"No mobile phones allowed on golf course."

This is Ireland?

Alas, it is. St. Margaret's is only one of at least twenty luxury golf developments that have been built in Ireland in the last decade, no small number for a place with a population smaller than Chicago's. For the most part they cater, not to foreigners, but to those who are benefitting somewhat disproportionately from Ireland's new prosperity.

Several of the new developments have adjoining hotels, and try to replicate the lifestyle enjoyed by those who gained most from the oppression of an earlier time. The brochure touting the charms of Slieve Russell, a new golf hotel in County Cavan, is a case in point:

> The Hotel has gracefully recaptured the opulence and charm of a bygone era. The marbled colonnade with its dramatic plastered ceiling provides a richly ornamented environment that mirrors our guests' *favourite era of the past*. An era of overscaled sofas, deep piled carpets and magnificent fireplaces—quite simply the era of luxury. Centred on the colonnade, a graceful marble staircase is surrounded by the blacksmith's art—a myriad of wrought iron with surprises around every corner. The mix of muted colour and textures, the generously proportioned seating spaces, recreate all that is the calm of an Irish country house (italics added).

The most opulent of the new resorts are essentially theme parks, a hybrid mixture of manicured American golf course luxury and ersatz English Manor that would not look out of place in Orlando. One half expects the staff to be dressed in period costume. For those in a hurry, the fanciest resorts may have a helicopter pad. Typically, the hotel will offer other pursuits, such as horseback riding, fishing, skeet shooting, tennis, swimming, croquet and an opportunity to join in a fox hunt.

You have to go back one hundred years—to the twilight years of the Ascendency—to encounter a comparable boom in luxury golf in Ireland. Several grand golf hotels were built before the turn of the century (Portsalon, Bundoran, Rosapenna and Lahinch among them) but they had disappeared or markedly declined by the end of the Second World War. By that time golf had become (with the exception of the exclusive clubs near Dublin and Belfast) an affordable if by no means popular sport. Almost all clubs were controlled by local members and expenditures on amenities were kept to a minimum. Only a few courses had paid professionals. Even today, many notable courses survive with two or three maintenance staff and a bartender who also collects green fees.

Change came in the late 1980s when two of Ireland's wealthiest men asked Jack Nicklaus and Arnold Palmer to design golf courses on former estates. The results were Mount Juliet and the K Club, playgrounds for the rich that featured exquisite accommodations at international prices. The almost-as-ostentatious Slieve Russell, strategically placed about equidistant from Dublin and Belfast, was built shortly afterwards, and in the 1990s many other courses have joined the list. The trend shows no sign of slowing down.

The common features of these new courses are entrepreneurial ownership, the use of American-style design and conditioning, luxurious clubhouse appointments and high green fees.

"The bottom line is that corporate golf is a huge growth industry," says St. Margaret's Denis Kane over some dainty sandwiches in the clubhouse bar. Kane works in a job that didn't exist in Irish golf ten years ago—as General Manager, he is responsible for stirring up business. Kane has years of marketing experience at first class hotels in North America, and he's obviously good at what he does.

"In the sales end of things," he tells me with quiet zeal, "you don't buy or sell to anyone you don't know. What better way to get to know them than on the golf course? You meet them at least fifty-four times— on the tees, on the fairway and on the greens."

Unlike Mount Juliet or the K Club, St. Margaret's has no hotel. Taking advantage of its location near Dublin's international airport, it specializes instead in corporate outings. Opened in 1992, more than twenty-five thousand rounds are played on the course annually, with about a quarter of the visitors from Great Britain, Scandinavia and Germany.

St. Margaret's also has two hundred corporate members, who pay almost £5,000 in initiation and £600 a year in membership dues— peanuts by the standards of London, New York or Tokyo, but stiff enough in Ireland. A major motivation for joining seems to be that the established clubs in the Dublin area discourage their members from entertaining large numbers of corporate clients.

The new clubs and resorts are following the example of similar enterprises in North America, and it is not surprising that the courses are about as Irish as Elvis. Admirably, St. Margaret's tries hard to create an Irish veneer, using the Celtic cross on its coat of arms, using the Gaelic word *slata* instead of yards on scorecards and making much of the fact that the two men who designed the course are Irish. But the course itself is unabashedly American in style, with elaborately shaped but shallow white-sand bunkers, huge tee boxes, man-made lakes and comprehensive watering systems that make the pitch-and-run obsolete. It is a homage to target golf.

American-style designs are still something of a novelty to Irish golfers, who have seen them on television, and they may be an enjoyable diversion for European and British visitors as well. It is also true that Mount Juliet, thanks to its hosting of the Carrolls Irish Open, has already become something of a landmark. North Americans are likely to be less than overwhelmed, however. Arguably, there are a dozen courses in Myrtle Beach (where the green fees are lower) as good as any of the new high-end layouts in Ireland. There are certainly a dozen better parkland courses (as the Irish call most non-links courses) around Toronto or San Francisco.

It's not that the fancy new courses in Ireland are *bad* golf courses—anyone with a few million pounds can afford to pay for a decent layout and keep it well-conditioned. They simply lack the qualities that bring golfers to Ireland in the first place—the spectacular natural landscape, the links terrain, the informality, the camaraderie, the sense of history, the value.

A serious golfer spending two weeks or less in Ireland could do worse than to avoid parkland courses altogether, except Killarney. If you want the pricey resort experience go to Palm Springs, the wonderful Pinehurst, the Costa del Sol or the incomparable golf hotels that dot the Canadian wilderness. When in Ireland stick to the links.

THE ISLAND

Founded: 1888
Designed by: Fred Hawtree and others

The Syndicate were very careful in whoever they invited to become annual ticketholders. The invited members were from the "best circles" and nobody who worked with their hands or whose religion differed was invited.

WILLIAM MURPHY, *A Century of Golf on The Island*

For close to one hundred years the only way to get to The Island was by row boat. And for the first half-century you needed an invitation. Originally the private preserve of a clutch of well-to-do Dublin bachelors, The Island almost went bankrupt in the 1950s, and has only reasserted itself as one of Ireland's premier courses in the last five years. But if you think The Island's history is topsy-turvy—wait until you play the links. It's an up-and-down journey over some of the world's most rambunctious linksland. Raw and stirring, The Island would not be out of place on Ireland's wild west coast, and there are a number of singular golf holes that burn into the memory.

~

IN 1887, FOUR OF DUBLIN'S MORE ELIGIBLE YOUNG MEN— frustrated at the prohibition on Sunday golf at the Royal Dublin Golf Club—rowed across a channel between the village of Malahide and a peninsula of all-but-deserted linksland known locally, if erroneously, as the "island." According to local lore, Jonathan Swift had used it for romantic outings in the seventeenth century, but for the most part the land was suitable only for grazing. Sure that the lumpy terrain would make for terrific golf, the four headed back to Dublin, and persuaded six other men to join them in forming a syndicate to secure the land and build a course.

143

The group consisted of five bankers, three lawyers, a soap-making industrialist and a brewer. All were bachelors. The attraction between man and linksland can rarely have been so strong, for six of the ten never did marry, satisfied, one presumes, with the pleasures of running their own little golf paradise.

Coming from the upper crust of Dublin society, it was no great strain for the bachelors to come up with the £10 necessary to rent the property, and for the next half-century The Island prospered as the preserve of the Syndicate—as they were known by all—and their well-off Protestant friends. Only the Syndicate had any say over the development of the club, though they invited a select few to become annual ticketholders. It was not just a question of keeping out Catholics and tradesmen, a common practice at other early clubs. The Syndicate's sense of caste was more refined than that. Distinctions were made, for example, between retailers, who where deemed to be not of sufficient social standing to play the links, and wholesalers, who presumably exerted themselves less and earned considerably more.

In the Syndicate's attempts to preserve the sanctity of the club, caddies presented a special problem.

"With a view to keeping the Links as private as possible, the club desires to discourage the use of 'caddies'," stated regulations published in 1897. "They are strictly prohibited on Sundays and may not be brought up on the links on that day by Club boats or otherwise, and on week days shall only be brought over when all other passengers are accommodated."

The sense of splendid isolation that the founders craved was enhanced by the fact that there was no road to the club. All visitors arrived in a large row boat—it could hold twenty people—that crossed the channel at regular intervals (an arrangement that lasted until 1971). Although women were not represented in the Syndicate, they made up almost half of the ticketholders, and The Island was known as much for its social scene as for its golf course.

"I think one of the great charms of the Island is the picnicking which precedes or follows the golf," a leading journalist of the time wrote. "There are no distracting elements such as liquor bars but this does not mean that a guest will be thirsty. There is no professional but the club enjoys the services of excellent boatmen, who also act as greenkeepers."

Irish independence altered the power structure that had made The Island possible. At first the Syndicate was unmoved and continued to run the club according to the old rules. But by the 1930s, as the original Syndicate members began to lose interest or die off, and as Ireland suffered economically, the condition of the course began to deteriorate. Ticketholders from other religions and professions were let in, but few resources were allocated for the upkeep of the course, which began to resemble, quite literally, a cow pasture, as cattle damaged greens and left their droppings everywhere.

Finally, after the Second World War, the Syndicate's heirs handed the club over to the annual ticketholders—the people who actually played the course. In the next two decades the new, democratically constituted club, which had far fewer resources than the original founders, desperately tried to keep The Island afloat. A proposal to reduce the course to nine holes in 1963 was only narrowly defeated, and in 1971 the membership gave serious consideration to selling the club to an American millionaire.

But the members persevered, and their fortunes truly changed with a brave decision to take out a sizable loan to build a new clubhouse in 1975, and to make enhancements to the course. Although the redesign was undertaken painfully slowly—taking fifteen years—it was also famously successful. Today The Island is like some long-neglected but lovingly renovated old building. It has quite suddenly blossomed into one of Ireland's golfing treasures. The rediscovering of The Island has really only just begun in earnest, even by the Irish. But with its proximity to the Dublin airport, it won't stop any time soon.

The Course

The Island has almost nothing in common with the classic Dublin-area links of Portmarnock, Baltray and Royal Dublin. Instead, its camel-hump dunes seem imported from Ballybunion. Whereas its Dublin neighbors are graceful, spacious and only moderately undulating, The Island is twisty, hilly, cranky and unpredictable. Although the redesign removed its zaniest and most anachronistic features, the comments of an Irish writer in 1908 hold just as true today:

> No one can walk around The Island and declare the course uninteresting. It is full of weird and wonderful interest which might assume the nature of nightmares to a golfer whose unlucky star is in the ascendent . . . . The hazards throughout are natural and fearful.

It is unclear who designed the original course in 1887, or who made the first set of amendments shortly before the First World War, although one can imagine the Syndicate members stalking their terrain in a waist-coat, flask in hand. Several holes remain, at least in part, from that time, including the fifth through the ninth, and the eleventh and twelfth.

The recent enhancements are a rare example of a historic course that has been made substantially better. The British architect Fred Hawtree mapped out the changes in 1973. These were slowly implemented with the assistance of Eddie Hackett. The revised layout respects the often crazy, natural terrain and thus retains some of the quirky and charming character of the original course. It also remains true that no two holes at The Island are much alike. Notable among the new additions are the rather grand first hole, an uphill par 4 cut through an enormous sand bank, and a strong finishing stretch. But some of the most memorable holes are leftovers from the previous course. The best may be the thirteenth, a cliff-side carry of 200 yards across an inlet. And next up is the notoriously skinny fourteenth—a short par 4 that slithers like an eel along the water's edge.

The two nines are quite different in character. The short front side—with eight tight par 4s and one par 3—is at once claustrophobic and charming. The fifth and the eighth, with their blind tee shots and zany, undulating fairways, have a strong nineteenth-century flavor.

The back nine is tougher and bigger, starting with Hawtree's long par-5 tenth; it's 100 yards longer than any hole on the front, and tempts long hitters to skirt dangerously with an out-of-bounds fence. The contrasting quality of the nines is compelling, and every round is made more memorable by terrific views of Ireland's Eye, and of sailboats in the harbor.

Word about the quality of golf to be found at The "New" Island has spread quickly, and the club feels able to charge visitors some rather stiff green fees. However, the air of elitism that characterized the club's early years has disappeared for good. After almost 110 years, you could say that The Island has finally come of age.

Location:	Four miles from Dublin Airport, take R126 east off the main road and keep asking for directions. You will get lost at least once.
Restrictions:	No visitors on weekends
Green Fee:	£27-30
Secretary:	Theresa Monks
Address:	Corballis, Donabate, Co. Dublin
	phone: (01) 843-6462 fax: (01) 843-6205

PORTMARNOCK

Founded: 1894
Designed by: W. C. Pickeman and others

The charm of Portmarnock is difficult to describe. There is little sign of artificiality and it is one of the most natural links in the world.

HAROLD HILTON, 1902

Only ten miles north of Dublin, Portmarnock is a world classic. Understated and enchanting, ever changing in the most natural of ways, yet full of energy, intelligence and beauty, Portmarnock is like a great piece of classical music—its genius seems to come from within. There is no reason to expect that such a course should evolve here—there are more interesting stretches of linksland, and there has been no famous architect to guide things. Yet the value of Portmarnock, like St. Andrews, seems only to grow over time.

AS ROYAL PORTRUSH IS TO THE NORTH, PORTMARNOCK IS TO the Republic—an undeniably great golf course that has been at the center of things since golf was established in Ireland. Even the land Portmarnock sits on has a famous pedigree—it was once owned by the Jamesons, the great distilling family, and for years a Jameson was president of the club. The club's flagpole came from the family yacht. To be at the center of Dublin society in the nineteenth century meant being Protestant, of course, so that's what Portmarnock was. The club's first professional was admonished for "compromising matters by taking an Irish wife."

It didn't take long for Portmarnock to acquire a reputation, both for the quality of its golf course and for being one of Ireland's most desirable clubs. By the turn of the century the great amateur Harold Hilton had called it the "most natural links in the world," and by 1905 there were 350 members and a waiting list to get in. In the same year the fine clubhouse, still in use, was built.

Women were not allowed to join, however. The first mixed foursome competition at the club was met with shock by many members, who argued that "the club had fallen from its high estate in sanctioning such a competition." In fairness, however, there has always been a gallant side to the club's chauvinism. Until 1905 no green fee was charged to women, who were allowed to play during the week, and Portmarnock has held the Irish Ladies' Championship three times. Portmarnock was also the site of the British Ladies' Amateur in 1931.

Although women are still not able to join, Portmarnock changed with the times in other respects. The honorary secretary in 1921, for example, was both Irish and a Catholic. But the club has remained, until this day, a refuge for Ireland's elite.

When Eddie Hackett became the professional at Portmarnock in 1939 he was told to remove his car from the parking lot and to eat his lunch in the kitchen.

"That's just the way it was in those days," he remembers. "The professionals saluted the members. I didn't mind, I loved the game so much."

If no one seems to hold a grudge against Portmarnock, despite its occasional airs, it is perhaps because the members have always known that the most important thing about the place is the miraculous golf course itself. The club has hosted countless Irish and international tournaments and visiting golfers have always been given a cordial welcome.

"The club is exceptionally hospitable to strangers," wrote Englishman Edward Markwick in the *Golfer's Magazine* of August 1900. "When properly introduced, you are accorded a week's free play; and your bodily comforts will be excellently looked after by a very obliging steward. If you are alone you will presently be accosted by some member and offered a game, and a drink, with the genial hospitality so peculiarly Irish."

There is an appealing air of mystery about the origins of the great links. It *is* established that William Chalmers Pickeman, a Scottish insurance executive, rowed over to evaluate the golfing potential of the peninsula on Christmas Eve in 1893. Pickeman designed a number of the very early Irish courses, and since Portmarnock was his pride and joy (he was honorary secretary until 1917) it is probable that he is responsible for getting the links on the right track. He certainly had a hand in early designs, and he may have been assisted by Mungo Park, who served as professional for one year.

On the whole, however, Portmarnock seems to have mostly evolved. The first greens were placed on the most natural sites available, and tees, fairways and hazards were more or less put where they had to be, given the impossibility of moving earth. Not that things remained static. As the decades passed the members added bunkers, extended tees, moved the odd green, and even added a hole or two (the last addition being the dramatic par-3 fifteenth, in the 1930s). But the course never underwent an extensive remodelling. The integrity of the original links, dictated by nature, seems to be intact.

Today, Portmarnock is over 7,000 yards from the championship tees, and has withstood challenges from the greatest players in the game. It is interesting that no fewer than seven Masters champions have won tournaments at Portmarnock (Sam Snead, Arnold Palmer, Ben Crenshaw, Bernhard Langer, Jose-Maria Olazabal, Seve Ballesteros and Ian Woosnam) for the course shares certain features with Augusta National—both have surprisingly generous, but undulating fairways, and each demands approach shots of uncommon skill to carefully guarded and difficult-to-hold greens.

In recent years, many of the world's great players have been introduced to Portmarnock at the Irish Open, played here on twelve occasions between 1976 and 1990. But while Portmarnock will undoubtedly remain the finest links course never to host a British Open, it has a surprisingly rich history of hosting other major competitions. In 1949, for example, one of golf's major championships, the British Amateur, was played at Portmarnock, a situation made possible due to southern Ireland's ambiguous status as a Free State within the British Commonwealth. Before the championship the Irish Prime Minister declared Ireland a Republic, but the tournament went ahead as scheduled, and was won by Max McCready.

In 1991 the Walker Cup was held at Portmarnock. The American team, led by Phil Mickelson, won by 14 to 10. Mickelson created a bit of a sensation in the practice round by hitting two balls onto the fifteenth green—one left-handed and one right-handed.

But the most important tournament ever played at Portmarnock was the 1960 Canada Cup (later renamed the World Cup). In the 1958 Canada Cup, played in Mexico, Portmarnock club professional Harry Bradshaw had teamed with Christy O'Connor to win the Cup. The victory caused great excitement in Ireland, where golf had been in the doldrums for many years, and the 1960 event at Portmarnock was played in glorious weather in front of colossal galleries. It didn't hurt, either, that Arnold Palmer was on hand to lead the United States to victory, in partnership with Sam Snead. Even today, that tournament is cited as a turning point for the popularity of golf in Ireland. Once again, Portmarnock was at the center of things.

THE COURSE

Portmarnock starts in a serene and welcoming way, with a short, easy par 4 along an estuary separating the peninsula from the mainland. It's the last time salt water comes into play on the course until the fifteenth, and for the most part Portmarnock's beauty is something you feel in your bones rather than see. Since the links is sealed off on three sides by the sea the impression is one of seclusion, and there are few elevated points to remind you of what is out there, beyond the linksland. Everything seems designed to help the golfer focus on the task at hand.

The next couple of holes are also short par 4s, but far more confusing and challenging. The fairways are less well defined and the greens are bunkered in a quirky and dangerous manner. Classic examples of holes that you just know you will birdie *next time*.

Now Portmarnock flexes its muscles, with three very long and splendidly natural holes through graceful dunes. The fourth and fifth have only one bunker between them. After the short seventh, there are four more classic par 4s.

By this time it will be clear that you will be playing low to the ground at Portmarnock—in the fashion of the older Scottish links—and that the view from the tee will tell you very little. When the drives aren't out-and-out blind, it is still difficult to see exactly where to play—the holes curl in one direction or another, and the landing area is often partially concealed by fescue-covered hills. The greens are just as unsettling—the quirky swales, formed by the elements, don't adhere to expected patterns, and the size or even existence of the pot bunkers is not always obvious.

Although all of the holes are good, the fourteenth and fifteenth have probably generated more praise than any others. Henry Cotton, so it is said, thought the fourteenth to be the greatest hole in golf, and while that is surely an exaggeration there are few holes where birdie looks so plausible and bogey is so much more likely. It is only about 380 yards from the men's tees, and the beautifully natural plateau green looks enticing from any position on the fairway. It is only when you get to the putting surface that you realize how tightly-guarded it is, with slopes that reject all but the best shots into severe pot bunkers.

The greatness of the fifteenth—a long but lovely par 3 along the shoreline—is apparent from the tee. The sudden view of the Irish Sea, after so many holes played in the middle of the linksland, is rather startling, and complicated by the knowledge that the ball could land on the beach. The rough to the left of the convex green is no treat either, and the wind is always stronger here than at any other place on the course.

If your nerves are still steady and you can avoid the panoply of fairway bunkers, then the short par-5 sixteenth offers a birdie opportunity. Don't expect similar chances on the final two holes, both par 4s, which are long and uncompromising.

Location:	Ten miles north of Dublin; just south of Malahide on R106
Restrictions:	Monday, Tuesday and Thursday are the best days for visitors
Green Fee:	£40-50
Manager:	J.J. Quigley
Address:	Portmarnock, Co. Dublin
	phone: (01) 846-2968 fax: (01) 846-2601

COUNTY LOUTH *(Baltray)*

Founded: 1892
Designed by: Thomas Gilroy, Tom Simpson

This is just about as fine a piece of linksland, ordained by nature for golf, as we have ever seen.

TOM SIMPSON, 1937

Although deeply respected in Ireland, the superb links beside the village of Baltray, an hour's drive north of Dublin, is little known elsewhere. Masterfully overhauled by architect Tom Simpson before the Second World War, Baltray (as the course is better known) demands accurate driving and an inspired short game. It may be the most intelligently bunkered course in Ireland, and each slick and undulating green presents a unique challenge. There is no breathtaking seaside scenery at Baltray. You will find few of the giant dunes and elevated tees so common on Irish links. But there is one entirely absorbing hole after another. Add one of the country's most commodious and friendly clubhouses (it doubles as a bed and breakfast) and you have one of Ireland's most satisfying golf experiences.

ARRIVE AT AN IRISH GOLF COURSE BY YOURSELF, AND THERE are two things that are gloriously uncertain—the weather and who you may end up playing with. The last time I played Baltray I hit the jackpot on both fronts. It was a Monday in temperamental November, but the morning was lovely and calm. I teed off just in advance of a large "society" of boisterous Dublin journalists, more than content to savor the joys of one of my favorite links in quiet solitude.

No one had hit off number one for some time (I had waited around for a possible playing companion), and the course seemed entirely empty before me, but on the fourth tee I ran into two gentlemen who were using that hole to start their round. They played twelve holes each day, they told me, beginning on the fourth, and cutting across from the eighth green to the twelfth tee. But would I like to join them until that point?

It was a fortuitous meeting, for one of my temporary companions turned out to be none other than Peter Lyons, a member of County Louth Golf Club for more than fifty years and a former President of the Golfing Union of Ireland. An astonishingly youthful eighty-three years of age, he moved and played in a dignified and graceful manner that could still be admired.

His memory turned out to be as crisp as his play and, to my delight, he vividly described the day, in 1937, that the great British architect Tom Simpson marched up the very same fairway. The fourth today, it was the opening hole of the old course then in use, and Lyons remembers Simpson saying, "If all the holes are like this, I won't have much to do." Simpson had been engaged by the club to update the course, and he did, in fact, leave the hole alone. It remains a decidedly old-fashioned and intriguing par 4 with no bunkers, but with a fairway that heaves and gyrates just before the green.

Simpson, however, changed every other hole in the links, which had been originally laid out in 1892 by Thomas Gilroy, the first captain of Royal Dublin. In his written report to the members of Baltray, Simpson was brutally frank:

> It would be idle to pretend that in its present form and condition it is a good golf course. . . . Unfortunately, those who were responsible for the design of the course as now planned, failed to observe and/or take advantage of the glorious possibilities that the ground afforded. . . . The bunkers on your course, so far as they exist, serve no useful purpose whatever in governing the play of the hole. The weakest point of all is your one-shot holes, they are featureless and badly sited.

As Peter Lyons, his friend Jim McCullen and I stood on the tee of the par-3 fifth, the efforts of Simpson and his assistant Molly Gourlay were plainly evident. Baltray's par 3s are now considered among the loveliest in Ireland (they may well be the work of Gourlay as she paid special interest to the short holes). The fifth calls for a precisely struck short iron to a pretty, elevated green that falls off on all sides. As we putted out,

Lyons pointed to the pot bunker that lies smack in the middle of the fairway on the long sixth.

"Simpson put that bunker there just to create controversy," he said. "He claimed that if you made a perfect course it would be of no interest. He told us that half the people will say that bunker shouldn't be there, and the other half will say it is perfectly placed!"

I avoided the bunker, and found the rough beside the green in two on the par-5 hole. But then I found my chips bouncing back and forth across the small, elevated green.

"The greens can be difficult," sympathized Lyons, who had hit four shots, all straight and accurate, to within ten feet of the flag. He holed the putt for a par, while I took an eight.

I knew from the club history book that Peter Lyons had left his mark on Baltray in a variety of different ways, over an astonishing number of years. A past captain and past president of the club, he donated the trophy for the inaugural East of Ireland championship in 1941. Played each year at Baltray, it is one of Ireland's most prestigious amateur tournaments. And here he was, more than fifty years later, three strokes better than I over four holes.

The last hole we played together was the eighth, a good, deceiving dogleg around some dunes. Lyons pointed out the spot where an over-zealous club captain (hoping to improve on Simpson's work!) built a new green. The members ignored it, and Simpson's original design remains intact.

Lyons had mentioned that he was also a member at Portmarnock, so as we shook hands I asked him about the difference between the two clubs.

"Well I score better there, for one thing," he said with a smile. "And I guess you'd say the social life is busier here. You don't see anyone after dark at Portmarnock."

With that we parted company, Lyons and his playing partner resuming their specially tailored round at the twelfth.

I played the ninth by myself, but started the back nine with two new companions—a man in his late twenties named Sean, I believe, and his mother. They were delightful companions and filled me in on what it was like to belong to Baltray today.

By now I had found some rhythm and somehow managed to outplay Sean, who seemed to want to impress me with his prodigious length off the tee. Baltray is the kind of course that rewards sober second thought, however, and nowhere is that more true than on the marvelous trio of successive par 4s that starts on the 410-yard twelfth.

The twelfth is the kind of complex dogleg that you find only on links courses. Thanks to dunes of various sizes and some well-placed bunkers, there are any number of possible lines on the drive, and the fairway narrows at the elbow of the dogleg to challenge the ambitious. The approach shot, which looks radically different depending on where you have hit the tee shot, is played rather thrillingly between the largest dunes on the course to a half hidden, saucer-shaped green.

The even longer thirteenth is one of the most attractive holes on the course, set picturesquely among the dunes that run along the ocean (the crashing surf is hidden but noisy behind them), while the 322-yard fourteenth is one of the most memorable short par 4s in Ireland.

With the wind in your face, the drive on the fourteenth is an intimidating, if short drive over a wasteland of dunes, setting up a pitch to a severely undulating green that rejects all but the most perfectly placed shots. Elsewhere on Baltray, Simpson has used bunkers to great effect, but on the fourteenth there are none. Instead, he has used the natural slopes of the land to create a gem that is tantalizing and frustrating for both long and short hitters alike.

The rest of the back nine is just fine—there are really no weak holes on Baltray—with more doglegs, well-placed and deep pot bunkers, and green sites that always make you think. Baltray represents Simpson at the height of his considerable powers. The intelligence of its layout and the challenge of its greens is reminiscent, in spirit at least, of his contemporary Donald Ross's work at Pinehurst #2.

Sean and his mother, who played in mixed competitions as a team, confirmed to me that Baltray's reputation as a sociable club was well intact. The family had been members for years, but with the recent golf boom the waiting list was now a mile long. Sean was hoping to be in good enough form to bag a turkey in the pre-Christmas competitions that are a tradition at Baltray and most other clubs in Ireland.

After only eighteen holes, I felt that my various companions had given me a taste of Baltray past and present. I entered the locker room with the immensely contented feeling generated by fascinating golf and warm, good-humored Irish conversation. In the summer, when there is more light, you will want to play two rounds at Baltray, although it is easy to get sidetracked by the comfortable bar. The clubhouse is a converted hotel, and still has rooms for rent. Some visitors use its bed and breakfast as a base for golfing trips up and down the east coast.

I was soon joined in the clubhouse by the Golfing Society that I had left behind on the first tee. Being journalists and Irish, they were eager interlocutors, and I was soon swallowed up in a grand debate about politics, the latest Dublin plays and, of course, the best courses in Ireland. One of the journalists, it turned out, had even written a successful golf thriller, *Operation Birdie*, about a fictitious IRA attack during a British Open at Turnberry.

It was a lovely end to a day that, like the course itself, took many unexpected twists and turns, all of them agreeable. The kind of day that makes travel anywhere, and especially in Ireland, so worthwhile.

Location:	Baltray, three miles east of Drogheda on R167
Restrictions:	Weekdays other than Tuesday are best for visitors
Green Fee:	£30-35
Manager:	Michael Delany
Address:	Baltray, Drogheda, Co. Louth
	phone: (041) 22329 fax: (041) 22969

MOUNT JULIET

Founded: 1991
Designed by: Jack Nicklaus

For those seeking the privacy of their very own country retreat, more secluded accommodation can be provided in the three luxurious suites at Ballylinch House. A favourite venue for small private meetings, it offers all that is best in traditional country living, including a personal housekeeper and a private room for your chauffeur.

MOUNT JULIET INFORMATION PACKAGE

Three hours' drive south of Dublin, the golf course at Mount Juliet is an immaculately groomed playground for the rich and chauffeur-driven. For North American visitors there is little reason to sample its expensive charms, unless you're fond of foxhunting or feel an urge to go all the way to Ireland to play a golf course you could play in West Palm (or even Myrtle) Beach. British or European visitors may enjoy the novelty of playing a Jack Nicklaus creation, although there is also a new one at Gleneagles in Scotland. Site for several years of the Irish Open, Mount Juliet is part of a luxurious resort that celebrates the leisured life of the aristocracy that the Irish spilled so much blood in their efforts to overthrow. Bring your helicopter—there's a landing pad on the grounds.

"DO YOU SMELL IT?" ASKED SEAN, OUR PLAYING PARTNER, AS we walked down one of Mount Juliet's immaculately groomed fairways. "There's a dog kennel over there. You can smell the dead meat they give to the dogs."

We tried not to inhale and asked Sean how he had come to be a member at Mount Juliet, one of Ireland's most expensive courses. He seemed out of place with his tattered golf bag (which he carried like a suitcase) and running shoes. He grew up in the area, as it turned out, and could remember the parties at the old estate (now turned into a luxury hotel), to which locals of his family's class were definitely not invited. Sean had joined the club as part of a corporate membership package—really just ten people banding together and sharing the fees. He was actually self-employed and lived in a fairly distant town. But he had the flexibility to drive down to Mount Juliet on a fairly regular basis, and could stay with his parents, who still lived nearby.

Mount Juliet was principally a resort, and somewhat out-of-the-way for the regular player. Membership was a bit thin.

"We don't have much of a club atmosphere," Sean said. "But it's our own fault really."

On the fourth hole, a terrific dogleg to a green that juts out into a pond, we passed a man sitting beside the green with a walkie-talkie.

"He's making sure that no one fishes balls out of the water," Sean explained. Apparently the chemicals in the pond could damage the green, and the Irish Open was only a week away.

Sean pointed out some other interesting sights. On the seventh hole, for example, we passed a controversial new house, apparently purchased by a rich Canadian. The neighbors (we couldn't see any—they must have been down the road a ways) had for some reason complained about an enormous skylight the owner was proposing.

Soon afterwards we saw a helicopter fly across the course.

"I think it's the prime minister of New Zealand," Sean said.

We played under the shadow of stands and caravans—the Irish Open is a regular stop on the European PGA tour—on a course that was in pristine condition. Despite our deep-seated objections to the gentrification of golf that such resorts exemplify, it was impossible not to enjoy the round. The design was more restrained than one might have expected from Nicklaus, and fit the estate surroundings rather well. A good job had been done with a lot of money. Sure, there are maybe fifty courses as good in the Carolinas, and the rather ordinary terrain could in no way compete with the majesty of Ireland's great seaside links. But it was a beautiful day and we felt rather privileged as we putted out and waved to the empty stands that surrounded the green on the finishing hole—a lovely par 4 that hugs the edge of a lake.

After the round we headed to the fabulously appointed change-room, showered, and took a late lunch in the courtyard café. There, for the first time in all our Irish travels, we found alfalfa sprouts next to our sandwiches and rock sugar with our tea. The staff were extremely friendly and unaffected, and didn't mind a bit when we ordered the cheapest thing on the menu. At a nearby table was the kind of Irishman we hadn't seen at Ballybunion or Enniscrone—dressed in a blue suit and expensive Italian loafers, he was making deals in a loud voice on a cellular phone.

Afterwards, we thought it our duty to tour the facilities and to fantasize about actually staying here (it would cost between £125 and £150 a night in the summer—golf is extra). There was the glistening museum quality to the furnishings common in such places, and we learned that there were plenty of non-golf attractions. Sean was right—there is an organized hunt most days in the winter months, as well as trapshooting, fishing and archery. And a spa, of course.

After driving out of the estate, we immediately picked up a hitchhiker. A sculptor, she was on her way to her home in nearby Thomastown, a crafts center that attracts artists from all over Ireland. We had an interesting, if brief discussion about the creative life in Ireland, and when she asked us if we were staying at the estate, it felt rather good to say no—we were on our way back to Dublin. It was a B&B for us.

Location:	Follow signs from Thomastown, about three hours southwest of Dublin
Restrictions:	None
Green Fee:	£60-65
Contact:	(Ms) Phil Lanigan
Address:	Thomastown, Co. Kilkenny
	phone: (056) 24455 fax: (056) 24522

THE KILDARE HOTEL AND COUNTRY CLUB

Founded: 1990
Designed by: Arnold Palmer and Ed Seay

This green was officially opened by Crown Prince Albert of Monaco during his visit to the K Club.

SIGN BY THE THIRTEENTH GREEN

The well-designed parkland course at the "K Club" has an exciting finish that features pond-side greens on the final four holes. The setting is opulent to the point of excess, and you have to live a millionaire's life to distinguish between the amenities at the Kildare Hotel and Country Club and those at Mount Juliet. Although plagued with drainage problems in its first few years, the Kildare golf course may eventually turn out to be the most interesting inland course in Ireland.

THE K CLUB IS THE DREAM-COME-TRUE OF DR. MICHAEL Smurfit, chairman of the Smurfit Group conglomerate, and a successful horse breeder. The Smurfit Group—which owns quite a number of things in Ireland—has done much to assist junior golf, and its chairman won't be the last person to spend millions on building a glamorous golf resort. But the K Club is nevertheless a queer distortion of the qualities and values that make golf in Ireland so attractive to the visitor.

Whereas the great links of Ireland have been laid out to fit in with the natural terrain, promotional literature from the K Club brags about reinventing the landscape by moving "a million tonnes of soil" and creating a cluster of man-made water hazards. Most golf clubs in Ireland take pains to be accessible to everyone, but the K Club caters to the hugely wealthy. And even though the Irish people were oppressed for centuries by the British ruling class, the Kildare Hotel and Country Club makes no apologies for romanticizing the lifestyle of the landed gentry.

The hotel, adjacent to the golf course, is crammed with some wonderful paintings, however, including a room devoted to the work of Jack Yeats, the poet's brother. If you have an interest in art, and decide to shell out the money necessary to play the golf course, the Yeats Room is worth checking out—time your visit correctly and you may be able to sample some sandwiches left over from afternoon tea.

For sheer irony, however, search out the corridor that has an exhibit on Irish revolutionary heroes. It is rather interesting, actually, if terribly out-of-place in this celebration of the aristocracy.

The golf course is a good one, though it is difficult to know whether Palmer and Seay have met the extraordinarily high expectations of their owner—the K Club bid to host the Ryder Cup even before the course was built. Smurfit did sponsor a European Tour event here in 1995 (the European Open), which Bernhard Langer won in a playoff after sinking a seventy-foot eagle putt on the eighteenth.

Despite the huge amount of earth that has been moved, the course has an intimate charm that recalls Killarney. There is a nice mixture of water and trees, and American-style mounds and sand traps are kept to a minimum. The K Club seems Irish in a way that Mount Juliet, for example, does not. As a designer, Mr. Palmer has had his critics but his two efforts in Ireland—Tralee and the K Club—have not done his reputation, or that of Ed Seay, any harm.

Location:	Straffan, seventeen miles southwest of Dublin off N7
Restrictions:	None
Green Fee:	£50-80
Director:	Ken Greene
Address:	Straffan, Co. Kildare
	phone: (01) 627-3111 fax: (01) 627-3312

ROYAL DUBLIN

Founded: 1885
Designed by: H. S. Colt
Made Possible by: Captain Bligh

By any standards, this is as good a traditional links as you will get.
CHRISTY O'CONNOR SR.

One of the oldest and most historic clubs in Ireland, and indeed the world, Royal Dublin is a subtle and intelligent links on an island that appeared magically in Dublin harbor in the nineteenth century. The island is also a bird sanctuary, and there is an unlikely sense of seclusion on this traditional and relatively flat golfing ground that today lies in the shadow of factory chimneys, only fifteen minutes from the heart of the capital. This used to be the most exclusive club in Ireland, but the staff and members at Royal Dublin are genuinely happy to see you.

~

NOT MANY CLUBS CAN CLAIM TO HAVE HELPED CHANGE THE course of golf history, but Royal Dublin is one of them.

The club's initial eighteen-hole course (the first in Ireland) was laid out on Easter Monday in 1885 by a Scottish banker named Lumsden who tramped around Dublin's Phoenix Park with eighteen jam jars and the same number of red flags. Golfers all around the world should be glad he did, because the next year the newly formed Dublin Golf Club was patronized by the most famous and influential golfer in the world at the time. Arthur Balfour wasn't a great golfer (he had an eleven handicap) but he was one of the most dashing politicians of his day. Ireland was still part of the United Kingdom, and Balfour had recently taken up the extremely sensitive position of Irish Secretary. A predecessor in the position had been assassinated in Phoenix Park by Irish separatists only two years earlier, and Lord Balfour's determination to play his weekly round of golf at the Dublin Golf Club, no matter what the risk, became the talk of Britain. He took a modest bodyguard of two detectives with him—one to carry his clubs and the other to act as forecaddie. This demonstration of golfing courage contributed to the Balfour legend and helped to ignite the golf frenzy that soon overtook the upper classes in England, Ireland and America. (Between 1885 and the turn of the century, the number of golf courses outside Scotland grew from a handful to over one thousand.)

Dubliners who used Phoenix Park for other purposes were baffled by the game. As was the fashion of the time, members of the Dublin Golf Club wore a red coat and knickerbockers as a kind of warning signal to passers-by, and members of the club were soon dubbed the "Red Loonies."

Though famous throughout the golfing world, Phoenix Park became soggy in the winter months and the indefatigable Lumsden persuaded the club to move to an island in Dublin harbor that owed its existence to, of all people, William Bligh. In the early 1800s, before the Bounty set out on its infamous voyage, Bligh helped to chart Dublin Bay for the British Admiralty. One of his recommendations was that a wall be built in Dublin harbor to prevent silting in the shipping lanes. Bligh's suggestion worked, and the soil that was displaced created an island on top of a submerged sandbank on the other side of the wall.

By 1890 North Bull Island had grown to 600 acres, with a sandy soil that was perfect for links golf. The course was laid out by Thomas Gilroy, Royal Dublin's first captain and unquestionably the best player in Ireland in the nineteenth century. Gilroy was so good that Ireland's first handicapping system used his scores as the definition of "scratch"!

Given the island's youthful age, the terrain for the new links was rather flat, but its beautiful turf (at a time when course maintenance was primitive) and proximity to downtown Dublin (only a fifteen minute ride by horse and carriage) made it the club of choice for Dublin's elite. Membership fees dwarfed those at most other clubs, and the members had the means to build Ireland's largest clubhouse, complete with staff quarters, clubmaking shop (the young Eddie Hackett, later to become Ireland's greatest architect, worked there in the 1920s) and a residence for the club professional.

More than a quarter of Royal Dublin's membership were lawyers, and the legal fraternity's fascination with the game was the subject of many jokes, including one printed in the *Irish Golfer* in 1899:

Judge: (to small boy whose head only tops the front of witness box). "Do you know the nature of an oath lad?"
Boy: "Yes, Sir, I used to be your caddie."

It was a golden age for Royal Dublin. Also known as Dollymount, after an adjacent neighborhood on the mainland, the club was patronized by a series of Royal Viceroys to Ireland, who underwrote tournaments that attracted the greatest players of the age. In 1910 the London-based writer Bernard Darwin called Dollymount one of his favorite courses, and Royal Dublin's young club professional, Michael Moran, was fast becoming one of the sport's dominant players. Moran won five straight Irish professional championships from 1909-1913, and at the age of twenty-five came third in the British Open of 1913, despite a third round of 89. His nickname of "Dyke" is still used today in Ireland to indicate a birdie.

Like so much in the world of the Anglo-Irish, Royal Dublin's golden age came to a crashing halt in 1914. The course was taken over by the British military as a training facility, and the grand clubhouse became an officer's mess. Michael Moran, just reaching the prime years of golfing life, died at the front.

By the time the members of Royal Dublin got their course back, the southern part of Ireland was independent and the country had endured a mean and bloody civil war. Royal Dublin quickly began the process of rebuilding. Before departing, the British military had paid the club £10,000 (an enormous sum at the time) to repair damage to the clubhouse, and the club's largely Protestant membership, though hardly thrilled at the prospect of Irish independence, were not as vulnerable to the winds of change as the landed aristocracy that had spearheaded the formation of golf courses in other parts of the country. There seems never to have been a thought to take the "Royal" out of the club's name, despite Ireland's new status.

There were enough resources to engage H. S. Colt, one of the premier architects of the age, to redesign the links. His work met with immediate acclaim, though some of his plateau greens wouldn't take, due to the extremely porous nature of the sandy soil on North Bull Island.

Disaster struck again during the Second World War, this time in the form of a fire that destroyed the fine old clubhouse. By some accounts, this may have been a blessing in disguise. The trials and deprivations of the war, combined with the intimacy of a temporary clubhouse, seem to have broken down social barriers. Though still an exclusive club (which did not admit women) Royal Dublin was perhaps more Irish than it had ever been before.

As the explosion in interest in professional golf took hold in the 1960s, Royal Dublin played host to several championships, including the Irish Open in 1984 and 1985. The course produced two memorable winners—Seve Ballesteros and Bernhard Langer. In fine weather, Langer finished 21 under par to win by four shots and he fired a course record 64 as well.

Through it all, Royal Dublin has retained its stature as a pre-eminent club. This is one reason why the club's refusal (along with Portmarnock) to allow women members has become a controversial issue in Ireland. Women are allowed to play as guests, but it is ironic that two of the most famous clubs in the country, which did so much to foster golf in Ireland (and elsewhere), should now find themselves behind the times.

THE COURSE

"We'll play a pound, pound, pound, then," we were informed by Pierce, who pulled a sweater over his rain jacket. The tone in his voice was not one that invited objections, and we were still a bit dazed from the overnight flight from North America.

We had just met Pierce, who joined us on the first tee. He had been a member of Royal Dublin for twenty-five years, he explained, but was recovering from a triple bypass heart operation. Then he asked us for our handicaps, calculated how many strokes we would give him, and pulled out a driver that looked at least sixty years old. After watching us butcher our first shots in Ireland, he stroked a low screamer right down the middle that seemed to roll forever.

The match was already doomed, of course, but we didn't mind. For Pierce was both a charming companion and an invaluable guide through Royal Dublin's hidden obstacles.

Writing in 1910, Bernard Darwin noted that at first Royal Dublin "looks a little flat, and bare, and even dull; we do not see where the holes are and whence and whither the players are going and what they are trying to do."

It is true that you seldom get a full perspective on what lies ahead at Royal Dublin. With so few spots of real elevation, the course's strategic strengths only fully emerge in retrospect, after you have played each hole.

The bunkers, for example, are often hidden, a feature that reminded Darwin of the world's oldest course.

"Save possibly at St. Andrews, I feel as if I have been in more bunkers at Dollymount than on any other course," he wrote. "This seems to be *the* feature at Dollymount, the amount of low cunning, if I may so term it, with which the bunkers are placed."

The sneaky bunkering remained a feature of Royal Dublin after Colt refashioned the course in the 1920s, and it is one of the charms of the links that you are never sure where the natural terrain ends and Harry Colt's design begins. Despite strong strategic elements, the course has a traditional look that seems entirely appropriate at such a historic club, and the lovely natural rhythm of the holes is a tribute to Colt's genius for creating a routing of great variety in a seamless, consistent style.

Though not as visually impressive as the more undulating Irish courses, there are many strong holes at Royal Dublin, beginning with the third. This 400-yard par 4 features an intimidating drive that must be struck boldly to the right side of a misleadingly narrow opening between sandhills. The green is ringed with bunkers, though one realizes afterwards that there is room to bounce the ball onto the green (a necessity in the summer months).

The fourth is the first of Royal Dublin's four par 3s—none are glamorous but all are long and difficult. Their severity is balanced by several short par 5s that reward accuracy off the tee as much as length. On the eighth, for example, cutting off some of the dogleg (while avoiding two insidious pot bunkers) gives you a chance to run the ball up to the green on the ever-narrowing fairway.

"The turf is light under your feet, isn't it?" Pierce exclaimed proudly as we reached the eighth green. "You have to pick them off the fairway clean."

The turf was, indeed, a delight, and we couldn't help but admire Pierce's ability to clip the ball off the grass without taking a divot.

The sense of tradition at Royal Dublin is enhanced by the old-fashioned out-and-back layout, and as we made the turn it was hard not to feel privileged to be playing golf in such a secluded and tranquil spot in the midst of an urban industrial center. Although factories loom next to the course on the mainland, the island itself is a bird sanctuary and biosphere reserve.

"They're manuring all the time," Pierce told us as we picked our way through some goose droppings. Long-legged hares were also out in force on the fairways, and we learned later that birds gather by the tens of thousands in marshes to the north of the course during the winter. There is an interpretive center beside the ninth green, and the beach on the south side of the island is a hugely popular public playground.

We lost our first pound on the ninth, of course, and fared little better on the tenth and eleventh, terrific driving holes that are pure H. S. Colt. The par-5 eleventh may be the best hole on the course. The tee is actually *out-of-bounds* and the challenge is to hit the drive back into play over a creek that runs parallel to the right edge of the fairway, while keeping the ball close enough to the creek to leave a manageable shot to the green. The putting surface slopes down from front to back, and overly-ambitious approaches can easily find thick rough behind the green.

The next two holes are brutishly long, but those who keep their score intact are rewarded with a very short par 5 and the quirky and tantalizing sixteenth. A par 4 of a mere 270 yards, it is much-complicated by the scattering of a dozen pot bunkers and an extremely undulating green.

Royal Dublin ends splendidly, with the most exciting finishing hole in Ireland, a right-angled dogleg around a piece of land called "the Garden" that is emphatically out-of-bounds. Though short for a par 5, it requires a brave shot over a huge chunk of the Garden to reach the green in two. It is here that Christy O'Connor completed a now legendary eagle, birdie, eagle finish to win an important professional tournament in 1965.

We also finished in triumph, securing a birdie and a par between us, but this was not nearly enough to dent the lead that Pierce had amassed. Perhaps feeling that this good-natured humiliation was sufficient, Pierce dismissed our determined efforts to make good on our debt. Instead, he showed us the way into the commodious Royal Dublin clubhouse, with its four comfortable bars, decent food, first-class snooker tables and lively hospitality. We stayed for dinner and then succumbed to the attraction of the pubs in downtown Dublin, which after all was only a few minutes away.

Location:	On North Bull Island in Dublin harbor, about four miles north of the city centre
Restrictions:	No visitors on Wednesday or Saturday
Green Fee:	£45-55
Secretary:	John Lambe
Address:	Bull Island, Dollymount, Dublin 3
	phone: (01) 833-6346 fax: (01) 833-6504

THE EUROPEAN CLUB

Founded: 1992
Designed by: Pat Ruddy

What I'm trying to do at the European Club is accelerated evolution. To do what St. Andrews did in 400 years, what Royal Dublin and Portmarnock did in 100 years, and do it in fifteen.

PAT RUDDY

A fascinating new links south of Dublin that was conceived, designed and developed by Irish golf writer and impresario Pat Ruddy, the European Club is a successful labor of love that makes wonderful use of one of Ireland's last stretches of muscular linksland. Although only a few years old, it is already one of the country's most challenging and satisfying links, with a host of classic doglegs through tall dunes, grand views from elevated tees, and a trio of exciting holes that hug the ocean. And for the most part, Ruddy has kept well within the boundaries of the Irish golf tradition. This is a modern course, but an intensely Irish one.

~

"I TRIED BEING A PRIEST ONCE, BUT I BELIEVED TOO MUCH IN golf," says Pat Ruddy, pausing just long enough to make you wonder whether he is pulling your leg. Then his face bursts into a big amiable smile that makes laughter irresistible.

"I'm on a high going to any golf course," he continues with his usual enthusiasm. "But going to special ones like Augusta [National], it's just where you want to be. To be there, and to look at the scenery and flowers and the goddamn grass. If it's in really good shape you want to get down and roll on the bloody thing. You know, the way a kid rolls down a hill."

There may have been obstacles and disappointments along the way (see p. 22 for a fuller account of Ruddy's colorful past), but to hear Pat

Ruddy tell it, his life has been one long roll on the grass. He is the kid who never had to grow up, who still can't quite believe that he has been able to make a living by immersing himself in the sport he loves so passionately. He has been a golf reporter, golf editor, golf promoter, golf publisher, golf architect and golf course developer. Now he is owner of one of the last championship links that will ever be built.

"I think we have a chance at a great links there." Ruddy says of the European Club at Brittas Bay, about thirty-five miles south of Dublin. "[How it will rank] on a world scale is very intricate, and the dividing factor at the end of the day will be the intangibles. You're talking about soul, about feel for the game. If it's a question of dollars the big men will win all the time, but the hungry fighter, the imaginative fighter has still got a chance in this world."

Ruddy is in a relaxed and expansive mood as we talk in his living room in the Dublin suburb of Dun Laoghire. There is a lively fire going and his wife Bernadine has spread out some tea and ham sandwiches. The day in 1988 when Ruddy showed up at Brittas Bay with a couple of shovels to begin work seems like ancient history. Golfers are flocking to the European Club, and Pat Ruddy can afford to dream a little.

"I have no doubt that it's a great piece of golf ground. I have no doubt I have done a reasonable job to start with. I have a committee of one, so I have the freedom to sit here and to think, and the freedom to do. You know when you get an examination paper you would always get a higher mark if you rework it. So there are more marks to be gained at Brittas Bay and that gives me great pleasure. All I have to do is live a while."

Ruddy's rambling house, built next to a golf course, is an entertaining place in its own right. It is part suburban home, part office (Ruddy edits his own golf magazines in the basement) and part golf museum, crammed full of amusing golf knick-knacks, musty golf books, old photographs and memorabilia. Although some of the golf antiques are undoubtedly quite valuable (they include a club with a wooden shaft and a tiny spoon-shaped head that Ruddy says was used to flick a putt over stymies) there is something engagingly artless about the house. Its contents seem to be an extension of Ruddy's personality, a three-dimensional expression of his overwhelming enthusiasm for the game.

"I've always tried to infect people with golf," he says. " I have a funny bent of mind, a mix of wild imagination but I'm an awful simple person as well. And I have a pretty analytical mind that can dissect situations."

Ruddy disguises his ambitions for the European Club in humor and self-deprecation, but he is constantly searching for those "intangibles" that will set his course apart. He has dedicated each hole to a famous golfer, and appointed an international advisory committee (called the Senate) of prominent figures in the golf world. He is toying with the idea of creating a lounge just for golf writers, and he has just finished building a giant replica of the dolmen that appears on the club logo. However, Ruddy has rejected the idea of constructing houses or another nine holes on the extra land that he has. Either option would make him a lot of money, but would jeopardize the sense of seclusion that Ruddy feels is the mark of most great courses.

"You can't build a golf course with a set square, it's an art form molding the thing into the landscape," he explains. "The developer who wants to fit in lots of roads and houses is thinking different. It's like asking me to run a four-minute mile shackled, trying to put in houses. It just can't frigging be done in my opinion."

In retrospect it seems that every road in Ruddy's life has been leading to the European Club, from the time he doodled course plans in his notebooks at school. Still only fifty, he is more than willing to take the long view.

"If you could get the European Club to be remotely as good as it can be then that would be a great life's work," he says. "The ranking of the top 100 courses [in the world is] constantly changing, and it's exciting to see if you can be part of it. If my family love the game as much as I do, we have a two-generation chance to get into the frame. Jerry [his son] is twenty-four, and he's looking at things as I do, his whole life is golf. And my daughter Sidon is twenty-one and also a slave in the fairways. So this gives us a chance. But it's such a big task, it gives you a chance and no more."

THE COURSE

For all of Pat Ruddy's charm and generosity of spirit, we are glad to have played the European Club before meeting him for the first time. Although it will be a few years before the course reaches peak condition, there is already a grandeur that is at odds with its designer's gregarious and down-to-earth personality.

The European Club comes into its own on the third, a lovely par 5 that meanders ever so naturally through high dunes down towards

Arklow Bay. The bunkering is restrained and strategic, rather than showy, and the effect is pure Irish links. The green is nestled in a natural amphitheater and partially protected by the sandhills.

The majority of the holes at the European Club take their cue from the third. While Ruddy has taken pains to provide a new twist to every hole, there is a satisfying consistency of style that will surely be called elegant when the course fully matures. Typically there is a drive from an elevated tee and an intriguing channel to be followed through the dunes. The channel usually narrows as you approach the target, and well-conceived slopes and bunkers make the greens more tightly guarded than they appear from the fairway.

"Archaic features such as the blind shot have been banished from the agenda," says the European Club's course guide, "with fourteen holes offering a tee-to-green vista; and the landing area for the drive is clearly visible on the others." Although we are rather fond of the many blind shots that distinguish Ireland's most venerable links, it must be admitted that few courses look as good from the tee as the European Club.

Midway through the back nine there is an exhilarating change of pace. The twelfth, thirteenth and fifteenth skirt the ocean, with the beach very much in play. The contrast between the holes carved through high dunes and the relatively flat, exposed seaside holes is invigorating. The walk to the extremely elevated twelfth tee, when the ocean suddenly comes into full view, is one of the most exciting moments on a very exciting golf course.

The sixteenth is a rather domesticated par 4 that doglegs around a farm fence, but the seventeenth is a wonderful return to natural duneland. It is a pretty and unaffected par 4 in its own little valley, lined with gorse and a variety of bushes and grasses.

On paper, the eighteenth is a good hole, too, but the artificial lake in front of the green is jarring on a golf course which, until this point, had made such a virtue of its Irish links heritage. This complaint is so common that Ruddy has turned it into something of a joke ("We'll let them concentrate on one mole—it will take the heat off everything else!") and there is, of course, a huge compliment embedded in the criticism. Most visitors believe that Ruddy's dream of building a modern course in a true links style has, for seventeen holes at least, come gloriously true.

"I'm trying to build a links for the next century, not just for today," Ruddy says. "Not through a giant of eight thousand yards, but through design principles that will withstand the great golfers over four rounds as the game evolves. We're not trying to build a bone-cruncher course that would crucify them to the 80s today. But one that will tease the pants off them forever."

Only time will tell if Ruddy has succeeded. Only when the greens and fairways reach true links speed will we know whether the course has the subtle charms to complement its visual excitement, whether it will ever be spoken of in the same breath as Portmarnock and Royal County Down, and whether it will be the kind of special place where some future Pat Ruddy will want to get down on his (or her) knees and roll on its fairways in excitement.

We wouldn't want to bet against it.

Location:	Brittas Bay, about thirty-five miles south of Dublin and five miles south of Wicklow
Restrictions:	None
Green Fee:	£25-30
Manager:	Sidon or Jerry Ruddy
Address:	Brittas Bay, Co. Wicklow
	phone: (0404) 47425 fax: (0404) 47346

DIVERSIONS
Dublin and the Southeast

DUBLIN IS ONE OF THE MOST ACCESSIBLE OF THE GREAT
European cities. Much of it is easy to walk around and its people are
famously easy and fascinating to engage in conversation. Founded by the
Vikings in the tenth century (the Millennia was celebrated in 1988)
Dublin is a city of satisfyingly monumental buildings, interesting museums, artistic activity and cozy pubs—and home to about a fifth of the
island's people. Working-class tenements and grand living have long
existed side by side in Dublin, which has been the home, at various points
in their lives, of the writers Swift, Wilde, Yeats, Joyce and O'Casey.
Dublin's energy and contradictions still foster the development of world-
renowned artists, although in keeping with the times they are as likely to
be rock musicians as serious writers.

Dublin was at its grandest in the eighteenth century, when the ruling
aristocracy had its own Parliament and a degree of autonomy from
London. Much of the most impressive public architecture dates from that
period.

The tourist attractions of Dublin are, by and large, contained in a
one square-mile block on the south side of the River Liffey. The famous
O'Connell Street Bridge is the main downtown artery for north-south
travel. If you are on foot, a more appealing option is the quaint **Ha'Penny
Bridge**, open to pedestrians only. Depending on the amount of time you
wish to take away from golf, Trinity College, the National Museum, the
Guinness Brewery museum, the National Gallery, St. Patrick's Cathedral,
the Grafton Street shopping mall, Christ Church Cathedral and Dublin
Castle are all worth a visit. On the north side of the river, take a quick
walk down the grand boulevard of O'Connell Street past the General
Post Office, an important site in the 1916 uprising. Note the statues of
Irish patriots and the ill-conceived Spirit of the River Liffey statue
(referred to by some Dubliners as "the floozy in the Jacuzzi").

The famous **Book of Kells** in the Trinity College Library is an illustrated version of the four Gospels of the New Testament created by the
monks of the monastery at Kells. The pages glow with the most intricate

of illustrations, done in luminous "paint" which was somehow fashioned from insects in the eighth century. The book is exceptionally fragile— only one page is on display per month. The college itself was an Anglican bastion from 1591 to 1873, when it was opened to Roman Catholics (though it remained largely Protestant until the 1960s). Guided tours are available in the summer months when classes are not in session.

The **National Museum** is worth a visit for its exhibits on the founding of Dublin by the Vikings, its material on the 1916 uprising and the War of Independence, and its collection of ancient gold objects, most notably the Tara Brooch. In the same complex of buildings, which is immediately southeast of Trinity College, are the **National Gallery,** the National Library and the Museum of Natural History. The National Gallery contains a decent collection of European painting from the Renaissance to the nineteenth century (the collection of Gainsboroughs is particularly strong), but is probably more interesting for its portraits of Irish literary giants Swift, Joyce, Shaw and Yeats.

A museum of an entirely different kind is the Guinness Brewery Visitors Center and museum at the **Guinness Brewery,** St. James Gate, just west of the downtown area. Although the brewery itself is not open for tours, the entire brewing process for Guinness stout is explained in detail, after which samples are provided. A visit here might start to explain the remarkable hold that this unique product has had over Ireland for two centuries. At the very least, you will find no larger collection of Guinness souvenirs anywhere in the world.

Dublin's two cathedrals are Christ Church and St. Patrick's. Christ Church is the older of the two, in the early Gothic style of the twelfth century. St. Patrick's was founded at roughly the same time but was almost completely rebuilt after a fire in the fourteenth century. It was built just outside the city walls in an attempt to evade municipal jurisdiction. It was the home of Jonathan Swift for thirty-two years, and he is buried here. It is a legacy of British rule in Ireland that both Christ Church and St. Patrick's are Protestant cathedrals—St. Patrick's is the national cathedral of the Church of Ireland, while Christ Church is the Church of Ireland cathedral for the diocese of Dublin.

Modern Dublin is perhaps best seen on foot in the **Grafton Street** shopping area. Between Trinity College and St. Stephen's Green the street is closed to vehicles. It has a collection of shops with the greatest variety of merchandise in Ireland—whether you wish to purchase Aran sweaters, Donegal tweed, Waterford crystal or heraldic items, they are all available here. And you're never far from a pub. Dublin is also one of the great cities of the English-speaking world for bookshops. Try in particular Fred Hanna, on Nassau Street opposite Trinity College, or any of Waterstone & Co., Hodges Figgis, Eason & Son Ltd. or the Trinity College Library Shop.

The district just south of the river and roughly between Trinity College and Christ Church is known as **Temple Bar.** It has been the focus of a major redevelopment in the 1990s, and is now a magnet for writers and artists, as well as tourists. It sports various galleries, boutiques, cafés and pubs, as well as the Irish Film Center. Late night dance clubs are attracting much attention in Dublin's answer to Soho.

Dublin castle was constructed by the Normans in 1204 and remained as the symbol, and usually the seat, of the English rule of Ireland until 1922. Much of the present complex dates from the eighteenth century, however. The State Apartments are the portion of the castle that is open to the public for tours when they are not being used for state occasions, such as the inauguration of the President of Ireland.

The Irish are passionate about sports, both the "international" sports of soccer and rugby and the Gaelic games, hurling and football. An All-Ireland final in either of the latter provides an excellent insight into Irish sporting culture. Both are held at Croke Park, on Dublin's north side, in September, but you may have to use your ingenuity to obtain a ticket. No less passionate are the supporters of the national soccer and rugby teams, especially given the remarkable success of the soccer team since the 1990 World Cup. Soccer and rugby internationals are held at Lansdowne Road stadium, south of the river in Ballsbridge. The main rugby union season (the Five Nations Cup) is from January to March. The national soccer team will have home matches throughout the year, either exhibitions (known as "friendlies") or qualifying matches for the World Cup or European Championship. Any home match for either team is a national event. A game against England is likely to bring Dublin to a near standstill.

Dublin also has an extensive theater scene, highlighted by the historic Abbey Theatre. The current Abbey Theatre was built in 1966, after the 1904 original burned down. W. B. Yeats was its first director. The Dublin Theatre Festival, held annually in September, is also excellent.

St. Patrick's Day (March 17) is, of course, a national holiday, but even in Dublin don't expect the raucous celebrations of Boston or New York. Bloomsday (June 16) is not an official national holiday, but it is a lively event just the same. It commemorates the travels around Dublin of the protagonist of James Joyce's *Ulysses*. Tourists and Dubliners alike turn out in striped blazers and straw hats to retrace Leopold Bloom's walk around the city, while readings and other events occur at various venues. Any day of the year may be made a personal Bloomsday by obtaining the *Ulysses* map of Dublin from Bord Fáilte. It sets out an extensive walk with twenty-two stops in all. True Joyce fans will also visit the James Joyce museum in the Martello Tower at Sandycove (also described in *Ulysses*).

To the south of Dublin (towards the European Club) stretches a coastline of some of the better beaches in Ireland, with the Wicklow mountain range rising in the background. The southeast region claims to be the sunniest part of the country, but it is doubtful that Bermuda feels particularly threatened. The valley of Glendalough, nestled between the Upper and Lower lakes, contains the ruins of one of Ireland's most important monasteries. It is worth a visit but can be heavily touristed in the summer months. Further southwest is the town of Kilkenny, perhaps Ireland's best preserved medieval town. It is also the home of the ubiquitous Smithwick's Ale, and tours of the brewery are available. Kilkenny's castle, the Black Abbey and St. Canice's Cathedral are the main medieval architectural attractions.

HIDDEN
TREASURES

IN GOLFING TERMS, THE NORTH AND SOUTH OF Ireland have never been separated. The Golfing Union of Ireland, founded in 1891, administers golf over the entire island, and is the oldest union of its kind in the world. That it decided to remain united after independence was no doubt partly due to the strong cultural ties among the Protestant elite which completely dominated golf at the time. In any event, the Golfing Union has had a salutary effect on the development of the sport in Ireland. With very few exceptions, golf clubs have escaped the violence that has plagued the North, and there is a genuine attempt to keep sectarian issues out of the game. If peace can be maintained in Northern Ireland, the great golfing treasures in the "six counties" will no doubt become even better known. Northern Ireland boasts two of the world's greatest courses—Royal County Down and Royal Portrush—and a number of other courses of real substance. The most interesting of these are found on the Causeway Coast, and make up the roster for the boisterous tournament of the same name that is described in the following pages. While the North is naturally influenced by culture in other parts of the United Kingdom, the Irish sense of hospitality is still very much in evidence. Northern Ireland is in most respects a cozy and friendly place, and first-time visitors are usually surprised at how much they enjoy it.

Golfing Through
the Troubles

It is almost impossible to remember how tragic a place the world is when one is playing golf.

ROBERT LYND (1879-1949), *Irish essayist and journalist*

THE OFFICIAL STARTER FOR THE twenty-seventh Causeway Coast Open carefully verifies my handicap certificate. Satisfied, he slips a four-ounce bottle of whiskey into my hands.

"You may need this out there today, lad," he says with a grin.

Outside the Starter's trailer, the wind is strong enough to knock you over. I stagger up a hill to the high perch that is also the first tee.

Fortunately, it is as sunny as it is windy, and the view is breathtaking. Below me to the right, Atlantic waves crash on a gorgeous curve of unspoilt beach. To my left are sun-dappled hills of green and yellow. Behind me, the town of Portstewart snuggles like a postcard against the thrashing sea. And straight ahead is one of the greatest opening holes in golf.

My reverie is interrupted by my playing partner, a spright, rosy-cheeked 60-year-old whom I have just met. He waves me over so that I can hear him properly through the howling gale.

"These courses would be no fun without the wind, don't you agree?" he shouts with a cheerful lilt. "It would be like playing snooker!"

I laugh with an abandon out of all proportion to the witticism. Golf will never get better than this, I say to myself.

And the crazy thing is—I'm in Northern Ireland.

Held each year in June in a string of four small towns on the northern edge of Ulster, and open to anyone with £60 and an eighteen handicap, the Causeway Coast Open is a hugely enjoyable, if often surreal experience. During the five days of the 1994 tournament, a funeral was held in Belfast for a dozen slain policemen, a man with a flamethrower attacked a high school during examinations, and a man was blown up—by mistake—in a revenge killing.

Since then there has been a shaky truce between the Irish Republican Army and the paramilitary Protestant groups. The new optimism in Northern Ireland about the prospects for peace has come none too soon. Since 1969, sectarian violence has claimed the lives of more than 3,000 people in Northern Ireland, which has a population of only 1.5 million.

Against this backdrop, the roaring success of the Causeway Coast Open is nothing short of astonishing. Each year a thousand golfers from a dozen countries ignore the depressing newscasts and descend on Ulster. We decided to join them to find out why.

The secrets begin to unfold during the engaging insanity that is the tournament's opening reception. When we arrive, the conversation (or "crack" as the Irish say) is already deafening, lubricated by an all-you-can-drink smorgasbord of complimentary Irish whiskies. There is no trace of food.

The lone Korean participant has been dragged to the microphone by tournament organizers. "If only Kim Il Sung played golf, the world would be a better place," he says in all seriousness to scattered applause.

His Worship, the Mayor of Portrush, whose enormous sash would make the North Korean leader envious, urges everyone "to go back home and tell people that Northern Ireland is a great place."

The ceremonies are overwhelmed, however, by the din of several hundred golfers talking golf. It is an invigorating, international mix. For this week, at least, the class lines that often divide golfers of rich and modest means have faded away. For the 300 or so from the Republic of Ireland, where golf is still a relatively inexpensive sport, the tournament is an affordable holiday. One group has changed hotels to save a pound a night. Several are staying in trailer parks.

At the other extreme are well-heeled North Americans and Japanese who will drop several thousand pounds in hotels, restaurants and sweater shops. There are also plenty of Scots, a couple of hundred English, and a smattering of Germans, Dutch and Scandinavians. Many have been coming for years. One regular, too ill to play, has come from London just for the "après golf."

The presence of so many foreigners is considered something of a miracle by the locals, given Northern Ireland's terrible image. "It's not like it is on TV, is it?" we are asked any number of times, despite the fact that we have only arrived the day before.

It doesn't take long for first-time visitors to shake their heads at their own good fortune, for the Causeway Coast Open is an outrageously pleasant mix of gorgeous surroundings, great hospitality and exhilarating golf.

The tournament itself is exceedingly well-run, consisting of four rounds on four different courses over five days. The Stableford scoring system (one point for a bogey, two for a par, etc.) is used and there are individual and team competitions. Team members never play together, however, and groups are changed half-way through to encourage camaraderie.

I stagger in with twenty-two points the first day, an appalling total but better than Scott and our teammate Jerry, who are overwhelmed by the wind. We are already well out of the running but are having too much fun to care. The Causeway Coast routine is taking shape—a round of golf on magnificent links followed by riotous conversation in the club bar, dinner, more drinks and more crack.

Since Portstewart and nearby Portrush are seaside resorts for Belfast and Londonderry, there are plenty of pubs, bars and nightspots. The food is mediocre, but the drink, the sing-a-longs and the jokes are world class. So is the hospitality—in Northern Ireland no one is exactly fed up with tourists. And just about everywhere we go there is a gaggle of golfers with intriguing backgrounds and a shared passion for the game.

If one had more time, there is plenty else to see. We feel obliged to tour the world's oldest whiskey distillery in the village of Bushmills (tournament participants get in free), but on this trip we miss the Giant's Causeway—the famous columns of black basalt lava that lie only a couple of miles from our hotel. We also drive by splendid old churches, ruined castles, deserted beaches, and picturesque towns that are rooted in a way that a North American finds remarkable (natives of Portrush and Coleraine, only five miles apart, claim they can identify one another by their different accents).

But it is the golf courses that are the area's most notable attraction. The Portstewart links, more than a century old but recently refurbished, is the best of the four courses played during the tournament. With its spectacular elevated tees, tremendous dunes and slick greens, Portstewart can now be compared favorably to the British Open courses in Scotland and England. The first hole—a steep descent into a fantasy of wild fescue-covered dunes—is one of the most dramatic anywhere.

Castlerock, Ballycastle and the Valley course at Royal Portrush are only a notch below Portstewart in quality. And on our "rest" day, tournament participants are encouraged to play the famous Dunluce course at Royal Portrush, site of the 1951 British Open and often ranked among the world's top ten courses.

All in all, it is a remarkable feast of golf on a twenty mile stretch of coastline.

For the 200 or so North Americans, the conditions take some getting used to. The week's most severe weather hits us on the third day at Castlerock. Flagsticks are knocked to the ground by a whipping rain that makes even putting difficult. Into the wind, it takes many of us four good shots to reach a long par 4.

"We don't golf in this &*%# in Orlando!" curses a swimming pool salesman from Florida who has taken refuge in a shack at the tenth tee that serves nothing but Bushmills and chocolate bars. He's on his fourth drink and has no intention of taking on the back nine.

For those of us who stick it out, the shared experience of surviving the elements further enhances the tournament's wonderful sense of camaraderie. Over hot whiskies in the bar afterwards, everyone has their favorite tall tale of 200-yard sand wedges downwind and putts that were blown off the green.

Any lingering anxiety about being caught up in violent "unrest" has long since dissipated. The golf clubs' claim to be rigorously non-sectarian seems genuine, and these lazy seaside towns have never really been a target for violence anyway.

Yet there are persistent reminders that this perfect golfing holiday is happening in a troubled place. There are police checkpoints, barricaded Legion halls, and warnings on the radio of "diversions due to a mysterious object on the road." (The truce in Northern Ireland was still a few weeks away.)

The contradictions become too much for Jim, an animated chemical executive from San Francisco. Jim and a Dubliner named Noel Kelly are my playing partners for two rounds.

"I don't understand how such wonderful people can get into such a terrible mess!" Jim yells at Noel, apropos of nothing, as we walk down the fourteenth fairway at Ballycastle. "All this violence and killing. It doesn't make any sense at all!"

Noel just shakes his head—whether at the truth or the absurdity of the outburst one isn't sure—and changes the subject. For the most part, the Troubles, like a death in the family, are only lightly touched on in conversation. It can't be ignored but it's the last thing anybody wants to talk about. It occurs to me more than once, however, that it is the proximity of the Troubles that gives the tournament its unique intensity. So close to the tragedy, we can't help but feel how lucky we all are.

From humble beginnings, the Causeway Coast Open now pumps a million dollars a year into the local economy, a substantial amount in an area with a population of about 50,000.

"I don't think people in Northern Ireland realize what has happened here," says John Dalzell, the unassuming but immensely popular tournament director.

Although Bushmills and the local tourist authority provide several thousand pounds in sponsorship, the tournament is essentially a volunteer effort. When Dalzell took over in 1982, only about fifty entries were from outside Northern Ireland. Now there are 700 and the waiting list is growing.

The tournament ends on an appropriately curious note. The prize presentations take place at a "cabaret" held in a colossal, charmless hotel with glittering decor. It is rural Ulster's version of Las Vegas and the entertainment consists of a lounge singer and a singularly tasteless comedian ("The best part of you went down your father's leg," he tells someone in the audience).

But the Guinness is as smooth as ever, and it's an opportunity to say goodbye to the characters we've met during the week. As we are leaving, a publicist for one of the sponsors asks our friend Jerry to pose for a fake presentation photo. He hasn't won anything, but he's of Chinese descent, and apparently it will look good in a brochure somewhere.

It is a perfect end to a strange but memorable week.

ROYAL PORTRUSH *(Dunluce Links)*

Founded: 1888   **Redesigned:** 1933
Designed by: H. S. Colt

[Portrush] is truly magnificent and Mr. H. S. Colt, who designed it in its present form, has thereby built himself a monument more enduring than brass.

BERNARD DARWIN, 1951

Site of the only British Open played in Ireland, the Dunluce links at Royal Portrush Golf Club is one of the masterpieces of golf architecture. Compared to some Irish links, the terrain is rather sedate, and the natural setting, while nice enough, is not in a league with County Down or even nearby Portstewart. It is the intelligence, precision and balance of the design that captivates at Portrush. Each hole presents a new and elegant challenge, yet each seems cut from the same cloth. Then there is Calamity, one of the world's most famous par 3s, and the glorious exclamation point that every great course seems to have.

NOW THAT SOLUTIONS TO THE UNREST IN NORTHERN Ireland seem conceivable, and the possibility exists that the British Open may return to the magnificent links in the busy seaside resort of Portrush, the number of visitors is sure to swell. Already the members feel able to charge green fees that are a small fortune by Irish standards. And although everyone is friendly and helpful enough, there is an air of we-are-doing-you-a-favor-just-letting-you-play-here that one doesn't normally find in Ireland. It is, of course, the kind of thing that descends on just about any place where demand exceeds supply.

It is hardly a new phenomenon for Portrush, which was one of the world's most popular golf courses *a hundred years ago*. In the roaring '80s and '90s—nineteenth-century variety—Portrush was a fashionable and hopping holiday destination. There were regular ferries from Glasgow, fast trains from Belfast, and a tramway that whisked visitors to the nearby Giant's Causeway ("Worth seeing? Yes; but not worth going to see," Dr. Johnson said of the famous attraction). Portrush was a "progressive" Victorian resort, meaning you could have a good time there, and the year-round population of 1,600 swelled several-fold during the summer months. Golf was exploding in popularity all over the British Isles, so when a couple of Scottish-born golf enthusiasts persuaded the Earl of Antrim to lease them ground for a links, it was an instant hit.

Golfers from Scotland, England and other parts of Ireland poured into Portrush. In 1900 a major British magazine described Portrush as the "St. Andrews of Ireland," and promised that the visitor would be treated with "plenteous kindness and whisky." By the turn of the century there were already 700 members (almost 300 of them women), making it the largest golf club in Ireland, and one of the largest in the world. Most members were from out of town—including one hundred from Lancashire! In 1908, no fewer than 7,000 paying visitors played the course—a colossal number for the time—and just as today there were moves to restrict play.

It was also a glorious time for women's golf at Portrush. There were more female members than today, and two of them—May Hezlet and Rhona Adair—were probably the two best women golfers in the world as the century ended. Between them they won the British Ladies' Amateur Championship, then the world title for women, four times in five years. Years later Rhona Adair made a celebrated trip to America and beat Margaret Curtis (who later donated the Curtis Cup) on the twentieth hole of an exhibition match at Merion.

The links used in the 1890s was nothing like today's, but by all accounts it was outstanding for its time. Its most notorious feature was the world's largest man-made bunker—150 yards across. In early photographs it resembles a meteor crater.

Despite the success of the club, members decided in the early 1930s to move the course to undeveloped linksland nearer the ocean. H. S. Colt was paid £212 for his design (a considerable sum for the day) and construction cost another £6,000. It was money well spent. Only eighteen years later the course hosted the British Open.

Bernard Darwin, reporting on the 1951 Open for the *Times*, had never before seen the Dunluce course. He was, to say the least, impressed.

"The first Open Championship ever held in Ireland was begun at

Portrush yesterday," he wrote, "and I must to my shame confess that I have never before seen this grand course. Let me at once pay it my respectful compliments."

The tournament was won by Max Faulkner, who never broke 70; he was to be the last British-born champion until Tony Jacklin in 1969. American stars were not present (this was before the Palmer revival) so the drama centered mostly on whether Bobby Locke would win his third straight Open. Locke failed, but did manage to lend his name to a famous corner of the golf world at the fourteenth.

A second of golf's major championships—the British Amateur—was played at Portrush in 1960, with the Irish star Joe Carr triumphant.

Like so many links, Portrush is in a constant battle with the elements. In the early 1980s, erosion threatened the fifth green and sixth tee, perhaps the most charming corner of the course and certainly the one with the best views. A £200,000 relief scheme was launched, and by the mid-1980s Portrush was peddling life memberships at $500 a pop to any American willing to help out.

That would have been quite a bargain, as Portrush now charges about one-sixth that for a single round. Golf is booming again in Ireland, and Portrush, with its British Open pedigree, has been the first in Northern Ireland to feel the benefit. The erosion problem seems well under control, and there is talk of the Open returning to the classic Dunluce links.

THE COURSE

Portrush's charms are not easily defined, and one is extremely hesitant to go where Bernard Darwin has gone before. In his report on the 1951 British Open, the dean of golf writers described the Dunluce course this way:

> The course does not disdain the spectacular, such as the one-shot hole called "Calamity Corner" with its terrifying sandy cliffs and its Gadarene descent into unknown depths to the right of the green; for the most part, the course does not depend on any such dramatic quality, but rather on the combined soundness and subtlety of the architecture. There is a constant demand for accuracy of driving, the more so at present as the rough is really worthy of its name and the approaches are full of varied interest. In par-

ticular there are one or two holes of the despised length called "drive and pitch" which are entirely fascinating, such as the fifth, with its green almost on the brink of the sea, and the fifteenth. The greens are full of interesting undulations and altogether I find it hard to imagine a more admirable test of golf.

Nothing has happened since to date Darwin's assessment. Colt's fairways remain elegant, clearly defined, well proportioned and full of purpose. Every tee shot presents a different challenge—the bunkers are never in the same place, the doglegs never turn at the same angle, and the elevation never seems quite the same. There is a dance-like quality to playing Portrush; it sweeps you along and swings you in a most rhythmic way, but never off your feet. The celebrated fifth hole is a good example. A short dogleg par 4 (after a long and straight hole) that offers all range of hitters increasingly risky ways to cut the corner, and a tricky seaside green. The way the fairway snakes through the sandhills—never very wide, with few steep descents or inclines, but never flat—is pure Portrush, and in this case there are no bunkers at all.

Of course none of this applies to Calamity, the mere sight of which can suck the air out of your lungs. Unless, of course, you hit a one iron like Jack Nicklaus. Colt set this 205-yard par 3 along the ridge of a deep chasm, leaving only a modest space to bail out on the left of the green, which has since become known as "Bobby Locke's Hollow." In the 1951 Open, Locke played to the spot each round, preferring to chip his second shot rather than risk disaster from the tee. Unfortunately, for most of us Bobby Locke's Hollow is not much easier to hit than the green itself. Calamity is a hole in the heroic mold, a great crashing of cymbals that only calls attention to the subtle charms that are more characteristic of Portrush.

Since Colt liked to test more than a golfer's length, the average player does not feel overwhelmed by Portrush and can fully appreciate its allure and challenge. There are six par 4s under 400 yards, and the four par 5s are all about 500 yards or less.

The most recent important tournament to be played at Portrush, the 1995 British Senior Open, was decided at the par-5 seventeenth. It features one of the largest bunkers in Ireland, sitting to the right of the fairway about 220 yards from the tee. It is terrifying for the slice-prone, but not in play for the professionals. The green may be reached with two good shots when the wind is calm or behind, but it is framed by insidious pot bunkers. Brian Barnes (who is the son-in-law of Portrush's Open champion Max Faulkner) made a spectacular eagle here on the third hole of a playoff to outduel American Bob Murphy.

The Valley Course at Portrush is by no means a weak test of golf, but it would be silly to argue that it is anything but an anti-climax to the Dunluce. Although there are some lovely natural holes, often with minimal bunkering, one is always aware that it has received less attention and care than its far more celebrated sister. It seems like a course with a lot of *potential*. Since the vegetation and terrain in the valley is quite different (the rough has more heather and the fairways, with the exception of an occasional steep descent or climb, are generally flatter) it doesn't really feel like Portrush at all.

Location:	Just east of town on Bushmills Road (the A2 highway)
Restrictions:	Best days for visitors are weekdays, except for afternoons on Wednesday and Friday. It may also be possible to play on Sunday afternoons.
Green Fee:	£43-50
Secretary:	Wilma Erskine
Address:	Bushmills Rd., Portrush BT56 8JQ phone: (01265) 822311 fax: (01265) 823139

PORTSTEWART

Founded: 1894
Designed by: A. G. Gow, Des Giffin, Willie Park Jr.

Men pretend that they go [to Portstewart] for golf, and better golfing they will not find anywhere, but in the depths of their hearts they go to the wind blown spaces in search of beauty and to hear the old music that has been played there for a million years—the lark's song, the sound of the waves, the curlew's call, the plover's flute—and inhale an air that is at once redolent of the mountains and the sea, the fragrance of flowers and the faint piquant incense of a thousand turf fires in the mountain homes across the Bann.

THE NORTHERN CONSTITUTION NEWSPAPER, 1933

With the addition of seven splendid new holes, the venerable links at Portstewart has finally begun to emerge from the shadow of its magnificent neighbor, Royal Portrush. With the green fees at Royal Portrush and Royal County Down spiralling out of control, Portstewart may be the best golf value in Northern Ireland. The front nine is among the best anywhere, and the first hole is in a class by itself. Wonderfully situated between a gorgeous stretch of Atlantic beach and the River Bann, Portstewart offers links golf at its thrilling and scenic best. Enjoy.

ALMOST FROM ITS FOUNDING IN 1792, THE SEASIDE RESORT of Portstewart has competed for holiday-makers with neighboring Portrush, only a few miles down the road. Two hundred years later, the fact that Portstewart usually came out second best has its rewards, for today it seems a more graceful and restful place than its relatively brash rival.

For its first century, Portstewart was more or less ruled by the Cromie family, who owned most of the town's land and leased it out to

189

residents. By all accounts, the Cromies were a rather moralistic and domineering lot who tended to put principle ahead of good sense. In 1855, John Cromie made the fateful decision to keep the railway from coming into Portstewart because it ran on Sundays. Portrush had no such qualms and immediately began to prosper at Portstewart's expense.

The introduction of golf in 1895 was just one in a long line of attempts to lure vacationers back to Portstewart. The civic chest-beating even made its way into the club's original constitution.

"Portstewart has been regarded as an old-fashioned Derry village, nestling quietly and quaintly by the seashore, beyond the sound of the rushing railway train," the document states. "Portstewart, like every other watering place of any pretensions, has [now] provided its visitors with a golf links. After all this, who can truthfully say that Portstewart lags behind?"

The early members at Portstewart were all well-to-do, but the first among equals was, naturally, the heir to the Cromie estate. Robert Acheson Cromie Montegu, the first captain and president, was also something of a sandbagger, winning more than his share of the handicap competitions.

Ulster's social structure gradually evolved and the club's membership broadened. The town's moralistic bent remained, however and it almost bankrupted the golf course in the cash-scarce years following the First World War. Each year at the annual meeting, a determined group of evangelical members would block motions to allow a bar in the clubhouse and golf on Sunday—reforms long since adopted in Portrush and the rest of Ireland, north and south. The motions finally passed in 1950, but not before opponents had cited everything from the Communist Menace to Creeping Materialism in their crusade to keep Portstewart dry and Sabbath-observing. In the records of the fierce debates one can get a taste of the kind of impassioned rhetoric that would fuel the Troubles two decades later.

The Portstewart links, like many in Ireland, has undergone constant evolution. The current course has its origins in a layout designed in 1910 by A. G. Gow, the greenkeeper at Portrush and formerly at North Berwick in Scotland. This routing appears to have stayed more or less intact until the 1960s. Bill Rodgers, a local historian, believes that Willie Park Jr., who is often given credit for the design, made only a few changes during his visit in 1913. The members themselves have been less reticent, and have fiddled with the course from the start—most notoriously in 1931 when dozens of new bunkers were dug in preparation for a tournament. The members spent the next decade gradually filling them in again.

To their everlasting credit, however, the members had a collective stroke of genius in 1951 when Portstewart was selected to be a site for qualifying for the British Open held at Royal Portrush. They decided to move the first tee high up on a perch overlooking the course, and to push the first green deep into the dunes. The result was one of the most satisfying first holes in all of golf.

By the 1950s Portstewart had gained a reputation as a first-rate, if not outstanding links, and members took pride in the fact that the British Open competitors actually found Royal Portrush easier than Portstewart. But next to the jewel that was (and is) the Dunluce course at Royal Portrush, Portstewart found it hard to sparkle. The club kept trying, but revisions in the 1970s to the back nine were not widely acclaimed. The only thing left to do was to extend the course into the wild terrain of Thistly Hollow.

Thistly Hollow was a particularly treacherous stretch of giant sandhills, covered by a thick layer of sea buckthorn, that had tantalized members for many decades. It had long been considered too expensive to develop the land, but modern earth-moving equipment had changed things. In typically Portstewart fashion, the task of designing the new holes was given to a local who had spent his childhood playing in the wild wasteland—the Greens Convenor and school teacher, Des Giffin.

The work was completed in 1992. Although it is still possible to find a particularly crotchety member in the bar who grumbles that the course was better in the old days, the new holes are splendid.

THE COURSE

If first impressions are important, it's no wonder that Portstewart has many friends. The first tee perches above the course and there is a terrific panorama of ocean, sandhills, the River Bann and even the hills of Donegal in the distance. Jogging down the steep incline you feel swallowed up by the linksland. Exposed to the wind, which is usually in the golfer's face, it takes a brave first shot to be long and straight enough to attack the green, which is guarded by dunes and is really but a rumor at the end of a marvelous vista.

The second hole is almost as breathtaking and every bit as nerve-racking—another steep drop from the tee to a narrow strip of fairway that rises up to a sloping green set in the sandhills. When the wind is howling there doesn't seem to be anything one can do to keep the ball in play (an illusion, actually). A professional could perhaps overpower the hole, but it's a stirring challenge for an average player.

The rest of the front nine is high-octane excitement, as you twist through Thistly Hollow via elevated tees and tricky, undulating greens. The fairways are narrow and hard and the rough unforgiving. The sixth is the best of a series of fine par 3s—a "Five Penny Piece" set up alone in the elements, and dropping off sharply on all sides. On a blustery day it can take a long iron to traverse its 127 yards, and it is always a thrill to see your tee shot land softly on the green. Many members hate the new eighth, a severe and downhill dogleg that seems to lean in all the wrong directions—like those funhouses at the fair where the floor moves. The lies are usually downhill *and* sidehill, the green slopes wickedly as well, and a couple of vicious pot bunkers swallow up the shots of anyone who bails out. We rather like it.

The back nine begins with two uphill, upwind slogs and another difficult par 3. But just when the fun is threatening to turn into an ordeal, everything changes in exhilarating fashion on the hugely elevated thirteenth tee. The towering dunes of Thistly Hollow are now behind you, replaced by the idyllic Bann, and you are likely to see fishermen casting picturesquely from the shore. The prevailing wind is, at last, right at your back and in front of you are two shortish par 5s that, relative to the tight terrors of Thistly Hollow, seem to be wide open. On a truly windy day you get almost light-headed, so drastic is the transformation—from hitting three good shots to reach an upwind par 4, to needing a good drive and an 8 iron to reach a par 5 in two. You return to earth with the fourteenth—a dandy par 3 into the wind, and three stiff par 4s that have been around for more than a century.

It's all terrific fun and certainly worth the green fee. At last, Portstewart need no longer feel it is "lagging behind."

Location:	Just west of town center on the Strand
Restrictions:	The best days for visitors are Tuesday and Friday, but it is possible to play any weekday if the course is not booked for a competition
Green Fee:	£25-35
Secretary:	Michael Moss
Address:	117 Strand Rd., Portstewart BT55 7PG
	phone: (01265) 832015 fax: (01265) 834097

BALLYCASTLE

Founded: 1890
Designed by: Various

Ballycastle lies at the foot of a very pretty glen in County Antrim, about fifteen miles to the east of the Giant's Causeway, and lately its already not inconsiderable attractions have been completed by that necessary adjunct to all well-regulated neighborhoods—golf links.

At times, Ballycastle just seems kind of slapped together—part parkland, part links, with fairways that run too close together, a couple of holes that appear too quirky by half, and a clubhouse that almost touches the eighteenth green. It shouldn't really work as a golf course, yet there is an undeniable exhilaration to be had in playing golf on the high linksland they call the Warren, which overlooks so much beauty, and so much Irish history. Amidst the views and legends you will also find many testing and intriguing golf holes.

IF YOU WERE A TEACHER TAKING STUDENTS ON A FIELD TRIP to discuss Ulster's history and lore you could do worse than to ask them to play a round at the Ballycastle Golf Club. The history lesson begins on the first three holes, which encircle the atmospheric ruins of the Bonamargy. It is in this sixteenth-century friary that the heroic figure of Sorley Boy MacDonnell is buried (hook the ball on the par-3 third and you may well end up in the graveyard). MacDonnell and his clan ruled this part of Ulster from his impressive Dunluce Castle along the coast at Portrush. After losing the castle in a siege to the English in 1589, MacDonnell somehow managed to reclaim it by raising his men in baskets up the cliffs.

The next history stop is the twelfth tee, high up on a cliff overlook-

193

ing the ocean, where a fine view can be had of the island of Rathlin. For such a rocky and barren place, Rathlin has been awfully busy over the centuries. This is where the Vikings first attacked Irish soil in 795, where Saint Columba performed a miracle in the sixth century, and where Robert of Bruce took refuge in 1306 before returning to Scotland to defeat the English at Bannockburn. According to legend, a diligent spider in one of Rathlin's caves inspired Bruce to coin the phrase, "If at first you don't succeed, try and try again." The island was also the site of a massacre in 1595 when an English fleet trapped the clan of the MacDonnells (who had been put on the island for safe keeping). On a more peaceful note, Marconi made his first successful transmission of the wireless between Rathlin and Ballycastle in 1898.

By then the golf course had been in use for almost ten years, on land provided free of charge by Miss Kathleen Boyd, a descendant of Colonel Hugh Boyd, one of Ulster's first industrialists. He developed the town of Ballycastle into something of an industrial center in the eighteenth century.

The Boyd family's legacy is clear to see from the bench at the hugely elevated seventeenth tee. There is a spectacular view of the golf course, the still-bustling town and Ballycastle's sweeping beach. In the distance are the massive promontory of Fair Head (with its 600-foot cliffs) and the famous Mull of Kintyre of Scotland.

There are any number of legends associated with the evocative landscape and the narrow channel that divides Ireland and Scotland. But while legend and history have been passed down with some precision, the origins of the Ballycastle Golf Club are something of a mystery. The club was all set to celebrate its centenary in 1991 when plans were set a flutter by a putter discovered in East Sussex. It had been presented to Naval Commander Alfred Malcolm Causton for his "indefatigable exertions in founding the club in 1890."

The centenary committee let out a collective "Oops!" and moved up their plans by a year.

If Commander Causton was the driving force in establishing the club, Kathleen Boyd must come a close second. Not only did she rent much of the land to the course free of charge, she was the club's Lady Captain for *forty-seven years* and often held women's committee meetings in her manor house. It was no doubt partly due to Boyd's example that Ballycastle had more lady members than men as late as 1953. The club's strong program for junior girls produced two national champions in the 1960s.

Boyd's long reign as captain is typical of the extraordinary continuity that marks Ballycastle's history and which is part of the charm of the course itself. Between 1894 and 1972, for example, the position of greenkeeper was held by only two men, which may explain in part why much of the original nine hole course used at the turn of the century has been preserved. Holes six to eleven survive in much the same form as they were in 1906, while the rest of the course dates from 1926 when two distinguished members of Royal Portrush—Major C. O. Hezlet and Sir Anthony Babington—were asked to suggest an extension.

The Course

Ballycastle consists of two entirely different sections. The first five holes are parkland in style and rather flat and sedate, although the opening hole does flirt with the River Margy. The most interesting hazard, of course, is the ruined Bonamargy, which comes into play on the third.

To cross the Cushendall Road back towards the clubhouse to the sixth tee is to enter a different golfing world. This is the Warren (you will still see a lot of rabbits), the linksland on which the course's original nine holes were first laid out. It is an unusual piece of golfing ground. Unlike most Irish linksland, the Warren has few high dunes; instead, it is creased with deep crevices that suck stray balls off the fairways and greens, which are typically on the highest ground and very exposed to the wind.

The sixth is aptly named Hog's Back, and if there is a way to keep the drive from rolling off the sides of the fairway into the rough we haven't discovered it. The seventh is a difficult dogleg par 4 that dips into a valley and then requires a heroic uphill approach reminiscent of the second at Ballybunion. It would surely be one of the best holes in Ireland if the tee did not straddle the sixth and eighteenth fairways. On a busy day you are likely to hear shouts of "Fore!" from all sides.

Claustrophobic layouts were common at the turn of the century, when there were far fewer golfers, and the holes on the Warren definitely have the feel of a "found course" that was up and running before golf architecture became a growth industry. One hundred years later the holes still seem fresh and unpretentious. The eighth is a formidable uphill par 3 over a gully, the ninth rolls along the beach and features an anxious and very beautiful downhill approach, while the tenth is a short and quaint par 4 up a hill to a knob of a green.

Holes eleven through seventeen are played on a higher piece of linksland across another road, and it is here that the views are bound to stop you in your tracks. The eleventh is the most theatrical hole on the course, requiring a semi-blind approach to a severely sloping green set high in the dunes, while the twelfth may be the windiest hole in golf. Only 111 yards, the tee is set out on the edge of a cliff. It is a breathtaking spot, and it doesn't really matter that the green is far too elevated for such a short par 3. Just remember to pack your hat away and batten down the hatches on your golf bag.

The next four holes are played up and down the side of a steep slope, and in the summer the most difficult challenge is inventing ways to keep downhill approach shots from bounding over the hard and well-guarded greens.

Ballycastle ends with a flourish. The seventeenth has perhaps the most elevated tee of any par 3 in Ireland (this is where you take out the camera) while the eighteenth is an excellent par 5 over rollicking terrain that features a green tucked in a rather dangerous position (for all concerned) next to the club's parking lot. Of course, when the hole was first laid out the motor car had only just been invented, and it is part of the attraction of Ballycastle that its oldest holes are also its most exciting.

Location:	One-half mile east of town, about twenty miles east of Portrush
Restrictions:	Weekdays are best for visitors
Green Fee:	£15-20
Secretary:	Hamilton Fraser
Address:	Cushendall Road, Ballycastle BT54 6QP
	phone: (012657) 62536

CASTLEROCK

Founded: 1901
Designed by: Ben Sayers

Hills and valleys alternate in the course . . . and the natural hazards pro-
vided in the rough ground, furze, bent, sand and drains render the links
exceptionally attractive to golfers who appreciate sporting chances. Some
of the holes, both out and home, Mr. Sayers described as "the best he had
ever seen."

BRITISH GOLF MAGAZINE, 1908

A true Irish-style links on the Causeway Coast, Castlerock may
be Northern Ireland's most rugged golf course, with a host of
long, demanding holes through impressive and intimidating
sandhills. When the wind is up, as it often is, Castlerock can be
a tiger—everything seems to be played uphill or upwind, and
approach shots bound off the hard and fast greens. An underrated
course and very enjoyable to play.

~

ALTHOUGH LITTLE-REMEMBERED TODAY, BEN SAYERS WAS
one of the most colorful characters in golf at the turn of the century. The
club professional at North Berwick in Scotland, Sayers was known to
cartwheel around the green after making an important putt. He competed in every British Open between 1880 and 1923, and was perhaps
the best player of the era never to win the championship. He was also a
famous club and ball maker. But his most enduring contribution to the
game may be the exciting links in the coastal village of Castlerock.
Despite a partial rerouting made necessary after the Second World War,
the links still takes its inspiration from the layout Sayers recommended
in 1908. It is one of only three remaining courses designed by the flam-
boyant Scot.

Any history of Castlerock, however, is incomplete without reference

197

to the august figure of Frederick Hervey, fourth Earl of Bristol and Anglican Bishop of Derry, who built an enormous castle just west of the present town in 1750. The only remnant of the estate is the Mussenden Temple, which the Bishop used as a library. In an unusual gesture of religious tolerance, he allowed Catholics to celebrate Mass in the temple, as there was no church nearby.

The Bishop had very fixed ideas about how the village that inevitably grew up around his estate should develop, and stipulated that no houses should be lower than three stories. The stone buildings in the town center are evidence of that edict.

Not surprisingly, the original golf course was built on lands owned by the Bishop's descendants, in 1901. The links was the main attraction of a recreation club established by a group of Anglican and Presbyterian ministers and local business and professional men. By 1908 the club was ready to invite Ben Sayers to completely revise the homemade nine-hole layout and expand it to a full eighteen holes. Enhancements were apparently suggested by H. S. Colt in the 1920s, and many of the present day bunkers and contours were the work of David Lyttle, the club professional and head greenkeeper. Five of the holes disappeared in the late 1940s when the landlords took back land for a housing development. In compensation, the club received ownership over the golfing ground that remained, and some additional land. Unfortunately, there wasn't much money in post-war Northern Ireland, and the cost of developing new holes put immense financial strain on the club. Soon the club started to sell sand from its most gigantic dunes in order to make ends meet (the contractors eventually hit the water table, and there has been a slight drainage problem on the first hole ever since). But the club persevered and the newly built holes (the first, second, eighth, ninth and tenth) were more or less in their present form by 1960.

THE COURSE

Despite the changes that have been necessary, there is no doubt that Ben Sayers deserves credit for moving the club in the right direction. Castlerock often has the feel of a championship layout, and its greens are known locally for their quickness. While driving is not nearly as strategic an exercise as it is at nearby Royal Portrush, the approach shots call for accuracy and courage. The prevailing wind at Castlerock is almost never helpful. The longest holes are usually upwind, requiring long and demanding irons to greens that are tucked between high dunes and fierce rough. Downwind approach shots are much shorter, but the green is often tightly trapped, perched on a devilish plateau, adjacent to a burn or out-of-bounds fence, or all of the above. On a truly windy day in summer, when the greens are hard and fast, even a wedge shot can be treacherous.

Castlerock's best known hole is the fourth, called Leg of Mutton. It combines a threatening creek on the left, a railway track on the right, and a raised green that is extremely difficult to hold. After a straightforward par 5, the front nine ends with four fine holes, usually into a stiff breeze. The sixth is a dogleg over a burn just in front of the green, while the seventh and eighth may be the best holes on the course—strong par 4s that feature greens set naturally and challengingly in the dunes. No bunkers are required. After the ninth, an extraordinarily difficult par 3 over 200 yards of gorse and rock, you will be ready to recuperate in the rustic halfway house.

The back nine offers more of the same, a mix of expansive and quirky downhill holes and formidable uphill ones. Against the wind, the par-5 fifteenth is perhaps the best, with its semi-blind tee shot and a narrow, twisting fairway that leads to an elevated green set in the dunes.

Castlerock finishes on an idiosyncratic note, a dogleg around an enormous mound to a sharply elevated green. It is the only green left from the original 1901 course, and if the eighteenth is unlikely to be copied by any modern architect, it is an engaging reminder of the club's turn-of-the-century origins. Castlerock has long had a reputation for being an informal and welcoming club, and the clubhouse, if not an architectural gem, boasts one of the friendliest bars in Northern Ireland.

Location:	In town of Castlerock, six miles northwest of Coleraine
Restrictions:	Monday to Thursday are best for visitors, though times may be available on other days
Green Fee:	£15-25
Secretary:	Geoffrey McBride
Address:	65 Circular Road, Castlerock BT51 4TJ phone: (01265) 848314

ROYAL COUNTY DOWN

Founded: 1889
Designed by: Old Tom Morris, George Combe, H. S. Colt

Many people know Newcastle and it is perhaps superfluous to say that it is a course of big and glorious carries, nestling greens, entertainingly blind shots, local knowledge, and beautiful turf . . . the kind of golf that people play in their most ecstatic dreams.

BERNARD DARWIN

Set dramatically in the foothills of the Mountains of Mourne, Royal County Down is recognized by all who have played it as one of the finest and most beautiful golf courses in the world. And best of all, even the paying customer can play it in blissful solitude. Ironically, much of the course's unique beauty comes from its fiercest hazard—the flowering gorse and heather that line its fairways. Then there is Slieve Donard, the graceful peak that rises up behind the town of Newcastle, creating a perfect backdrop for a course that seems to have been created with a postcard in mind. As striking as they are, photographs don't do County Down justice. On a sunny day, when the gorse is in full bloom and the scent of peat fires is on the breeze, the combination of scenic splendor, world-class links golf and the marvelous sense of isolation can be transporting. These are the links of heaven. You won't want the day to end.

"PLEASE TAKE THE LOCK OFF THE DOOR, AND CLOSE IT ON your way out—thank you." We still have that handwritten note, which had been tacked to the door of the visitors' locker room. Our rental was the last car in the parking lot, the professional's shop was shut, and the caddies had long since gone home. Dusk was just beginning to fall. We

200

had played twice through eighteen of the most magical holes imaginable, in mid-September, and had the course to ourselves. We were the luckiest people alive.

That was in 1988. Since then the volume of visitors has increased (and the green fee has soared) and if a stable peace holds in the North, Newcastle may one day see the hordes of visitors that overrun Ballybunion. For now, Royal County Down is still a blessedly tranquil place where golf, on a warm summer day, can turn into a kind of dream.

County Down is just far enough off the beaten track to keep the bus tours from rolling in. Yet the course is easily accessible for even the slightly determined—three hours from Dublin and forty-five minutes from Belfast. Although the surrounding countryside is attractive, it is not of overpowering interest to overseas visitors, and the town of Newcastle is a rather glum beach resort for Belfast's middle class, chock full of poker machines, tawdry bars and uninspired B&Bs. After playing County Down the first time we wanted to move Newcastle somewhere else, and replace it with an idyllic village with thatch-roofed cottages, horse-drawn wagons and—why not?—leprechauns.

Newcastle's shortcomings and the standoffishness of the club (visitors are quarantined in a pleasant new addition—it's just about the only place in Ireland, North or South, where visitors are not welcome in the clubhouse proper) may actually contribute to County Down's hold on the visitor. There is nothing else to do but admire the links itself.

In common with all Irish clubs established before the turn of the century, the miracle began with a cluster of well-to-do Protestants—this time from Belfast—who wanted to spread the game of golf into Ireland as an upper-class pastime.

They hired Old Tom Morris of St. Andrews to design the original eighteen holes in 1889, but by 1902 only six of his holes were left. George Combe, an early captain and one of the leading figures in Irish golf, made a series of alterations. Combe was something of a golf pioneer, introducing metal cup-liners to Ireland, inventing a wooden teeing box to protect the turf in wet weather, and devising a new handicapping system, parts of which were adopted worldwide.

Combe also brought over luminaries such as Harry Vardon from England to play the links and to comment on the design. As head of the greens committee until 1913, Combe has to be given much of the credit for nurturing County Down into a great links. Finishing touches were made on the advice of H. S. Colt in the 1920s, and today Royal County Down is generally recognized as one of the top ten courses in the world.

One of the course's champions was the great golf writer, Bernard Darwin. Reporting in 1957 for the *Times* on a tournament held at Royal County Down, Darwin was full of praise:

> I am ashamed to say that I had not recognised Royal County Down as one of the world's greatest seaside courses. I now say that I have seen nothing finer, either as a test of the game or from the point of scenic splendour.

Although it has never hosted a major professional tournament, Royal County Down was the site of the British Amateur championship in 1970, the 1968 Curtis Cup matches between the United States and Britain and Ireland, and no fewer than seven British Ladies' Amateur championships.

Within Ireland, Royal County Down has a reputation of being among the most elitist of clubs and its membership, naturally, has largely consisted of devout Loyalists. Granted its Royal designation at the turn of the century, the club named the Duke of Edinburgh as its patron in 1953. With a Who's Who of Protestant Ulster society in its membership, it is not entirely surprising that the club should get caught up in the Troubles. On a Sunday morning in 1977 a car-bomb attack caused some damage to the clubhouse. In a show of bravado of which the club is still proud, the debris was cleared up and the day's tournament went off as scheduled.

Although the bombing was by far the most serious and potentially tragic attack, the club's centenary book rather tantalizingly reports that a band of suffragettes vandalized the club back in the 1920s without providing any more details. If the members' chauvinism was at the root of the incident, there was undoubtedly some cause. Though women have been active at the club since its inception, female members were not, until recently, allowed into the clubhouse unaccompanied by a man. Although a much less glamorous Ladies' Course was built in 1909, all women had to allow men to pass them on the main course until 1962.

If it is disappointing that visitors are not encouraged to mix with the members, County Down at least encourages visiting golfers to play. And after some initial resistance, it also allowed Newcastle locals to form a second club—called the Mourne—which has rights to play on the championship links. It is in the Mourne club's bright and brassy clubhouse that you will find a beer after the round (just ask someone to sign you in).

THE COURSE

In addition to a beautiful setting, County Down has its own unique architecture, characterized by blind tee shots, some of the fiercest rough in Ireland, and deep pot bunkers that are set back a bit from the greens. Although the course has changed since the days of Old Tom Morris, the strategy for surviving at Royal County Down has not—don't miss the fairway. The knee-high fescue and ball-swallowing gorse make "U.S. Open rough" seem tame by comparison.

Royal County Down is the world's greatest advertisement for the return of the blind shot from the tee. In the nineteenth century, when there were no bulldozers to level the undulating duneland where golf was first played, it was common for the drive to be played over a sandhill onto a fairway unseen from the tee. The following description of a long-since rearranged hole at County Down was published in the Irish *Golf Annual* of 1895:

> The tee of the "Alps" (233 yards) is in the centre of an arena surrounded on all sides by towering sandhills. Right in front, and at a distance of 100 yards from the tee, stretches a terrible bunker. There is no playing round it; you must take your trusty club in hand and go for it; and who shall describe the feelings of that player who gets away a "bonnie lick" as he stands and watches his ball rise straight over the guide-post and fall out of sight beyond. Crossing the "Alps" by the steps the ball is seen lying on beautiful turf at the foot of the sandhills.

After the first round at County Down, the blind shots seem more like a challenge than a trick. They often provide lovely moments of surprise— the natural beauty of the course unfolds in a series of revelations as you climb over each rise. Besides, as Tommy Armour once said, "a blind hole is only blind once to a golfer with a memory." In tune with the modern golf sensibility, there are no completely blind approach shots—the play to the green is usually clear and dazzling—and when surrounded by flowering gorse and heather, the greens are exceptionally beautiful.

Like any great golf course, Royal County Down is more than the sum of its parts, and much of its charm is intangible. The course has a pace of its own—each hole seems to tilt and bend in a different way, with the fairways narrowing and widening at unexpected and strategically interesting moments. The level of difficulty also ranges widely—from the short par-4 sixteenth that dares you to reach it with a decent drive, to the terrifying par-3 fourth, that requires a picture-perfect carry of 217 yards over a stunning expanse of whins and bunkers.

There is only one water hazard at County Down, a rather irrelevant little pond on the seventeenth that somehow cost Bernard Darwin a berth in the quarter-finals of the Irish Amateur in 1931. But the fierce rough makes every hole feel as if it is lined with danger. In the summer, the fairways and greens are firm and the ball will roll great distances. In the tradition of true links golf there is almost always one line that enables you to avoid bunkers and run the ball onto the green. Keep the ball in play and you will be able to savor everything that County Down has to offer. If you have a wayward driver, leave it in the car.

If you really wanted to be picky, you could point out that the finishing two holes are not the most memorable, and that the course's wonderful seclusion is somewhat marred by some ill-conceived holes from the second course that come a little too close. But to dwell on such details is a little like parsing a haunting lyric for its grammar. As with a beautiful poem or song, Royal County Down is best appreciated in its glorious entirety.

Location:	Golf Links Road, Newcastle (behind the Slieve Donard hotel)
Restrictions:	Visitors are permitted Monday, Tuesday and Friday; it may also be possible to play on Sunday afternoon
Secretary:	Peter Rolph
Green Fee:	£30-60
Address:	36 Golf Links Rd., Newcastle BT33 0AN phone: (013967) 23314 fax: (013967) 26281

DIVERSIONS
Northern Ireland

MAKE NO MISTAKE ABOUT IT, NORTHERN IRELAND IS LESS dangerous for tourists than Amsterdam, Paris or Florence, let alone Miami, New Orleans or Los Angeles. Even before the ceasefire in the Troubles, tourist-related crime was extremely rare. More and more people are coming to recognize this fact. The number of visitors to the North is increasing dramatically. What they are finding, besides the not-to-be-missed links of Royal Portrush, Portstewart and Royal County Down, are superb coastal and mountain scenery, the only UNESCO world heritage site in Ireland, and natives who are eager to encourage tourism.

The character of the Province, as it is sometimes called, is both Irish and something less definable, unique unto itself. The distinctions may be too subtle for the first-time visitor, but they are there. The roads are a little better, the amenities a little fresher. There are no bilingual road signs. The breakfast is more classically British (the ubiquitous Ulster fry), lacking, for instance, the tasty Irish breads. While still extremely open and accessible by North American standards, the golf clubs are somewhat less egalitarian (Royal County Down is the only club featured in this book which bars visitors from its main clubhouse). Even a pint of Guinness can taste slightly foreign on this soil.

Belfast is a city of history and substance. Its greatest glories were in the last century, built chiefly on textiles, shipbuilding and its excellent harbor. There are many examples of fine Victorian architecture in Belfast, including the City Hall, Belfast Cathedral, St. Mark's Church and the Grand Opera House. Perhaps best of all though is the wonderfully preserved Crown Liquor Saloon, located at the outset of the "Golden Mile" of Great Victoria Street. Its gas lights, snugs and snob screens, intricate woodwork and ornate granite bar, preserved as a National Trust monument, transport drinkers one hundred years into the past.

Travelling south, Great Victoria Street becomes University Road at Queen's University. The university area, also home to the beautiful Botanic Gardens, is an excellent one for restaurants and bed and breakfast accommodation. The north and west ends of the city (especially the infamous Shankhill and Falls Roads), along with the dock area, are to be avoided after dark.

There are many interesting towns near Belfast. Carrickfergus will be familiar to anyone with even a passing interest in Irish music, and boasts the oldest castle in Ireland, built by the Normans in 1180. Hillsborough is a pretty and affluent village to the southwest of Belfast. If you go, don't miss the Hillside and the Plough, two of the best pubs in Northern Ireland.

The **Ulster Folk and Transport Museum** makes an excellent day out for those travelling with children. It is located about five miles east of Belfast, at Cultra. It is an open-air museum, which documents the traditional way of life of Northern Ireland. Actual buildings, such as a thatched cottage, a schoolhouse and a shoe shop have been dismantled and reassembled on the grounds to form a village. The attendants are informative and interesting.

After the folk museum it may be convenient to continue to Bangor, a picturesque resort east of Belfast along the prosperous south shore of Belfast Lough. Directly south from Bangor is the **Ards Peninsula,** separated from the rest of the Province by Strangford Lough. Strangford Lough is a renowned migratory bird sanctuary. The peninsula also contains several charming fishing villages. Once at the southern end, a short ferry ride from Portaferry and a twenty-mile drive along the coast will bring the visitor to Newcastle and Royal County Down.

Halfway to Newcastle, however, a stop at Downpatrick may be in order. The town is the capital of County Down, and the main attraction is Down Cathedral, the burial place of St. Patrick, patron saint of Ireland. Interestingly, this is not a Roman Catholic cathedral, but one of the Church of Ireland.

Newcastle has precious little to recommend itself except its famous golf club. But it does enjoy a lovely backdrop in the Mountains of Mourne. Slieve Donard is the tallest peak, and hiking trails to its summit are well laid-out. The beach is also excellent, but the weather doesn't always cooperate.

Proceeding north from Belfast along the coastal A2 road brings you to the beautiful **Glens of Antrim,** nine enchanting valleys which extend from the Antrim Mountains down to the sea. The town of Cushendall, at the foot of Glenballyemon, is perhaps the most convenient base for exploration of the nine glens.

The **Causeway Coast** is stunning. It is a string of villages nestled under imposing cliffs, each more dramatic than the last. It culminates with the Giant's Causeway, the only UNESCO World Heritage site in Ireland. The Giant's Causeway is made up of a series of black columns which protrude step-like from the sea. They are said to have been created as a walkway across the Sea of Moyle to Scotland by the mythic giant Finn MacCool (hero, incidentally, of the recent novel of the same name by Morgan Llywelyn). In fact, the Causeway was formed by volcanic eruption of basalt lava, which cooled slowly (probably by sea water) to form the columns. It is likely the most famous attraction in Northern Ireland, and really shouldn't be missed. Despite its popularity, it is admirably preserved in a natural state and only accessible on foot.

Many elevated points along the Causeway Coast offer dramatic vistas. Even for non-golfers, the park bench by the seventeenth tee at Ballycastle Golf Club must provide one of the most glorious views on a sunny day. The entire Causeway Coast, Rathlin Island and even the coast of Scotland are in sight. Further west, from Portstewart for example, the Donegal coastline is plainly in view.

Just to the west of Ballycastle is the Carrick-a-rede rope bridge, a precarious walkway from the mainland to Carrick-a-rede Island. Only the brave will attempt to cross it when the wind is blowing. Do not look down in any event. There is boat service to the island for the sensible. The island provides a unique perspective back on the Causeway Coast, as well as housing a fish hatchery and copious sea-birds. The rope bridge is open only in the summer.

Londonderry (a.k.a. Derry) is easily avoided thanks to the new Foyle bridge. For the adventurous, though, a historic but troubled city awaits. It is divided by the River Foyle, with Protestants (for the most part) to the east and Catholics to the west. Highlights are the city walls, the last constructed in Europe (in the seventeenth century), and St. Columb's Cathedral, the first built in the British Isles after the Reformation. Both figured in the unsuccessful siege of the city led by James II in 1689.

For anyone with energy to spare after golf the Ulster Way is a hiker's dream. It is five hundred miles long, encircles the entire Province, and passes through the Glens of Antrim, Mountains of Mourne and Giant's Causeway, to name but a few highlights. It is accessible at a myriad of locations and thoroughly documented; details are available from the Northern Ireland Tourist Board and many other sources.

CONTEXTS

EQUAL PARTNERS?
Women's Golf in Ireland

When we played with men we had to have a chaperon. We had either
ninepenny or shilling chaperons. The ninepenny ones were small boys
and the shilling ones were slightly older.

MAY HEZLET, *British Ladies Champion, 1899, 1902 and 1907*

ANYONE WHO THINKS THAT sport's first Battle of the Sexes
had something to do with Bobby Riggs and Billie Jean King does
not know enough about the history of women's golf in Ireland.
More than seventy years before the wacky tennis match at the
Astrodome, a far more interesting cross-gender tussle occurred in a far
more dignified location.

"[I will] no' be licked by a lassie," Old Tom Morris reportedly
vowed before his challenge match at St. Andrews with the Irish phenom,
Rhona Adair. It was July 1899. Morris was seventy-seven years young at
the time, but apparently thought nothing of the prospect of a one-day
thirty-six-hole match.

His opponent was only seventeen. But Rhona Adair was already
known to be able to hit the ball further than any woman ever had, and
she would win the British Ladies' Amateur title the very next year.

"She stands up to the ball in a manner quite worthy of the sterner
sex," wrote the great English amateur Harold Hilton. "There is a determination and firmness in her address which is most fascinating to watch.
Lady players, as a rule, appear to persuade the ball on its way; Miss
Adair, on the contrary, avoids such constrictions on her methods by hitting very hard indeed."

It must have been quite a sight—the white-bearded golfing icon and
the teenager in her long dress and stiff white collar. It was certainly quite
a match. After the first round, Morris led by one hole. He extended his
lead to three after twenty-seven holes, and fended off a late challenge to
win on the last green.

It is a tribute to the strength of women's golf in Ireland at the turn of the century that Adair, despite her celebrity, was probably not even the best woman player *in her own club*. For Royal Portrush was also home to the great May Hezlet. Between them, Adair and Hezlet appeared in the finals of five straight British Championships (then the undisputed world title) from 1899 to 1903, winning four of them, and Hezlet won another for good measure in 1907. Hezlet and Adair were also avid badminton, tennis and field hockey players, and they introduced a new athleticism to women's golf. Although the steady Hezlet had slightly the better record, Adair seems to have caused the greatest sensation due to her startling power.

After winning her second British title in 1903, Adair made a historic visit to North America, playing in a long series of challenge matches in the United States and Canada, and losing only once. Her tour was followed with intense interest. The *Illustrated Sporting News* trumpeted the fact that Adair would compose a copyrighted column for the paper during her visit, "the only one she will write for any American publication, [in which] she gives her impression of America's leading women players and best courses, and tells of the advantages of the game as an important aid to good health." Adair's feat of clearing a water hazard of 170 yards (a considerable shot with the equipment of the time) was greeted with astonishment, and she brought home no fewer than sixteen gleaming trophies. The trip also made an enormous impact on the young American player Margaret Curtis, who would later launch the Curtis Cup, the most important international match in women's golf.

Adair and Hezlet were by no means the only women playing golf in Ireland. Only a decade after the game took root there were an astonishing 290 lady members of the Portrush Golf Club. Several clubs had as many lady members as men, and Royal County Down found it necessary to establish a separate ladies' course in 1909.

"Golf undoubtedly owes much of its popularity to the enthusiasm with which it has been taken up by what men are pleased to term the weaker sex," wrote the editor of the *Irish Golfer* in 1899. "Many conscientious fathers of families can now take their families to the seaside and enjoy their rounds of golf, because their womenfolk also pursue the game, instead of boring themselves to death in seaside lodgings talking scandal or reading trashy novels."

Needless to say, women put a slightly different spin on the same phenomenon. In the first issue of *Ladies' Golf*, a writer pointed out that before golf "the comings and goings of . . . more or less attached husbands, who golfed, fished and shot, were veiled in mystery."

In the early days, golfers of both sexes came from the Protestant upper classes. Typical attire for women consisted of elaborate hats, stiff collars, petticoats, ankle-length skirts and corsets. That so many Victorian women and girls were taking up the sport despite these obstacles was considered by some a trend of the first importance.

"The whole hearted adoption by women of the Royal and Ancient Game marks an epoch in the history of the sex," reported *Ladies' Golf.* "Without unduly straining a point, it may be said that golf has been a factor of no small importance in the mental, as well as the physical, development of the modern girl."

In those days golf was an outdoor adventure with limited clubhouse amenities, and women and girls were given equal access to Irish courses. If the enormous galleries depicted in photographs from the era are any indication, interest in women's competitions in Ireland, especially in Ulster, was substantial. The exploits of Adair and Hezlet undoubtedly added to the credibility of women's golf in Ireland. It is perhaps no coincidence that the British Amateur Ladies' Championship has been played in Ireland no fewer than fourteen times, including once at Portmarnock, one of the few clubs which admits no women members.

There has been a steady flow of outstanding Irish players over the years, the best being Philomena Garvey, a seven-time Curtis Cup player from County Louth. But one of the most celebrated never won a major championship. Bridget Gleeson was born in 1963 and raised in the lodge beside the fifteenth green at Killarney's Mahony's Point course. She started hitting balls at the age of two-and-a-half and by five she was a BBC television celebrity and played in exhibition matches as far away as Canada. She won the club championship at ten. An injury interrupted her career, though she has returned to competitive golf and has hopes of competing internationally.

Although there have been individual highlights, it seems that the proportion of women players (compared to men) began to decline along with the aristocratic lifestyle that allowed some women considerable leisure time. There is also evidence that men began to exert increasing control over the sport as it became institutionalized (and more elaborate clubhouses were built). In an arrangement common in other parts of the world and all but universally applied in Ireland, women were redesignated as "associate" members at significantly reduced membership fees. As associates, women were denied voting rights at annual meetings and faced some restrictions on playing time. It is not exactly clear how resentful women were of these changes, although it may not be completely coincidental that Killarney and Royal County Down were both targets of suffragette attacks before the First World War.

This is not to say that women golfers were treated less fairly in Ireland than their counterparts in England and America. Indeed, the degree of participation of women in golf clubs in the Republic is somewhat surprising, given the traditional role espoused for women by the Catholic church and the early nationalist governments. The 1937 Irish constitution stated that "by her life within the home, woman gives to the State a support without which the common good cannot be achieved." It was not until 1977 that it became illegal to require women to resign from civil service jobs upon getting married. Divorce and abortion remain illegal.

By the late 1980s women's rights had become a central issue in the Republic, and were given further impetus by the election of Mary Robinson as President (a largely ceremonial yet influential post) in 1991. The winds of change have begun to sweep through golf clubs as well, with clubs such as Killarney and Ballybunion offering full membership privileges to women. It will take longer elsewhere, but the trend seems irreversible. The new courses for executives—such as St. Margaret's—make no distinction between men and women, though few women as yet are using golf as a business tool. It doesn't help, of course, that two of the most important clubs for networking—Royal Dublin and Portmarnock—don't allow women members.

Today about forty thousand women golf in the Republic and in Northern Ireland, double the figure of ten years ago. Many Irish women played robust sports when they were young (including camogie, a version of hurling), but were encouraged to quit when they married in order to focus on raising a family. Although there are many exceptions, the majority of women golfers began playing when their children were old enough to enjoy a measure of independence.

"A friend and I took up golf just a few years ago," says Eileen, a fiftyish member at Dooks in County Kerry. "We thought that if something happened to our husbands it would be the only socializing we could do in mixed company."

Happily, there are few additional obstacles to be faced by women travellers wishing to golf while they are in Ireland. Restrictions on visitors almost always apply to men and women equally, and indignities such as male-only lounges in clubhouses are largely a thing of the past. While many handicapped golf tournaments (such as the Causeway Coast Open) are aimed at men, the Open Weeks held by the clubs usually have mixed and ladies' competitions that are open to all comers.

Given that men represent the overwhelming majority of golfing visitors to Ireland, those women who do make the trip can expect an especially warm welcome.

TRY THE BREAD
A Golfer's Survival Guide to Irish Cuisine

THE MOST SURREAL PLACE IN all of Ireland is the food section of a fancy book shop. Here you will find glossy, full-color books celebrating the glories of Irish cooking.

The sheer *chutzpah* required to publish and market such products is breathtaking. You half expect to see *John Daly's Book of Manners* next to it.

Guidebooks to Ireland, published outside the country, are usually not so brazen as to celebrate Irish cuisine. They limit themselves to a few paragraphs brimming with euphemisms. One popular guide, for example, comments that "the cooking can be variable," "the Irish still eat quite a lot of potatoes," and "the baking of bread is almost always reliable."

Of course there are some very good historical reasons for the plainness of Irish cuisine. The lords and ladies of the Anglo Ascendency could afford to experiment with exotic tastes. But for millions of Irish peasants the main challenge was survival. In 1845 it was estimated that fully one-third of Irish families relied *entirely* on potatoes (mixed with buttermilk) for their food. This reliance on one staple had devastating consequences during the potato blight of the following year and led directly to the Great Famine.

Food is a very personal subject. We all swear by that casserole dish our mother made when we grew up and will become incensed when someone (a spouse, for example) suggests it is but a slightly more elaborate version of Kraft dinner. Those who grew up in Irish households, took their honeymoon on the Ring of Kerry, scored a hole-in-one at Ballybunion, or have some other very solid reason for thinking fondly of *everything* Irish, should read no further.

It is an inescapable fact that mealtime can be a disappointing and surprisingly expensive experience for the first-time visitor to Ireland. After, say, thirty-six glorious holes at Ballybunion or Royal County

Down, you will enter a perfectly respectable and charming little restaurant with a nautical name, and prepare to satiate that hunger you had so luxuriously developed walking for several hours along the seashore. You will have a pint of Guinness and order your food—say mussels followed by something called a Seabake—and think this has been a perfect day.

And if you have prepared yourself the day will remain perfect. You will smile knowingly when the mussels are served shell-less in a puddle of butter, simply chuckle when the £10 Seabake turns out to be a gluey custard with a couple of shrimps dropped in, and remain unconcerned when the vegetables are so overcooked they could be eaten with a straw. After all, you will remind yourself, french fries come with everything (even the boiled potatoes).

Those with a lot of money can avoid such adventures. In the major centers, at least, it is possible to seek out one of the frighteningly expensive restaurants that feature a respectable standard of international cuisine. But even for the rest of us an Irish meal need not be an entirely negative experience. The Guinness is always superb, and waiters and waitresses in Ireland are terrifically friendly, if not particularly well organized. In Ireland a restaurant is not a place to sample innovative dishes. It's a place to talk with your friends and perhaps a few strangers. And the talk, needless to say, is usually excellent.

Here then are some tips to help you make the most of Irish cooking.

WHERE TO EAT

Breakfast—At your B&B use up the packaged, cold cereal, which is just like at home. And the milk in Ireland is fine. At first, you may be able to handle the bacon and eggs as well—it is, after all, the perfect pre-golf ritual. One of our favorite B&Bs in Dublin fries *one* mushroom and *one half* a cherry tomato with each egg. But after a few days of super-cholesterol you may wish to switch to the poached eggs on unbuttered toast. One option is to ask for the porridge when available, though it's often rather runny. Yes, in some places you can get soda bread in the morning. By all means eat it, and count your blessings. You are just as likely, however, to get slices of cold, unbuttered white toast, especially in Northern Ireland.

Lunch—Eat at the golf club. It's the one place where you may be pleasantly surprised. It is convenient, prices are usually modest, and you will have an appetite. Toasted sandwiches are as reliable as Ireland gets, and we had a fabulous chicken soup in Portsalon of all places. The dining room at Royal Portrush is particularly noteworthy for its reasonable prices (given the high green fee) and its "carvery" with Yorkshire pudding. Wherever you are, beware of the Golfer's Grill—fried eggs, fried bacon, fried sausages and, if you're lucky, fried bread.

Dinner—Dinner is problematic for the golfer in Ireland, due to the discordant mix of long summer days and early-closing kitchens. You will quickly realize that the food served so laboriously in hotel dining rooms is the same stuff they slap in front of you in the bars, only there's too much of it in the dining room version and it costs an arm and a leg. The most economical place to eat is a pub or hotel bar, but the pubs stop serving food at a very early hour, often at eight o'clock. After that you are stuck with full-fledged restaurants, and many of these close early as well. On a Sunday night in a small town, a hotel dining room can be your only option.

THE MENU

For those who don't like to choose, Irish menus are pleasingly straightforward. Although often disguised under different names and typefaces, there is really only one menu in Ireland. It goes something like this:

Soup of the Day
Shrimp Cocktail

Gammon Steak with Pineapple
Plaice and Chips
Chicken and Chips
Lasagna and Chips
Salmon Steak

Dessert

There are local specialties of course—a sausage and chips here, a shrimp and chips there, and in the pubs you will indeed find Irish stew. But the consistency of selection is quite remarkable.

The Soup of the Day is almost always vegetable broth. It is reasonably priced, tastes okay and has the virtue of not being fried.

In Ireland it is not a question of whether there will be potatoes with your meal, it is the combination of potatoes you are going to get. The first time it happens you may think some kind of mistake has been made, as in "I already have three sizable boiled potatoes on the plate, what is the waitress doing with those french fries!" The quantities of potatoes will astonish even Texans. A word of warning for North Americans—if you try to order sour cream with your baked potato you are apt to be responsible for befuddled looks, discussions in the kitchen, and an attempt to find *cream that has gone sour*.

The menus in Dublin and a few other larger towns are sometimes more ambitious. This is not necessarily a good thing. In Dublin, where you can actually get mussels in a shell, Mussels Meuniere may well be suffocated with the tasteless white sauce that gets put on everything. Even in the swishest bistro you may find a slice of processed cheese floating on the top of your French Onion Soup. And don't expect your lamb chops to come medium rare.

One nice thing about the lavish use of potatoes in Irish cooking is that you often have no room for dessert. You can get ice cream and pudding-like things, often with huge amounts of whipped cream and an umbrella on top.

The tea is good. The coffee is usually instant. Dublin is an exception—it has had a thriving café society for centuries, and its coffee shops are apt to have a literary history and flair, especially near the universities. The pastries are not nearly as good as they look.

FAST FOOD AND ETHNIC CUISINE

You know how Japanese restaurants often put a plate of exquisite looking food (or its plastic replica) in a window box to entice you to order? Irish "takeaways" do the same, but instead of delicately crafted sashimi or deftly prepared tempura you are likely to encounter fatty hunks of battered sausages and battered hamburgers. Many takeaways actually deep-fry the patty (or the sausage) for a greasy sensation that is guaranteed to take several hours off your life. (For a hilarious account of the evolution of a Dublin chip wagon read Roddy Doyle's *The Van*.)

In the less interesting culinary areas of Scotland and England a visitor can always take refuge in Indian restaurants. They are fewer in number in Ireland. Even in small towns there is the inevitable Chinese takeaway, where you may be able to find a vegetable that still crunches. But these, as in the rest of the world, are hit and miss affairs.

Pizzas are less greasy than they used to be, but you should expect some typically Irish toppings, such as boiled egg and sausage. Your best fast-food bet is always french fries.

VEGETARIANS

If the golf courses were all in downtown Dublin, vegetarians could survive quite nicely in Ireland. As it is, it's a struggle. There are potatoes of course, and vegetable broth soup, but the salads are unimaginative in the extreme—iceberg lettuce, tired looking coleslaw, and tasteless mixtures of corn and beets. Cooked vegetables are soggy. Once again there is, unfortunately, no escaping the need for french fries.

SNACK FOOD

On a windswept, rainy day on a seaside links, you may want to put a bit of solid sustenance in your bag along with your bottle of amber liquid. A good rule of thumb is to avoid anything you've never heard of before. Open the local version of flavored potato chips, for example, and the aroma is apt to cause severe discomfort to any non-Irish golfer several fairways away. In an emergency, however, the "Scampi" flavor can perhaps be used in place of smelling salts. Then there are the little packages of cooked pancakes that you find next to the Twinkies.

On the other hand, we have a German friend who insists that chocolate bars are *the best food available in Ireland*. We wouldn't go that far, but it is nevertheless true that after a few days in Ireland a Mars Bar begins to taste like a Belgian truffle. And chocolate bars are inexplicably cheap.

It is our theory that the quality of Irish food—like the quality of the weather—is simply nature's way of balancing things out. Otherwise you would never want to go back home.

GUINNESS IS GOOD FOR YOU
A Guide to Drinking in Ireland

MUCH OF THE CHARM OF drinking in Ireland derives from the characters encountered in the typical pub. With the same three beers and four or five whiskies available in virtually every pub in the country, an Irishman is said to choose his pub on the quality of the "crack" or conversation and banter. The Irish are nothing if not lovers of a well-told joke and masters of the ruthless witticism. As well, due to the immense number of expatriate Irish around the world, someone is invariably interested in or familiar with your home town or its environs, no matter how obscure. But proceed with caution. The Irish, especially in rural areas, can be conservative and quite proprietary about their local. Ease yourself into the conversation with tact; you will be rewarded many times over.

The pub remains at the heart of the community in most rural areas. It is also the typical focus of the local music scene, be it "traditional" Irish music or modern folk, jazz or rock. Impromptu sessions where local musicians bring their instruments and perform are still quite common. Ask the bartender or a local member before you leave the golf club—they will point you in the right direction.

Like many things Irish, the opening hours of pubs are not exactly set in stone. Officially, they are 10:30 a.m. to midnight in the Republic (11:30 p.m. in winter) and 11:30 a.m. to 11:00 p.m. in the North. Many pubs will close for an hour or two in the middle of the afternoon (euphemistically known as the "holy hour"). Pubs will open later and close earlier on Sundays. In the Republic, closing time is extended for a myriad of local festivals and race meetings, so one can never be sure when last call will be. As well, it is far from unknown for a rural publican to draw the blinds and lock the front door at "closing time" and continue to serve for an hour or more. Hotels with bars are obliged to serve residents at any hour; it is not unheard of to circumvent closing time by being "mistaken" for a resident in the lounge of a larger hotel. Indeed, a pub can encounter difficulty in enforcing the letter of the law when it comes to closing, and it is not uncommon for staff to spend thirty minutes herding the drinkers towards and ultimately out the front door. If all else fails, certain other types of licensed establishments, such as clubs and discotheques, serve alcoholic beverages—often for a stiff cover charge— after the pubs close. Just ask a likely-looking local.

Previously all but ignored, drinking and driving is now taken seriously in Ireland. In order to reduce the rate of road fatalities, which was among the highest in Europe, random police checkpoints have begun to appear, and the legal blood-alcohol limit for drivers has been reduced.

BEER

A great many people think Guinness is the best beer in the world. Certainly it is the most recognizable, its name synonymous with *dry stout* on every inhabited continent. It is Ireland's most famous export; no one seems to mind that the national symbol, the harp, is also a Guinness trademark. Like many things Irish, its history is bound up with that of England.

In the 1700s, the principal styles of beer in England were brown ale, old ale and pale ale (the Irish were primarily drinkers of a distinctive reddish-brown ale). In London, the practice of a drinker blending the three types of ale in his glass became popular. Over time, this blend became known colloquially as porter, thought to be so named because it was favored by the porters in London's markets. Enterprising breweries began to do the blending themselves, and porter was born as a distinct product. Porter quickly became London's most popular beer, and as a product of the industrial revolution it was exported far and wide, including to Ireland. It seems it was warmly embraced by the Irish, first in Dublin, and later in the countryside. In 1759 the Arthur Guinness brewery was established in Dublin; by 1799 it was strictly a brewer of porter.

In the 1800s, Guinness produced two porters of varying strengths (plus an even stronger version for export). The stronger of the domestic porters became known as "extra stout porter" and was eventually known universally as "stout." The weaker porter was simply called plain.

Domestic porter reached its zenith in England in the 1800s and was all but extinct by 1935. The Irish, however, had other ideas. Some put it down to their natural conservatism; others say they sensibly realized they were drinking the greatest libation man could devise. In any event, plain porter survived in Ireland until 1974, while stout took firm hold as the national drink. It also became a huge success as an export product to much of the world including, ironically, England, the place of its birth.

The period from 1925 to 1955 saw Guinness establish itself as one of the world's great trade names. In the late 1920s a British advertising agency was commissioned to determine what Guinness drinkers liked about the product. The response appears to have been that it was "good for you." Thus was born one of the most successful advertising campaigns in history. "Guinness is good for you" passed into everyday language. The campaign continued through the 1930s with such slogans as "Guinness gives you strength" and "my goodness my Guinness." Various animals were introduced, including a seal, an ostrich and a toucan. By 1953 the animals appeared in uncaptioned advertisements, with no further explanation or corporate logo necessary.

A good pint of Guinness is a drink like no other. It is intensely bitter, with strong grapefruit flavors, but with aspects of burnt toast and roasted nuts. At times it is slightly smoky. Although very bitter, it is also quite smooth, even creamy, with little carbonation evident. This is due to its method of dispense. Despite the strong taste, Guinness (in Ireland, at least) is not a particularly alcoholic drink. It contains approximately 4.2% alcohol by volume ("regular" American beer is 4.5%). So have another; the Guinness served in Ireland, because it is only lightly pasteurized, is a much richer and fuller tasting drink than the beers of the same name exported around the world.

Guinness is available everywhere in the Republic and Northern Ireland. Because it is filtered and kept chilled, quality rarely varies. Nevertheless, the Irish are inordinately concerned with "pulling a good pint." Guinness is kept under gas pressure and dispensed through a tight sparkler. No actual pulling is required. Rather, the glass is quickly filled to about the two-thirds mark and left to sit. A dense, creamy head will "mushroom up" through the beer. When the beer has settled fully, the glass is filled to the brim and again set aside, allowing the mushroom effect to occur anew. A classic tourist *faux pas* is to drink from a fresh pint before it has fully settled; nothing will bring more scorn from the barman or any of the pub's regulars.

Of much greater effect than how the pint is pulled is the temperature at which it is consumed. A slightly cool Guinness will taste altogether different, and better, than a cold one. Unfortunately, in order to fight the popularity of Budweiser and other bland international lagers (especially with teenagers and young adults) Guinness is served much colder than it was twenty years ago and about ten degrees colder than the ideal.

Two other stouts, Beamish and Murphy's, are available in parts of Ireland. Both are produced in Cork and are principally available in and around that city and in certain pockets in the north. Beamish tastes much more of roasted coffee beans and cocoa and is less bitter than Guinness. Its head is noticeably whiter. Murphy's is similar to Beamish in character, with more of a roasted, toasty flavor. Neither Beamish nor Murphy's is as intensely dry as Guinness.

Of course, true beer connoisseurs, led by Britain's Campaign for Real Ale (CAMRA) would point out that, even in Ireland, Guinness is "flash" pasteurized, filtered and dispensed with the aid of gas, which detracts from the ultimate product. While this is undoubtedly true for British-style ales, it may be off the mark for Irish stout. It is hard to imagine a more intense-tasting Guinness, even if a cask-conditioned version were available. CAMRA has a point when it comes to bottled Guinness, however. In 1993 bottle-conditioned Guinness (i.e., that which contains a sediment of yeast to enhance the beer's flavor) was discontinued in Britain and Ireland. It was replaced with the mediocre "draught Guinness in a can" which is also available in the United States and Canada.

It may not seem so at first blush, but dry stout matches extremely well with seafood. Although many novice drinkers will describe stout as "heavy," it is actually an appetite enhancer (in moderation) because it is so dry. It is particularly good with oysters, and both Guinness and Murphy's sponsor oyster festivals in County Galway in September. Some famous places to try the oyster and stout combination are The Oyster Tavern in Cork and Moran's of the Weir, near Kilcolgan, Co. Galway, which faces directly onto some of Ireland's best oyster beds. Oyster season runs from September to December.

Traditional Irish ale, once a thriving product, has all but vanished. A true Irish ale is slightly red in color and has a sweet and rounded taste. The ubiquitous ale of present-day Ireland (brewed, naturally, by a Guinness affiliate) is Smithwicks. Irish Smithwicks is quite different from the export version available in North America. It is noticeably drier, with a good hoppy flavor and a toffee-like finish, and is about 4% alcohol by volume (export Smithwicks is 5.5%). The Guinness family of beers is rounded out by Harp, a bland lager of no particular distinction.

Northern Ireland, due to its continuing links with Britain, enjoys a greater selection of ales than the Republic. The first is Macardles, brewed by Guinness at its Dundalk plant, but available exclusively in the north.

It is a better beer than Smithwicks, rounded and much fuller tasting. Ireland's finest ale, however, is made by the tiny Hilden brewery. It has been the only cask-conditioned "real ale" produced in Ireland for some time, and is worth seeking out but extremely difficult to find (try the Hillside pub in Hillsborough or the brewery itself in Lisburn, which has a pleasant reception centre and wood-panelled bar). After years of neglect, at least two of England's real ales (Draught Bass and Theakston Best Bitter) are available in a few Belfast pubs.

WHISKEY

After dinner, another pint of "the black stuff" may not appeal. Guinness is sometimes just too voluminous to fit in a satiated stomach. Fortunately, the Irish have invented the perfect solution, in the form of the other national drink, Irish whiskey.

Irish whiskey pre-dates Scotch, at least as a commercial product. No one knows for sure which nation had the first backyard still, but they were prevalent in both countries. It is thought that the process of distillation was introduced to Ireland by missionary monks as early as the sixth century. Bushmills, licensed in 1608, is the oldest commercial distillery in the world, and markets itself as such. It is known that there has been a distillery in the village of Bushmills since at least 1276.

Thus the Irish regard Scotch as something of a latecomer, despite the fact that it supersedes the native drink in worldwide popularity. Most Irish are happy to assume that the modern world is misinformed in the matter—in previous centuries it was the Irish style which predominated. In his 1750 dictionary of the English language, Dr. Johnson defined whiskey as "a compounded, distilled spirit . . . the Irish sort is particularly distinguished for its pleasant and mild flavor. In Scotland it is somewhat hotter." In the nineteenth century Irish whiskey dominated the spirits trade: there were more than 400 brands, produced by 160 distilleries, for sale worldwide. Now, however, there are but two distilleries, producing the five principal brands: Bushmills, Jameson, Power, Paddy and Tullamore Dew. Prohibition in America, coinciding with the Irish War of Independence and a trade war with England which followed, are thought to be the principal causes of the dramatic contraction.

The difference in taste between Irish and Scotch is readily apparent, even to the beginner. Irish whiskey has none of the smoky, peaty flavor of Scotch and is slightly sweeter. The Irish, at least, would regard it as more delicate, refined and sophisticated. It is triple distilled, as opposed to just twice for Scotch, which undoubtedly contributes to the smooth body. It is also variously described as "perfumy," "fruity," "malty" and "rounded."

Differences between the main brands are subtle but can be detected. Jameson is the most popular Irish whiskey worldwide, and is light and smooth. Jameson also makes two older, premium whiskies: Crested Ten and Jameson 1780. Paddy has a huge following in the south and west of Ireland. It was named after Paddy O'Flaherty, who worked with such success as a salesman for Cork Distilleries in the 1920s that the practice of simply asking for "Paddy's whiskey" became widespread. The name was eventually adopted on the label. Paddy is dry and crisp. Tullamore Dew is the lightest tasting of all Irish whiskies, and has its greatest popularity in France, where it is pronounced "tous l'amours"!

John Power & Sons (Power) is the largest selling whiskey within Ireland, and justifiably so. It is drier than Jameson or Black Bush, with malty complexity and a smooth finish. It is known colloquially as "three swallows" and, inevitably, there is an elaborate story behind it. Power was the first Irish whiskey to be sold in miniature "airplane" bottles, which the Irish apparently felt contained about three swallows of whiskey. The bottles became so popular, and the three swallows reference so prevalent, that three small birds, swallows, found their way on to the label at the neck of the bottle where they remain to this day, a classic Irish pun.

All of Ireland's whiskies are distilled at Midleton, County Cork, with the exception of Old Bushmills and its premium brands Black Bush and Bushmills Single Malt ("Bush Malt"). The Bushmills distillery is located on the banks of the River Bush in County Antrim and is recognized by its pagoda-style malting towers. Guided tours are available year round. Old Bushmills is a standard Irish whiskey, tending towards the sharp side. Black Bush, which is aged in sherry casks, is very smooth and slightly sweeter. Bush Malt is a fine drink, firm and dry yet very smooth. It is one of the very few "single malt" Irish whiskies (not blended with grain whiskey), and is so marketed to compete with the famous malts of Scotland.

Irish whiskey is meant to be consumed straight up or with a small amount of water. Ice is often available (but rarely needed by the travelling golfer). Far more likely will be the need for a restorative "hot whiskey" to combat the effects of eighteen holes of wind and rain. A hot whiskey is made by adding boiling water, lemon, clove and sugar to a generous measure of Irish whiskey. At the right time in the right place it is a superb drink.

A GOLFER'S HISTORY OF IRELAND

It is hard to escape history in Ireland—there are few places where the echoes of the past resound so loudly and meaningfully. We recommend that you read one of the excellent books on the subject listed in the Appendix. What follows is in no way meant to substitute for more complete and authoritative accounts, although it will give you a thumbnail sketch, at least, if you are already descending into Dublin, Shannon or Belfast.

G OLF IS A SOCIAL GAME, so it is no surprise that its progress in Ireland has been shaped by the political and economic currents that have so buffeted Irish society in the last century. In fact, golf may have been introduced to Ireland as early as 1606 by a Scottish "laird" named Hugh Montgomery. A good friend of James I, Montgomery secured much of the Ards Peninsula to start a plantation after the latest of what was already a long line of Irish rebellions against English rule. Montgomery built a school not far from present-day Belfast which included "a green for recreation at goff, football and archery." The success of the Montgomery estates encouraged many more English and Scottish Protestants to settle in Ulster, with consequences that reverberate to the present day.

Until that point Ireland had managed to survive or assimilate its invaders. A bewildering array of autonomous Celtic "kings" jockeyed for power and territory with each other and with foreign intruders. The Celts themselves had arrived in Ireland at least a thousand years before, and established a civilization full of magic and myth in which a learned caste of poets, historians and druids were revered and powerful. They built the impressive hill-forts that still dot the Irish landscape, and you will find that golf clubs are particularly proud of archeological discoveries on their golfing grounds.

St. Patrick and the Golden Age of the Irish Church

Given that St. Patrick has become almost a mascot of Ireland in the eyes of many foreigners, it is worth pointing out that he was a real human being. An English-born missionary who travelled widely in Ireland in the fifth century, St. Patrick was a pivotal figure in the introduction of Christianity to Ireland, and became even more important in legend.

The three centuries following St. Patrick's death were in many ways the golden age of Irish influence abroad. The remote and fortified monasteries of Ireland—beyond the reach of the marauding tribes which overran most of Europe and England—became renowned outposts of learning. The Book of Kells, an astonishing illustrated manuscript on display at Trinity College in Dublin, dates from the early part of this period. Irish missionaries and scholars reintroduced Christianity to much of Europe, established monasteries in Germany, France, Switzerland, Italy and Austria, and became the wise men of European courts.

"Almost all of Ireland, disregarding the sea, is flocking to our shores with a flock of philosophers," complained a European writer in the year 870.

Although Ireland was later invaded by the Vikings and the Normans in turn, Irish kings remained powerful and influential, continually forging alliances with foreign forces (Brian Boru became the first and only Irish king to assert control over all of Ireland when he defeated the Vikings in 1014; but he died in the final battle). Indeed, it was an Irish chief's request for assistance in a local squabble in 1166 that brought an English king (Henry II) onto the Irish political stage for the first time. During the next four hundred years English monarchs gradually increased their control over Ireland, distributing land and power to the English nobility.

Henry VIII's break with Rome in 1533 added an ominous religious dimension to the power struggle between Irish chiefs and the English intruders, and eventually led to Oliver Cromwell's invasion of Ireland in 1649. Battle-hardened, religiously zealous and eager to avenge a particularly bloody Irish uprising in Ulster, Cromwell's army overwhelmed all resistance and killed many thousands, often indiscriminately. Afterwards Cromwell ordered all Irish landowners to migrate to inhospitable lands west of the Shannon river or face death or slavery in the West Indies. It was the beginning of two hundred years of repressive English rule—the percentage of land owned by Irish Catholics plummeted to just 22 percent by 1685 and to 5 percent by 1800.

There was a brief reversal when a Catholic monarch ascended to the restored English throne in 1685, but five years later James II was forced to flee after his defeat by William of Orange at the Battle of the Boyne.

Ulster's Loyalists reserve their most enthusiastic marches to commemorate that day.

THE PENAL LAWS

It is difficult to exaggerate the degree of discrimination that Irish Catholics endured for the next century at the hands of the Anglican "Ascendency"—the all-powerful ruling class that owed their good fortune to the seizure of millions of acres of Irish land. In an attempt to make this power permanent, they passed a series of draconian measures through the Irish Parliament (which was loyal to the English sovereign). Known as the Penal Laws, they deprived Catholics of the right to vote, to receive a formal education, to hold any kind of public office or to buy land or even a horse. To a far milder extent, Protestant settlers in Ulster also faced discrimination—those who were Presbyterian rather than Anglican could not hold government office or run for Parliament.

One consequence of this oppression was the first wave of emigration. Remnants of the old Irish nobility fled in huge numbers to France and other parts of Europe, where many enjoyed highly successful military careers. Thousands of Irishmen fought in "Irish Brigades" in Europe and beyond in the eighteenth century. Fourteen generals in the Austrian army were Irish, as was the founder of the American navy (John Barry) and the liberator and first president of Chile (Bernardo O'Higgins). In addition, no fewer than ten American presidents are descendants of the thousands of Ulster Presbyterians who emigrated to the United States.

The success of Irishmen abroad contradicted Ascendency propaganda, which justified the Penal Laws by depicting the Irish as uncivilized. Jonathan Swift, an Anglican Dean and author of *Gulliver's Travels*, wrote that it "ought to make the English ashamed of the reproaches they cast on the ignorance, the dullness and the want of courage of the Irish natives; those defects, wherever they happen, arising only from the poverty and slavery they suffer from their inhuman neighbours."

The arrogance of the Ascendency eventually gave rise to an opposition that crossed religious and class lines. The Great Rebellion of 1798, inspired partly by the example of revolutions in America and France, attracted a mix of Ulster settlers, Catholic peasants and Anglican revolutionaries, with support from the French government. Though the rebellion was ruthlessly suppressed, its leader Wolfe Tone became an enduring symbol around which future nationalists could rally.

The Irish Parliament's decision to agree to a complete union with Britain in 1801 and the elimination of legal discrimination against Catholics in 1829 did little to address underlying grievances. The next century saw the birth of popular movements in support of land reform, the formation of underground groups (such as the Fenians) which favored armed revolt, and endless intrigues around the "Irish Question" in the British parliament in London.

THE FAMINE

The most profound and devastating event, however, was the Great Potato Famine of the 1840s. In the early nineteenth century potatoes had become the sole food of a third of the population and the livelihood of millions more, and the Irish peasantry was helpless when a potato blight destroyed crops on a huge scale in 1846 and several succeeding years. At least one million people died of starvation and related diseases, and about the same number emigrated to the United States and other countries (seventeen thousand died aboard transatlantic ships). Although the British authorities under Prime Minister Robert Peel reacted swiftly in the early stages to set up relief operations, Peel was defeated later in 1846 and replaced by a government grimly committed to a *laissez-faire* ideology.

"The matter is awfully serious, but we are in the hands of Providence, without a possibility of averting the catastrophe if it is to happen," declared the civil servant in charge of famine relief.

The consequences of the depopulation of Ireland were profound, changing the agricultural economy, creating a culture of emigration (and huge and influential Irish communities abroad) and delivering a death blow to the Irish language. Today the population of Ireland remains 20 percent lower than it was in 1845.

Though large landowners felt the pinch of land reforms which followed the Famine, the upper classes were largely insulated from the catastrophe. What did sweep through high society was the new fad of golf. No fewer than 110 clubs were founded in Ireland between 1885 and 1900, a rate of growth not equalled since. Golf was for the privileged—wealthy Protestant merchants, aristocrats and Scottish officers sent to Ireland to enforce British rule. In 1901 the *Irish Times* reported that the relative paucity of golf enthusiasts in the southeast of Ireland was due to "the great amount of time devoted to hunting and the numerous packs of hounds that there are to follow."

Political change was on the horizon, however. For the first time large numbers of Irish Catholics could vote and be represented in Westminster, and by voting as a block Irish nationalist MPs soon found they could influence British politics. Greater autonomy for Ireland in the form of "Home Rule" was first proposed in 1886 by Prime Minister William Gladstone (who needed the support of Irish MPs to stay in power) but the legislation faced an endless series of setbacks, not the least of which was the public disgrace faced by Charles Parnell—the parliamentary leader of the nationalists—who admitted to an adulterous affair. The machinations in London also raised emotions in Ulster, where most Protestants feared the prospect of rule from Dublin.

INDEPENDENCE AND CIVIL WAR

Still, self-government of some kind seemed inevitable as the First World War started, and it was with some shock that Dubliners woke up on Easter Sunday in 1916 to find their city the site of an armed revolt. Led by Patrick Pearse, the hopelessly undermanned uprising resulted in the deaths of about one hundred people and caused extensive damage to downtown Dublin. The initial reaction of the populace was indignation—at the rebels. However, the heavy-handed response of the British government—fifteen rebel leaders were executed and thousands were arrested who had nothing to do with the rebellion—turned public opinion around completely, and the rebels soon became martyrs to a rejuvenated nationalist cause.

When the British government did not act swiftly to meet nationalist demands after the First World War, a guerrilla-style War of Independence developed and enjoyed widespread popular support. Once again, the British government was its own worst enemy. Ill-disciplined troops from the war against Germany were deployed, and these "Black and Tans" became notorious for indiscriminate revenge killings and destruction.

International opinion turned against the British, and hastened negotiations. In 1922 a treaty was signed that created an Irish Free State within the British Commonwealth. However, the six counties in Ulster where Protestants were in the majority were to remain part of the United Kingdom. Not all revolutionary leaders accepted the deal, and the next two years saw Irish shooting Irish in a brief, but mean civil war between nationalist factions. Ultimately pro-treaty forces prevailed. Several hundred people were also killed in riots in Northern Ireland, as Loyalists formed their own Parliament and police forces.

What many assumed would be a temporary partition of Ireland quickly became solidified. Unsure of their positions, politicians on both sides played the "religion card" to shore up support. In Northern Ireland, the minister of agriculture (and future prime minister) went so far as to dismiss 125 Catholics working on his estate "to set an example to others."

ECONOMIC DOLDRUMS

After the heady patriotic fervor of the early 1920s, the rest of the period between the world wars was comparatively dull. Voters in the Free State were overwhelmingly rural and Catholic, and heartily sick of violence and turmoil. A series of conservative governments stressed symbolic measures—reviving Irish-language teaching in schools, introducing high tariffs on imported goods from England, and welcoming the influence of the Catholic Church over all aspects of Irish life.

Schools were controlled by the church, abortion and divorce were banned, and the state censorship board prohibited thousands of books from being distributed in Ireland, including many by internationally respected Irish writers. As one historian has remarked, the list of banned books made up "a respectable list of modern classics."

On the other hand, it was also a time of idealism. There was a surge of interest in Irish music, folklore and culture, and Irish missionaries once again roamed the world—this time administering to impoverished populations in the emerging nations of South America, Africa and Asia. The mixture of conservatism and idealism was reflected in a radio speech to the nation by the dominant politician of the era, Prime Minister Eamon de Valera:

> The Ireland which we dreamed of would be the home of a people who valued material wealth only as a basis of right living, of a people who were satisfied with frugal comfort and devoted their leisure to the things of the spirit; a land whose countryside would be bright with cosy homesteads, whose fields and villages would be joyous with sounds of industry, the romping of sturdy children, the contests of athletic youths, the laughter of comely maidens; whose firesides would be the forums of the wisdom of serene old age.

Economically, however, the picture was bleak. In Northern Ireland, unemployment rose to 25 percent and as late as 1938 more than 85 percent of rural homes in Ulster had no running water. Things were just as bad in the Free State.

The gap between rich and poor was nowhere more obvious than at golf clubs, many of which continued to thrive despite the prevailing hardships. Many of the best-known clubs (including Royal Portrush, County Louth, Lahinch, Killarney, Royal Dublin and County Sligo) had enough money to pay the foremost architects of the age to redesign their courses. Some also built elaborate clubhouses. Though members of the middle class (Protestant and Catholic) began to penetrate what had been an upper-class domain, golf retained its aristocratic air between the wars.

The sport's elitism did have one salutary effect. Since most golfers shared the same religion, class and point of view, there was no incentive to break up the Golfing Union of Ireland. The sport continues to be administered on an island-wide basis today, and Ireland sends united teams to international events.

The divisions between Northern Ireland and the Free State deepened during the Second World War, when the Irish government declared itself neutral (though it cooperated quietly with the Allies). The war years revitalized Ulster's shipping industry, but Belfast suffered from German bombing raids. Throughout Ireland horse-pulled carts made a return to country roads, and golf clubs all but closed down as there was no petrol to transport golfers to the course. Golf balls were rationed and golfers used paint (until it ran out) and glue to keep them together.

POST-WAR IRELAND

Things did not get much better after the war, and social pressures were only eased by emigration. Each year during the 1950s some forty thousand people sought better lives in the United States, Canada, England and Australia. The influence of the Church in what was now the Republic (declared in 1949) declined very slowly, and the Catholic hierarchy was able to stop a government plan for socialized medicine, arguing that a welfare state was against Church doctrine. Women's rights fell short of those enjoyed in other Western democracies. The constitution declared that the State had to ensure "that mothers shall not be obliged by economic necessity to engage in labour to the neglect of their duties in the home."

The 1950s were the Dark Ages for many golf clubs. The aristocrats were now all but gone, but the elitist image of the sport remained. For the young, golf couldn't compete with the attractions of hurling, Gaelic football or (in the North) soccer. And the average person could not afford even the few pounds necessary for a golf membership. Not a single golf course of distinction was built in Ireland between 1940 and 1965.

Ireland finally began to modernize in the early 1960s. A new prime minster, Sean Lemass, oversaw policies of economic liberalization and cultural pragmatism, and the notorious censorship board was emasculated. For the first time, the Republic embarked on a prolonged period of steady economic growth. Those looking for work headed to Dublin instead of overseas. A growing middle class began to discover golf, aided by the introduction of television and the heroics of Irish golfers.

Within golfing circles the achievements of Jimmy Bruen, Fred Daly (who became the first and thus far only Irishman to win the British Open, in 1947) and Joe Carr reached mythical proportions, but their performances were less important to the general public. In 1958, however, news reached Ireland that Christy O'Connor and Harry Bradshaw had won the Canada Cup (the forerunner to the World Cup). When the tournament was held in Ireland two years later, tens of thousands of spectators flocked to Portmarnock (it didn't hurt that Arnold Palmer and Sam Snead represented the United States). Suddenly it was okay to be a golfer in Ireland.

Slowly, golf clubs began to grow again. The Irish Tourist Board helped matters by supporting golf course construction in places such as Westport and Killarney. Community-run clubs in Ballybunion, Tralee, Enniscrone, Dingle and Connemara followed suit and built new links of their own, sometimes with glamorous architects such as Arnold Palmer and Robert Trent Jones.

THE TROUBLES

These efforts to attract tourism were undermined by the Troubles. The violence that began in the late 1960s in Northern Ireland followed the first real thaw in relations between Protestant and Catholic groups. A new prime minister of Northern Ireland, Terence O'Neill, began to dismantle discrimination against Catholics in employment and housing, but the reforms came too slowly for young Catholics inspired by civil rights movements in America and elsewhere. Street demonstrations turned into violent confrontation with Protestant militants. This led to O'Neill's res-

ignation and a bloody crackdown by his successors. This in turn ener-
gized militant factions of the Irish Republican Army (which had more or
less given up armed struggle). The new "Provisional" IRA rushed to
defend Catholic neighborhoods. Some Protestants, who feared the IRA
was behind the civil rights movement, became even more militant in
response. What began as a struggle for civil rights became a rigidly sectarian cycle of violence.

The escalation of terrorism in Northern Ireland led, in 1972, to the
disbanding of the Northern Ireland parliament by the British government
and the implementation of direct rule, an arrangement that has been in
place ever since.

More than three thousand people died in the Troubles, which
became regular fodder for television newscasts around the world. Given
the many aborted attempts at starting a peace process, the announcement
of a unilateral ceasefire by the IRA in late 1994 (followed by similar commitments from the Protestant paramilitary groups) caught many of the
most knowledgeable observers by complete surprise. One result was that
tourism to Ireland, north and south, began to soar, jumping by more than
25 percent in 1995 alone.

THE GOLF BOOM

The remarkable rebound of golf in Ireland has not been caused by
tourism, however, but by the enthusiasm of the Irish themselves. In the
1970s and 1980s the standard of living increased markedly in Ireland
(though there were growing disparities). For the Republic, membership
in the European Community helped to diversify trade and proved to be
both a psychological and economic boost—Ireland could move out of the
shadow of Britain.

Due partly to this new prosperity, Ireland caught the wave of the
international golf boom of the 1980s like few other countries. Television
helped to fuel the growth, and a new generation of heroes—Christy
O'Connor Jr., Philip Walton, Ronan Rafferty, David Feherty, Des Smyth
and others—reinforced the sport's popularity in the Republic and in
Northern Ireland. In 1988 and 1990 there were new international tri-
umphs for Ireland—at the heavily televised Dunhill Cup at St.
Andrews—and Irish players have sunk match-deciding putts at two
recent Ryder Cups.

The number of golfers in Ireland has doubled in the last decade, to
over 300,000. Even in remote areas, green fee revenues are soaring, while

it is a struggle for new golfers in the major cities (there are few public courses in Ireland) to find any place to play at all. Sensing a business opportunity, entrepreneurs have started building golf courses aimed at the corporate market.

"Golf used to be a middle-aged person's sport," says Pat Ruddy, who has written about golf in Ireland for more than thirty years. "Now thousands of young people are coming out of big office blocks, all going to play golf by the busloads. In the public houses you used to talk women, horseracing and football, but now they're talking golf as well."

PLANNING
YOUR JOURNEY

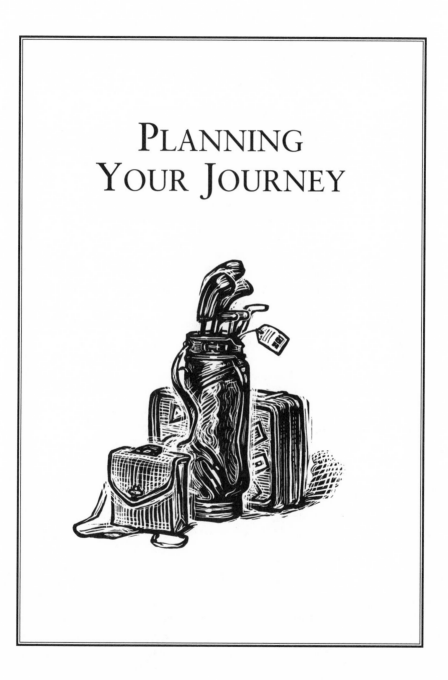

PLANNING
YOUR JOURNEY

GOLFING IN IRELAND IS rather different than spending a week in Scottsdale or the Costa del Sol. You are not patronizing a golf resort—instead, you are accepting the hospitality of fellow golfers. You are not staying put in a villa or hotel for a week—instead, you are travelling the narrow, unfamiliar roads and staying in cozy bed and breakfasts that often double as people's homes. If you are on a tight schedule or consider the words "vacation" and "surprise" to be incompatible, the many tour companies which arrange golf holidays to Ireland are worth investigating. Many specialize in "self-drive" holidays—they arrange for accommodation, starting times and a rental car, and the rest is up to you. Some also offer guided tours, in which you travel in a small bus with a number of other golfers. Differences in price between various packages have little to do with golf and everything to do with accommodation. The most expensive tours use large hotels, while the cheapest will likely use bed and breakfasts. It is always a good idea to talk to someone who has used the company before—not merely to check on the company's reliability but to help you decide which kind of tour is best for you. The advantages of a guided tour are obvious. Little advance planning is necessary on your part, there are few surprises and you will travel with a bunch of like-minded people with whom you may well make fast friends (a guided tour holds particular attractions to those who may be travelling on their own). The disadvantages are just as obvious. You are somewhat insulated from your Irish hosts, there's little flexibility should you want to stay in one place for an extra day (or if poor weather spoils your round), you won't experience the thrill of finding the perfect pub or bed and breakfast on your own and you may find yourself cooped up with that one obnoxious character you can't stand. Self-drive tours offer more flexibility and privacy within a reliable itinerary and are used by about half of the North Americans who travel to Ireland specifically to play golf. But for a real cultural experience there is nothing like the excitement and pleasure of planning, and taking, your own journey. This section will help you do just that.

WHEN TO GO

There is no reason to think of Ireland as a summer destination only. One of our most enjoyable trips was taken in early November. The weather, such as it is, does not change all that much throughout the year (especially in the southern part of the country). It is rare for the temperature to fall below forty degrees Fahrenheit or climb above seventy-five degrees Fahrenheit. The links courses are generally open year-round, and spring and fall are the driest (least wet) times of the year. In November and March the courses are not in as fine condition as they are in the summer, but as compensation you will often have them to yourself. One important difficulty with off-season golf travel is the amount of light available. In June in Portrush it is light until 10:30 p.m., but dusk begins to fall at 4:00 p.m. in the winter months. For first-time visitors, the best times to go are probably mid-April to mid-October.

GETTING THERE

We have set out below several itineraries for golf journeys in Ireland which vary according to the number of days available and the arrival and departure points used. Each begins and ends at a course which is convenient to one of Ireland's three international airports (British visitors may choose to arrive by ferry at Larne or Rosslare). Many of the itineraries rely on booking an "open-jaws" flight (where you arrive at one airport and depart from another). Most, if not all, of the airlines which service Ireland offer this feature, usually for no extra charge. Apart from charter operators (of which there are several, but many tend to be seasonal), Aer Lingus and Delta fly directly to Ireland from the United States. Aer Lingus has daily flights to Dublin and Shannon from New York (JFK) and a daily flight from Boston in the summer months. In winter, the Boston service is reduced to three times per week. In 1995, Aer Lingus began twice-weekly flights direct to Belfast for the summer months only. Delta Airlines flies daily to Dublin and Shannon from their base in Atlanta. Several airlines (including British Airways) offer flights to Dublin and/or Belfast via London. There is no regularly scheduled, direct service to Ireland from Canada.

GETTING AROUND

When booking your flight, have your travel agent book a rental car as well. Irish rental cars are usually cheaper when booked from North America, and it is not unheard of for all available cars to be rented out at Shannon Airport, say, in the busy summer months.

If this is your first time in Britain or Ireland, there is really not much you can do to prepare for driving "on the wrong side of the road." You will likely become accustomed to it quickly. Although you are driving on the "wrong" side of the road, the steering wheel is also on the other side of the car. Just keep in mind "driver towards the middle" and you will never find yourself heading into oncoming traffic.

A detailed map is a necessity in Ireland, especially if you are intent on finding some of the more remote links we have described. The Michelin road map of Ireland is excellent. Even with a map, however, you will get lost from time to time. When you are reviewing the map and estimating the amount of time it will take to drive from point A to B, count on progress of thirty to forty miles per hour. Of course, it is possible to make better time on some of the main highways, but narrow and twisting country roads lead to many of the great Irish links. Most roads pass through a string of towns which will slow your progress. In many rural areas, livestock on the road remains a real possibility. Also, note that road signs in the Republic can give distances in either miles or kilometers. The old white signs express distances in miles, while newer, green signs give distances in kilometers. But there are also new white signs which give distances in kilometers—these will have a small "km" above the number. To add to the confusion, the locals often don't refer to a road by its "official" name, especially in rural areas. Asking for directions can sometimes be a gamble.

ADVANCE STARTING TIMES

Tee times, at least for the "championship" courses, should be arranged in advance. This is particularly true if you are planning to travel between June and September, when demand is at its greatest. Courses to which we would recommend writing well in advance for starting times in the summer months are Waterville, Killarney, Ballybunion, Lahinch, Rosses Point, Royal Portrush, Portstewart, Royal County Down, Baltray, Portmarnock, Royal Dublin and The Island. Remember that a green fee in Ireland is often payment for a day's play, not just one round. Be sure to specify if you wish to play one round or two and request tee-off times for both rounds if you are going thirty-six. If you are, be sure to leave yourself enough time for lunch—Irish clubs will often estimate a pace of play that is quite fast. If you plan to hire a caddie, this should also be specified to the club in advance. Some Irish clubs claim to require a letter of introduction (from your home club) and/or a handicap certificate. We have never been asked to produce either of these items in Ireland, but carry one along just to be on the safe side.

What To Take

As the departure day approaches, try to pack as lightly as possible. Rental cars in Ireland are not big (even the station wagons) and four golfers sharing one car will have problems if they have brought more than one suitcase and a medium-sized golf bag each. Having said that, there are certain essentials. The first is a reliably waterproof rainsuit and either one pair of comfortable, waterproof golf shoes or a second pair to wear when the first becomes waterlogged. On links courses, umbrellas are more often than not a nuisance in the ocean wind. Two or three all-weather golf gloves will be useful. Bring one wool and one cotton sweater, and one cotton turtleneck shirt, even in July. A sports jacket and tie is required apparel in certain parts of some clubhouses, and worn more frequently than in North American clubs. Finally, bring enough golf balls to see you through your trip, and lots of wooden tees and pencils. These will not always be available.

What It Costs

Budgeting is a very personal matter. By North American standards, food is rather expensive and alcoholic drink is quite reasonable. Travellers planning to stay at bed and breakfasts should budget for £25-35 per day for golf, £20-25 per day for accommodation, £25-30 per day for food and £5-10 per day in the pub. There are, of course, high-end hotels (sometimes in grand castles) and restaurants in Ireland where it is possible to spend five times this amount. Green fees have been rising steadily, so you are best advised to use the green fees listed in this book for comparison purposes only. Competitive and up-to-date prices for air fare and rental cars are easily obtained from any reputable travel agent.

The currency of Northern Ireland is the pound sterling, while that of the Republic is the Irish pound, also known as the punt. In recent years its value has been very close to one pound sterling, and both the pound sterling and punt have been worth around U.S. $1.50 to $1.70. Be sure to change at least some of your money into either currency before you leave home. Banks do not tend to be open beyond the "traditional" banking hours—the hours you will want to be playing golf. In rural areas, banks are few and far between. Traveller's checks in pounds sterling are virtual cash equivalents at hotels and restaurants (neither American Express nor Thomas Cook has traveller's checks in Irish punts). Carry the amount of cash you are comfortable with in punts, and put the rest in pounds sterling traveller's checks. Credit cards are also widely accepted. Automatic teller machines are becoming more common, but not all of them have access to an international network.

COMMUNICATIONS

Throughout the book we have given telephone and fax numbers for the various golf clubs. Note that all of the area codes (called "city codes") which precede the actual phone numbers begin with "0". When in Ireland, the "0" must be dialled, but if you are calling from North America or Great Britain, the "0" is ignored. When dialling from overseas, the country code for the Irish Republic is 353; for the United Kingdom (including Northern Ireland) it is 44. Therefore, to call Ballybunion from North America, one would dial: 011-353-68-27146. To call Portstewart, the number would be 011-44-1265-832015. If, however, you are in Dublin and wish to call Ballybunion, dial 068-27146.

SOME SUGGESTED JOURNEYS

HERE ARE SOME ITINERARIES for golf journeys in Ireland. These itineraries are quite golf intensive—they can, of course, be modified to intersperse some non-golf days or to provide for longer stays in fewer places. What we have set out here is what, from our experience, is possible for travellers who want to play as many of the great courses of Ireland as they can in the time available. There will be little opportunity for sightseeing for anyone following these itineraries. It is always a good idea to be flexible when following an itinerary—you might make some new friends and be invited to participate in some unforeseen adventures.

JOURNEY #1—THE GRAND TOUR
Shannon to Dublin—Two Weeks

arrive Shannon, depart Dublin

Saturday	arrive Shannon, drive to Killarney (option: afternoon round at Killarney)
Sunday	Killarney: Mahony's Point (morning); Killeen (afternoon)
Monday	Waterville
Tuesday	Tralee (option: substitute Dooks)
Wednesday	Ballybunion Old (morning); New (afternoon)
Thursday	Ballybunion Old (option: New in afternoon)
Friday	Lahinch
Saturday	drive to Sligo Town; afternoon round on Enniscrone
Sunday	Donegal
Monday	County Sligo

Tuesday	drive to Portrush, afternoon round on Portstewart
Wednesday	Royal Portrush (Dunluce)
Thursday	Royal County Down
Friday	Portmarnock
Saturday	Mount Juliet (option: substitute European Club or sightsee)
Sunday	depart Dublin

The tour begins with the most "American-style" of the great courses of Ireland, Killarney. Since flights from overseas usually arrive in the morning, keeners will head for the course after checking into their B&B.

Waterville and Tralee are within driving distance of Killarney, for those who do not wish to be constantly changing accommodations. There is much to be said for moving each night, however, as there is an excellent post-round atmosphere in the bar at Waterville, which may only be properly enjoyed without the prospect of a two-hour drive at its conclusion. Tralee is well worth playing, both for the spectacular scenery and an insight into how a modern American player and designer (Arnold Palmer, with Ed Seay) sees links golf. But for an off-beat treat, the extremely friendly and old-fashioned Dooks is also recommended.

Even though the object of this tour is to play as many of the great Irish courses as possible, Ballybunion merits a stay of two days. There are, after all, two fine courses here. Again, take the opportunity to compare the modern vision of Trent Jones with the classic Old Course. Decent accommodation can be scarce in Ballybunion—this may be one night's stay that should be booked in advance.

Lahinch is an easy ninety-minute drive to the north, which can be undertaken on Friday morning before the round. A longer drive is in store between Lahinch and Sligo. Get it out of the way as early as possible on Saturday and set up a base for the next three days. Despite the fact that it is a weekend, tee times may be available on Saturday afternoon at Enniscrone and Sunday at Donegal (or Rosses Point, for that matter) if you enquire in writing prior to your departure.

It is to be hoped that your swing is grooved and your energy remains high, for the heart of the trip is just ahead. Make the three-to-four hour drive to the Portrush/Portstewart area and book accommodation for a couple of nights. Royal Portrush and Portstewart are only about fifteen minutes apart—and could both be played in one day—but each is clearly worthy of a day to itself. Do not confuse the second course at Royal Portrush, the Valley course, with the championship Dunluce links.

Next is the beautiful and imposing Royal County Down. While any of the courses on this tour are worth playing twice, this is the one place you should definitely play thirty-six if you have the energy. Besides, there's nothing else to do in Newcastle. Get out of town after your rounds and head for Dublin, establishing a base for the final weekend of the tour. The majestic Portmarnock is within thirty minutes of downtown Dublin. Mount Juliet (a resort course) may be played on Saturdays, but it is a considerable drive southwest of Dublin. With some luck and enough advance planning, a late afternoon tee time at Baltray or Royal Dublin might be possible, but don't count on it. Safer options are the European Club or one of the newer courses such as the K Club, St. Margaret's or Seapoint, a new links beside Baltray. If all else fails, take a day to sightsee in Dublin, and leave Ireland with the memory of elegant Portmarnock lingering.

JOURNEY #2—THE GRAND TOUR
Dublin to Shannon—Two Weeks

arrive Dublin, depart Shannon

Saturday	arrive Dublin, sightsee
Sunday	European Club (option: substitute Mount Juliet)
Monday	Portmarnock
Tuesday	Royal County Down
Wednesday	Portstewart
Thursday	Royal Portrush
Friday	County Sligo
Saturday	Enniscrone
Sunday	Donegal
Monday	Lahinch
Tuesday	Ballybunion Old and New
Wednesday	Ballybunion Old (option: New in afternoon)
Thursday	Tralee
Friday	Waterville
Saturday	Killarney (option: substitute Dooks)
Sunday	depart Shannon

Here is an alternative itinerary for a grand tour which begins in Dublin and ends in Shannon. Check with your airline as to which city the plane lands in first and departs from last to save yourself from two annoying "commuter" flights across the country. This tour starts off with a bang, with Portmarnock, Royal County Down, Royal Portrush and County Sligo in the space of five days. It will be tempting to play thirty-six every day this week, but try not to exhaust yourself (physically or mentally) before the trip is even half over. As above, the middle weekend is spent in or around Sligo Town. The second week centers on a tour of the great courses of the southwest. Try to conserve enough energy to play Ballybunion Old twice and the New course at least once. If you haven't had enough of links golf, the intriguing Dooks could be substituted for the parkland (though admittedly beautiful) courses at Killarney.

JOURNEY #3—THE GREAT SOUTHWEST—One Week

arrive and depart Shannon

Saturday	arrive Shannon, drive to Killarney, play Mahony's Point or Killeen
Sunday	Dooks
Monday	Waterville
Tuesday	Tralee
Wednesday	Ceann Sibéal
Thursday	Ballybunion Old
Friday	Ballybunion New
Saturday	Lahinch
Sunday	depart Shannon

For those who have only one week, and who do not wish to change accommodations nightly, a week in the southwest of Ireland is very appealing. All of these courses, with the exception of Lahinch, are within driving distance of a centrally-located base in the Killarney or Tralee areas.

If, for some reason, you do not fancy the trip to Lahinch, either of two new parkland courses in County Cork could be substituted: Lee Valley, designed by Christy O'Connor Jr., is at Ovens; while Fota Island, venue of the 1995 Irish Amateur, is somewhat further afield at Carrigtwohill.

JOURNEY #4—
UNDISCOVERED GEMS OF THE WEST—Ten Days

arrive and depart Shannon

Saturday	arrive Shannon; drive to Connemara
Sunday	Connemara
Monday	Carne
Tuesday	Enniscrone
Wednesday	County Sligo
Thursday	Donegal
Friday	Narin and Portnoo
Saturday	Rosapenna
Sunday	Portsalon; drive to Lahinch
Monday	Lahinch
Tuesday	depart Shannon

Here is a tour for those who like their golf peaceful and undisturbed. Undertaken at any time other than the height of summer, this tour will likely yield nine rounds played in splendid solitude. There are two lengthy drives involved—about three hours from the airport to Connemara, and perhaps four hours from the extreme northwest of the country (Rosapenna and Portsalon) back down to Lahinch. Do not be intimidated, however, as Rosapenna and particularly Portsalon are unlike any other links in the country and worth the extra effort.

JOURNEY #5—DUBLINERS—One Week

arrive and depart Dublin

Saturday	arrive Dublin, sightsee
Sunday	The European Club
Monday	Royal Dublin
Tuesday	The Island
Wednesday	Baltray
Thursday	Portmarnock
Friday	Royal County Down (option: substitute St. Margaret's)
Saturday	The K Club (option: substitute Mount Juliet)
Sunday	depart Dublin

There has been an explosion of golf courses in and around Dublin. Still, the classics should not be missed, just interspersed with some of the better recent layouts. A week of outstanding golf can be had in the vicinity of the capital. Choose a hotel or B&B to the north of the city, if possible, as all of the courses are in that direction with the exception of The European Club and the K Club. The only trip of a substantial distance is the two-and-a-half hour drive to Royal County Down—a must if you have never been before. Fans of modern parkland golf could substitute with St. Margaret's or Mount Juliet.

The Dublin area is one part of the country where visiting golfers may be restricted to certain days of the week. Portmarnock, for example, prefers visitors on Monday, Tuesday and Thursday, while Baltray allows visitors any weekday except Tuesday, and The Island and Royal Dublin welcome guests weekdays other than Wednesday. The European Club and the K Club, being newer courses, will take visitors every day of the week, for the time being at least. Realistically, with a little perseverance and enough advance warning, an early morning or late afternoon tee time should be possible at any of these clubs on any weekday, and even on some weekends.

JOURNEY #6—THE CAUSEWAY COAST—One Week

arrive Belfast, depart Belfast/Dublin

Saturday	arrive Belfast, drive to Portstewart, afternoon round at Portstewart
Sunday	Royal Portrush (Dunluce) (option: play Valley course in afternoon)
Monday to Friday	play in tournament: Ballycastle, Castlerock, Portrush (Valley) and Portstewart; off-day: Royal County Down
Saturday	depart Belfast

if additional days can be added:

Saturday	Portsalon (option: afternoon round at Rosapenna)
Sunday	Donegal
Monday	County Sligo
Tuesday	Portmarnock (option: substitute Malone)
Wednesday	depart Dublin

The Black Bush Causeway Coast Open is one of the great experiences in Irish golf. The tournament is played in four rounds over five days (Monday to Friday, with one of the days being an "off" day) at Portstewart, Castlerock, Ballycastle and the Valley course at Royal Portrush. While free practice rounds are available during the week on each of these courses in the late-afternoons, we recommend that you forego these. They will impede your ability to socialize with the (mostly Irish) tournament participants, which is at least half the point of going in the first place. Better to arrive on the Saturday prior and take a look at Portstewart and Royal Portrush before the tournament begins. Take your time, as it stays light past ten o'clock in Northern Ireland in June. Much of the membership of Royal Portrush hails from Belfast, and by noon on Sunday the course is often all but deserted.

For your off-day (tournament organizers will let you know which day this is), be sure to have made a booking at Royal County Down. It's only a two hour drive away. If you have only one week available, bid your new friends adieu on Friday night and head home from Belfast on Saturday. If you are able to squeeze a few more days into your vacation, we recommend a visit to the Republic. The drives between courses are all under two hours, with the exception of the final Sligo to Dublin (Portmarnock) trip. But it is an easy drive of 120 miles, following the N4 highway straight across the country. Count on three-and-a-half hours. If you are unable to arrange an open-jaws departure from Dublin, play Malone or Belvoir Park on your final day and depart from Belfast.

Details on how to enter the Causeway Coast Open can be found on p. 289. Of course even if you can't attend the tournament, this is a great place to spend a week, and the above itinerary can be easily adapted.

ACCOMMODATION

OBTAIN BORD FÁILTE'S ANNUAL accommodation guide ("the official guide to all registered and approved hotels, guest houses, town and country homes and farmhouses, youth hostels, holiday hostels, caravan and camping parks, self-catering group schemes, specialist accommodation and pubs"—*phew*) and you will have all the information you need. For Northern Ireland, get the annual *Where to Stay in Northern Ireland* guide to hotels and guesthouses. Addresses for both tourist boards are provided at the end of this chapter.

Both "guest houses" and "town and country homes and farmhouses" are essentially bed and breakfasts (B&Bs). The difference is that a guest house must have at least five bedrooms for rent. A large guest house is pretty much indistinguishable from a small hotel. A town and country home or farmhouse may have fewer than five bedrooms and can be more intimate—you will often have breakfast in the proprietor's own dining room, and they will invariably take a personal interest in your journey. The quality of tourist-board-approved B&Bs in Ireland is consistently good, and we recommend them over hotels as a means of experiencing and understanding the local community.

Hotels have certain advantages though. They may have more amenities, like a bar which is required to stay open as late as you wish (see "Drinking in Ireland"), a television in your room, an en-suite bathroom and the flexibility of coming and going as you please.

A third option is to rent an entire house or cottage. There are some very good properties available at reasonable prices, but the obvious disadvantage is that you are restricted to the area in which your cottage is located. Bord Fáilte publishes the *Ireland Self-Catering Guide* which lists all of the houses available (including photographs) and gives details on how to book. Bookings are generally made by the week.

If you arrive in Dublin by air and do not have sleeping arrangements booked, try visiting the Bord Fáilte's excellent information and room-booking service at the airport. They will find and reserve bed and breakfast or hotel accommodation according to your specifications, for a modest fee. A B&B on the less-glamorous north side of Dublin will be more convenient for access to the airport, Portmarnock, The Island, Royal Dublin and Baltray.

Here are some B&Bs and hotels situated in or near the principal golf-ing areas. Many hotels have various rates depending on the season. We have based our price descriptions on the high-season rate.

Inexpensive: under £20 per person per night; **Moderate:** £20 to £50 per person per night; **Expensive:** over £50 per person per night; double occupancy in all cases.

SOUTHWEST

Near Killarney

Hotel Europe, Fossa, Killarney (064) 31900; fax: (064) 32118
luxury resort hotel right on Lough Leane, fitness center, pool, sauna, etc., 205 rooms, *expensive*

Aghadoe Heights Hotel, Killarney (064) 31766; fax: (064) 31345
luxury hotel with fine views of the lakes, 57 rooms, *expensive*

The Nineteenth Green, Lackabane, Fossa, Killarney
(064) 32868; fax: (064) 32637
guesthouse adjacent to the courses with its own putting green, 10 rooms, *moderate*

Belvedere Hotel, New St., Killarney (064) 31133; fax: (064) 36093
town-center hotel, 18 rooms, *moderate*

Foley's Townhouse, 23 High St., Killarney
(064) 31217; fax: (064) 34683
nineteenth-century coaching inn on the High Street with seafood restaurant attached, 12 rooms, *moderate*

Near Waterville

Waterville House, Waterville (066) 74244; fax: (066) 74482
Jack Mulcahy's hotel to accompany the famous links, 10 rooms,
expensive

Butler Arms Hotel, Waterville (066) 74144; fax: (066) 74520
hotel overlooking Atlantic which has Charlie Chaplin connections, 31
rooms, *expensive*

Smugglers Inn, Cliff Rd., Waterville (066) 74330; fax: (066) 74422
guesthouse adjacent to the links, 10 rooms, *moderate*

Near Dooks

Hotel Ard-na-sidhe, Caragh Lake, Killorglin
(066) 69105; fax: (066) 69282
Victorian mansion on Dingle Bay three miles from Dooks, 20 rooms,
expensive

Ocean Wave, Glenbeigh (066) 68249
bed and breakfast with tremendous views of Dingle Bay and the links,
6 rooms, *inexpensive*

Near Tralee

Grand Hotel, Tralee (066) 21499; fax: (066) 22877
town-center hotel with restaurant, 44 rooms, *moderate*

Kilteely House, Ballyard, Tralee (066) 23376; fax: (066) 25766
large nineteenth-century guesthouse, 11 rooms, *moderate*

Barnagh Bridge Country Guesthouse, Cappalough, Camp
(066) 31045; fax: (066) 30299
B&B in lovely setting about ten miles west of Tralee on Dingle peninsula, 5 rooms, *inexpensive*

Near Ceann Sibéal

Dun An Oir Golf Hotel, Ballyferriter (066) 56133; fax: (066) 56153
modern hotel adjacent to the links, 20 rooms, *moderate*

Dingle Skellig Hotel, Dingle (066) 51144; fax: (066) 51501
modern hotel situated on Dingle Bay, 110 rooms, *moderate*

Bambury's Guesthouse, Mail Rd., Dingle
(066) 51244; fax: (066) 51786
new home built specifically to be a B&B, 9 rooms, *inexpensive*

Near Ballybunion

Marine Links Hotel, Sandhill Rd., Ballybunion
(068) 27139; fax: (068) 27666
Ballybunion's best hotel and also closest to the famed links, nice bar, 11
rooms, *moderate*

Eagle Lodge, Main St., Ballybunion (068) 27224
town-center guesthouse with restaurant, 8 rooms, *moderate*

Teach de Broc, Links Rd., Ballybunion (068) 27581; fax: (068) 27919
fine B&B very close to the links, 6 rooms, *moderate*

The Manor Inn, Coast Rd., Doon, Ballybunion
(068) 27757; fax: (068) 27793
modern, golf-friendly B&B just out of town, 5 rooms, *inexpensive*

Doon House, Doon Rd., Ballybunion (068) 27411
typical B&B in town, *inexpensive*

Near Lahinch

Aberdeen Arms Hotel, Lahinch (065) 81100; fax: (065) 81228
large hotel with formal dining room in village center, 55 rooms,
moderate

Sancta Maria Hotel, Lahinch (065) 81041; fax: (065) 81529
low-rise hotel on edge of links, 18 rooms, *moderate*

Greenbrier Inn, Lahinch (065) 81242
ranch-style B&B on outskirts of Lahinch, 7 rooms, *moderate*

NORTHWEST

Near Connemara

Ballynahinch Castle, Ballinafad, Recess (095) 31006; fax: (095) 31085
for many years was private retreat of Indian prince His Highness the
Maharaja Jam Sahib, *expensive*

Abbeyglen Castle, Sky Rd., Clifden (095) 21201; fax: (095) 21797
castle hotel with beautiful gardens and fine views of the Twelve Bens
and the coast, 39 rooms, *moderate*

Ardagh Hotel, Ballyconnelly Rd., Clifden
(095) 21384; fax: (095) 21314
secluded hotel on Ardbear Bay, 17 rooms, *moderate*

Rosleague Manor, Letterfrack (095) 41101; fax: (095) 41168
Georgian house overlooking Ballinakill Bay set in thirty acres, 15
rooms, *moderate*

Erriseask House Hotel, Ballyconnelly (095) 23553; fax: (095) 23639
on Mannin Bay with own beach, 13 rooms, *moderate*

Murlach Lodge, Ballyconnelly (095) 23921
adjacent to golf club, 4 rooms, *inexpensive*

Near Carne

Western Sands Hotel, Belmullet (097) 81096
small hotel with bar and food service, 10 rooms, *inexpensive*

Near Enniscrone

Downhill Hotel, Ballina (Co. Mayo) (096) 21033; fax: (096) 21338
about ten minutes from Enniscrone, health club, indoor pool, 50 rooms, *expensive*

Benbulben House, Enniscrone (096) 36185
basic hotel, color TV in all rooms, 14 rooms, *inexpensive*

Links Lodge, Ballina Rd., Enniscrone (096) 36628
modern home overlooking course, 5 rooms, *inexpensive*

Near Rosses Point

Ballincar House, Rosses Point Rd., Sligo (071) 45361; fax: (071) 44198
country house hotel with tennis and sauna, located between Sligo and Rosses Point, 25 rooms, *expensive*

Yeats Country Hotel, Rosses Point (071) 77221; fax: (071) 77203
large hotel with tennis court, basketball, 79 rooms, *expensive*

Sea Park House, Rosses Point (071) 45556
overlooks Sligo Bay, 6 rooms, *inexpensive*

St. Martins, Cummeen, Strandhill, Sligo (071) 60614
better-than-average B&B with very considerate proprietor, 4 rooms, *inexpensive*

Near Donegal

Hyland Central Hotel, Donegal (073) 21027; fax: (073) 22295
large town-center hotel, 74 rooms, *moderate*

Drumcliffe House, Donegal (073) 21200; fax: (073) 22667
period home with antiques, 5 rooms, *inexpensive*

The Arches Country House, Lough Eske, Donegal (073) 22029
views of Lough Eske and mountains, 5 rooms, *inexpensive*

Haywoods, Donegal (073) 21236
B&B run by avid golfing family, *inexpensive*

Near Narin & Portnoo

Nesbitt Arms Hotel, Ardara (075) 41103
one-hundred-year-old hotel 5 miles from course, 22 rooms, *moderate*

Bay View Country House, Portnoo Rd., Ardara (075) 41145
turf fires, award-winning bread, 6 rooms, *moderate*

Hazelwood House, Narin (075) 45182
near course, turf fire in lounge, 3 rooms, *inexpensive*

Thalassa Country Home, Narin (075) 45151
overlooks ocean, 4 rooms, *inexpensive*

Near Rosapenna

Rosapenna Hotel, Rosapenna (074) 55301; fax: (074) 55128
hotel which owns the golf course, spacious lounges with fires, fine
breakfasts, 43 rooms, *moderate*

Arnold's Hotel, Dunfanaghy (074) 36208; fax: (074) 36352
overlooking Sheephaven Bay, 34 rooms, *moderate*

Hill House, Dunmore, Carrigart (074) 55221
overlooks Downings Bay, 4 rooms, *inexpensive*

Near Portsalon

Rathmullan House, Rathmullan (074) 58188; fax: (074) 58200
elegant country house in beautiful grounds stretching to Lough Swilly,
antiques, 23 rooms, *expensive*

Fort Royal Hotel, Rathmullan (074) 58100; fax: (074) 58103
pitch & putt, tennis court, extensive grounds, 15 rooms, *expensive*

The Old Rectory, Rathmullan (074) 58226
Victorian house overlooking beach, 5 rooms, *inexpensive*

Ardeen House, Rathmelton (074) 51243
old country home overlooking Lough Swilly, 4 rooms, *inexpensive*

DUBLIN AND THE EAST

Dublin and environs

Davenport Hotel, Merrion Square, Dublin
(01) 661-6800; fax: (01) 661-5663
formerly Merrion Hall, beautiful Georgian building is now a luxury
hotel, 116 rooms, *expensive*

Shelbourne Hotel, St. Stephen's Green, Dublin
(01) 676-6471; fax: (01) 661-6006
famous hotel at heart of Dublin, 142 rooms, *expensive*

Bloom's Hotel, Anglesea St., Dublin (01) 671-5622; fax: (01) 671-5997
hotel at heart of vibrant Temple Bar district, 86 rooms, *expensive*

Portmarnock Hotel and Golf Links, Strand Rd., Portmarnock
(01) 846-0611; fax: (01) 846-2442
formerly the Jameson estate, now includes The Links Portmarnock
course, 19 rooms, *expensive*

Barry's Hotel, 1/2 Great Denmark St., Dublin
(01) 874-6943; fax: (01) 874-6508
one of the city's oldest, in the heart of Dublin off O'Connell St.,
28 rooms, *moderate*

Staunton's on the Green, 83 St. Stephen's Green, Dublin
(01) 478-2300; fax: (01) 478-2263
Georgian house on St. Stephen's Green, 26 rooms, *moderate*

Howth Lodge Hotel, Howth (01) 832-1010; fax: (01) 832-2268
seaside hotel in Howth, convenient to the north-side courses, 46 rooms,
moderate

Sea View House, Strand Rd., Portmarnock
(01) 846-2242; fax: (01) 846-2008
fine views of the Irish Sea and Ireland's Eye, 9 rooms, *moderate*

Marymount, 137 New Cabra Road, Dublin (01) 868-0026
typical Dublin B&B, well-located for north-side golf, 4 rooms,
inexpensive

St. Brendans, 41 Home Farm Road, Drumcondra, Dublin
(01) 837-0263
friendly and accommodating B&B on north side, 3 rooms, *inexpensive*

Wesley House, 113 Anglesea Rd., Ballsbridge, Dublin (01) 668-1201
south-side B&B in upscale area with above-average furnishings,
3 rooms, *inexpensive*

Elmhurst, 27 Herbert Av., Dublin (01) 269-1225
friendly and quiet B&B on south side, *inexpensive*

Near Co. Louth

Boyne Valley Hotel, Drogheda (041) 37737; fax: (041) 39188
large country house-style hotel with pitch-and-putt course, 37 rooms,
moderate

Westcourt Hotel, West St., Drogheda (041) 30965; fax: (041) 30970
town-center hotel about three miles from Baltray, 37 rooms, *moderate*

Aisling House, Baltray (041) 22376
B&B overlooking the estuary and adjacent to the links, 4 rooms,
inexpensive

Near Mt. Juliet

Mount Juliet Hotel, Thomastown (056) 24455; fax: (056) 24522
extremely luxurious hotel with equestrian center, shooting and fishing
as well as the golf course, 65 rooms, *expensive*

Abbey House, Jerpoint Abbey, Thomastown
(056) 24192; fax: (056) 26275
country house adjacent to Jerpoint Abbey, 7 rooms, *moderate*

NORTHERN IRELAND

The Causeway Coast

Bayview Hotel, Bayhead Rd., Portballintrae
(012657) 31453; fax: (012657) 32360
seafront hotel with outstanding views over bay, three miles from
Portrush, 16 rooms, *moderate*

Ballymagarry Country House, 46 Leeke Rd., Portrush (01265) 823737
country house with fine coastal views, once home to Earls of Antrim,
4 rooms, *moderate*

Bushmills Inn, Main St., Bushmills
(012657) 32339; fax: (012657) 32048
former coaching inn refurbished in 1987, turf fires, 11 rooms,
moderate

Causeway Coast Hotel, 36 Ballyreagh Rd., Portrush
(01265) 822435; fax: (01265) 824495
centrally located between Portrush and Portstewart, fine Atlantic views,
21 rooms, *moderate*

Magherabuoy House Hotel, 41 Magheraboy Rd., Portrush
(01265) 823507; fax: (01265) 824687
hotel set high on hill with distant coastal views, 38 rooms, *moderate*

Blackheath House, 112 Killeague Rd., Blackhill, Coleraine
(01265) 868433
Georgian country house built in 1791 with two acres of gardens,
5 rooms, *moderate*

Brown Trout Golf and Country Inn, 209 Agivey Rd., Aghadowey
(01265) 868209; fax: (01265) 868878
fine inn which caters to golfers and has its own nine-hole course, 17
rooms, *moderate*

Edgewater Hotel, 88 Strand Rd., Portstewart
(01265) 833314; fax: (01265) 832224
adjacent to Portstewart links with fantastic view from the bar, 31
rooms, *moderate*

Golf Hotel, 17 Main St., Castlerock
(01265) 848204; fax: (01265) 848295
village-center hotel very close to links, 16 rooms, *moderate*

Marine Hotel, 1 North St., Ballycastle
(012657) 62222; fax: (012657) 69507
seafront hotel overlooking Rathlin Island, leisure center, 32 rooms,
moderate

Radisson Roe Park Hotel & Golf Resort, Limavady
(015047) 22212; fax: (015047) 22313; USA toll free: (800) 333-3333
luxurious new hotel and golf complex within thirty minutes of the
Causeway Coast, 65 rooms, *expensive*

Near Royal County Down

Slieve Donard Hotel, Downs Rd., Newcastle
(013967) 23681; fax: (013967) 24830
dramatic red-brick hotel overlooking the links not what it once was,
but you can't beat the location, 120 rooms, *expensive*

Glassdrumman Lodge, 85 Mill Rd., Annalong
(013967) 68451; fax: (013967) 67041
elegant former farmhouse with fine sea views, 10 rooms, *moderate*

Burrendale Hotel, 51 Castlewellan Rd., Newcastle
(013967) 22599; fax: (013967) 22328
centrally located hotel with restaurant, 50 rooms, *moderate*

Brook Cottage Hotel, 58 Bryansford Rd., Newcastle
(013967) 22204; fax: (013967) 22193
hotel with large garden at foot of mountains, 8 rooms, *moderate*

Enniskeen House Hotel, 98 Bryansford Rd., Newcastle
(013967) 22392; fax: (013967) 24084
hotel in fine eleven acre setting at base of Mountains of Mourne,
12 rooms, *moderate*

TOURIST BOARD ADDRESSES

Irish Tourist Board (Bord Fáilte)
United States
345 Park Ave.
New York, NY 10154
tel: (212) 418-0800
fax: (212) 371-9052
(212) 371-9059

Canada
160 Bloor St. E.
Suite 1150
Toronto, ON
M4W 1B9
tel: (416) 929-2777
fax: (416) 929-6783

Great Britain
150 New Bond St.
London W1Y 0AQ
tel: (171) 493-3201
fax: (171) 493-9065

Northern Ireland Tourist Board
United States
551 Fifth Avenue, Seventh Floor
New York, NY 10176
tel: (212) 922-0101
(800) 326-0036
fax: (212) 922-0099

Canada
111 Avenue Road
Suite 450
Toronto, ON
M5R 3J8
tel: (416) 925-6368
fax: (416) 961-2175

Great Britain
11 Berkeley St.
London W1X 5AD
tel: (171) 355-5040
fax: (171) 355-5040

100
MORE GOLF
COURSES

ONE HUNDRED MORE GOLF COURSES

T HE COURSES HIGHLIGHTED in the previous chapters are the ones that set Ireland apart and offer attractions that you will not get at home, in our opinion. However, Ireland has dozens of other full-length courses that are certainly worth playing if you find yourself in the area, or can't get on one of the more highly recommended courses. Here is a selected list of noteworthy layouts. Those of particular quality are designated with an asterisk (*).

SOUTHWEST

Cork

* Cork Golf Club (Little Island)
Little Island, Co. Cork
tel: (021) 353451; fax: (021) 353410
Redesigned by Alister Mackenzie in 1927, part of the course is routed through an old quarry. There are also lovely views of Cork harbor. Has hosted the Irish Open.

Harbour Point Golf Complex
Clash, Little Island, Co. Cork
tel: (021) 353094; fax: (021) 354408
New course with modern driving range on banks of River Lee.

Douglas Golf Club
Douglas, Cork, Co. Cork
tel: (021) 891086; fax: (021) 895297
Well-maintained parkland course which is easy to walk, three miles from city center.

* Fota Island Golf Club

Carrigtwohill, Co. Cork
tel: (021) 883700; fax: (021) 883713
This new Christy O'Connor Jr. layout in Cork harbor hosted the 1995 Irish Amateur.

* Lee Valley Golf Club

Clashenure, Ovens, Co. Cork
tel: (021) 331721; fax: (021) 331695
Another Christy O'Connor Jr. design in the upscale, inland mold.

Monkstown Golf Club

Monkstown, Co. Cork
tel: (021) 841376
Well-bunkered course with very difficult closing stretch.

Fernhill Golf Club

Fernhill, Carrigaline, Cork
tel: (021) 372226; fax: (021) 371011
Course overlooking Owenabwee valley, which is owned by Fernhill Country House hotel.

Mallow Golf Club

Ballyellis, Mallow, Co. Cork
tel: (022) 21145
Long parkland course twenty-one miles north of Cork which dates from the 1940s.

Youghal Golf Club

Youghal, Co. Cork
tel: (024) 92787; fax: (024) 92641
Founded in 1898, the course presents commanding views of the town and the sea.

Water Rock Golf Course

Midleton, Co. Cork
tel: (021) 613499
Pay-as-you-play facility featuring fearsome 240-yard par 3 over a swan-filled lake.

Muskerry Golf Club
Carrigrohane, Co. Cork
tel: (021) 385297
Undulating course northwest of Cork with River Shournadh much in play.

Kerry

Beaufort Golf Club
Churchtown, Beaufort, Killarney, Co. Kerry
tel: (064) 44440; fax: (064) 44752
New course set in an estate near Killarney, opened September 1994, designed by Dr. Arthur Spring.

Killorglin Golf Course
Stealroe, Killorglin, Co. Kerry
tel: (066) 61979; fax: (066) 61437
Eddie Hackett parkland layout overlooking Dingle Bay, very close to Dooks.

Limerick

✓ Limerick Golf Club
Ballyclough, Limerick
tel: (061) 415414; fax: (061) 415946
Parkland course just south of town, founded in 1891.

Limerick County Golf & Country Club
Ballyneety, Limerick
tel: (061) 351881; fax: (061) 351384
New Des Smyth-designed course five miles from Limerick.

* Adare Manor Golf Club
Adare, Co. Limerick
tel: (061) 396566; fax: (061) 396124; USA toll free tel: (800) 462-3273
Upscale hotel complex with Robert Trent Jones course which opened in September, 1995.

Castletroy Golf Club

Castletroy, Limerick
tel: (061) 335753; fax: (061) 335373
Mature, tree-lined parkland course three miles from town.

Clare

Shannon Golf Club

Shannon, Co. Clare
tel: (061) 471849; fax: (061) 471507
An ordinary parkland course, built in 1966, adjacent to the airport at mouth of the Shannon, promotes itself as "Greg Norman's favorite Irish golf course".

Dromoland Castle Golf Club

Newmarket on Fergus, Co. Clare
tel: (061) 368144; fax: (061) 363355
Set in grounds of magnificent castle hotel, water much in play on back nine.

Woodstock House Golf & Country Club

Ennis, Co. Clare
tel: (065) 29463; fax: (065) 20304
Undulating course featuring several elevated greens, just fifteen minutes from Shannon airport.

* Kilkee Golf Club

East End, Kilkee, Co. Clare
tel: (065) 56048; fax: (065) 56041
Clifftop quasi-links dating from the turn of the century, with spectacular Atlantic views.

Tipperary

Co. Tipperary Golf & Country Club

Dundrum, Co. Tipperary
tel: (062) 71116; fax: (062) 71366
New course attached to the Dundrum House Hotel, designed by Irish professional Philip Walton.

Clonmel Golf Club
Lyreanearla, Clonmel, Co. Tipperary
tel: (052) 24050
Hilly course by Eddie Hackett with clubhouse of Alpine design.

Ballykisteen Golf & Country Club
Monard, Co. Tipperary
tel: (062) 51439; fax: (062) 52457
Another of Des Smyth's recent efforts, stretching to 7,000 yards from the tips.

NORTHWEST

Galway

Galway Golf Club
Blackrock, Galway
tel: (091) 22033
Alister Mackenzie-designed course, but not his most interesting work, first four holes are links-style, then course moves inland.

* Galway Bay Golf & Country Club
Renville, Oranmore, Co. Galway
tel: (091) 90500; fax: (091) 90510
Christy O'Connor Jr. design, surrounded on three sides by the Atlantic but inland in character. Ireland's first golf course surrounded by a Florida-style real-estate development.

Oughterard Golf Club
Oughterard, Co. Galway
tel: (091) 82131
Parkland design on road to Connemara, extended to eighteen holes in 1985.

Tuam Golf Club

Barnacurragh, Tuam, Co. Galway
tel: (093) 28993
Course whose crest features a crow with a golf ball in its beak—the crow is said to have a preference for tee shots on the eleventh fairway.

Mayo, Roscommon and Sligo

* Westport Golf Club

Westport, Co. Mayo
tel: (098) 25113; fax: (098) 27217
Very long, testing, Fred Hawtree design in magnificent isolation of Clew Bay, has hosted Irish Amateur, back nine is particularly fine.

Athlone Golf Club

Hodson Bay, Athlone, Co. Roscommon
tel: (0902) 92073; fax: (0902) 94080
Inland-type course in magnificent setting on peninsula jutting into Lough Ree.

Strandhill Golf Club

Strandhill, Co. Sligo
tel: (071) 68188; fax: (071) 68428
Sligo's "other" links, with views of Atlantic and Ox Mountains, founded 1931, a bit short at 5,950 yards.

Donegal

* Bundoran Golf Club

Bundoran, Co. Donegal
tel: (072) 41302
Historic seaside course redesigned by Vardon in the 1930s, home to Christy O'Connor Sr. for a time in the 1950s.

Letterkenny Golf Club

Barnhill, Letterkenny, Co. Donegal
tel: (074) 71150; fax: (074) 22606
1968 Eddie Hackett parkland layout on shores of Lough Swilly.

Dunfanaghy Golf Club
Dunfanaghy, Co. Donegal
tel: (074) 36335
Ancient par-68 links with just one par 5, opposite Rosapenna across
Sheephaven Bay.

* North West Golf Club
Fahan, Lifford, Co. Donegal
tel: (077) 61027
Rather tight and intriguing links course dating from nineteenth century
with strong membership from Londonderry.

* Ballyliffen Golf Club
Ballyliffen, Carndonagh, Co. Donegal
tel: (077) 76119
Ireland's most northerly links, recently expanded to thirty-six holes with
addition of Glashedy Course designed by Pat Ruddy; the Old Course features very undulating fairways and the Tank, the unique par-3 fifth.

Cavan and Longford

* Slieve Russell Hotel Golf & Country Club
Ballyconnell, Co. Cavan
tel: (049) 26444; fax: (049) 26474
Splendidly conditioned parkland course opened in 1992, midway
between Dublin and Sligo, Paddy Merrigan design.

Co. Longford Golf Club
Glack, Longford
tel: (043) 46310
Remodelled in 1970s with fine views of Longford Town.

DUBLIN AND THE EAST

Monaghan, Meath and Louth

Nuremore Hotel & Country Club
Carrickmacross, Co. Monaghan
tel: (042) 64016; fax: (042) 61855
Parkland course featuring water on many holes, high-end hotel complex
with tennis courts, sauna, gymnasium, etc.

Greenore Golf Club
Greenore, Dundalk, Co. Louth
tel: (042) 73212; fax: (042) 73678
Course dating from 1897 with some links holes overlooking Carlingford
Lough, spacious new clubhouse built in 1994.

* Seapoint Golf Club
Termonfeckin, Co. Louth
tel: (041) 22333; fax: (041) 22331
A new links (adjacent to Baltray) designed by Irish professional Des
Smyth, includes real-estate development.

Dundalk Golf Club
Dundalk, Co. Louth
tel: (042) 21731; fax: (042) 22022
Recently remodelled by Peter Alliss and Dave Thomas, excellent views of
Dundalk Bay.

Laytown & Bettystown Golf Club
Bettystown, Co. Meath
tel: (041) 27170
Seaside course with outstanding junior program and reputation for
friendliness.

Dublin area

Malahide Golf Club
Beechwood, The Grange, Malahide, Co. Dublin
tel: (01) 845-3533; fax: (01) 846-1270
Twenty-seven hole Eddie Hackett layout.

* St. Margaret's Golf & Country Club
St. Margaret's, Co. Dublin
tel: (01) 864-0400; fax: (01) 864-0289
Well-designed and well-conditioned parkland course, three miles from the airport, which will be terrific when the trees grow in. Designed by Pat Ruddy and Tom Craddock.

Luttrellstown Castle Golf & Country Club
Clonsilla, Dublin
tel: (01) 821-3237; fax: (01) 821-3241
New parkland course set in 560-acre estate aimed at rich tourists and corporate outings.

Corballis Public Golf Course
Corballis, Donabate, Co. Dublin
tel: (01) 843-6583
Short at just over 5,000 yards, but nevertheless a delightful links bordering on The Island. Usually in excellent condition, and excellent value.

Beaverstown Golf Club
Beaverstown, Donabate, Co. Dublin
tel: (01) 843-6439; fax: (01) 843-6721
Eddie Hackett design in former orchard near The Island.

* The Links Portmarnock
Portmarnock, Co. Dublin
tel: (01) 846-1800; fax: (01) 846-1077
New links (opened June 1995) on former Jameson estate adjacent to Portmarnock Golf Club. Designed by Bernhard Langer—his first course in Ireland.

Howth Golf Club
Sutton, Dublin
tel: (01) 832-3055; fax: (01) 832-1793
Hilly course on Howth Peninsula with fine views of Dublin Bay.

Deer Park Hotel & Golf Courses
Howth, Dublin
tel: (01) 832-2624; fax: (01) 839-2405
Also on Howth, this public complex comprises an eighteen-hole course, another nine, a twelve-hole short course and a pitch-and-putt.

Forrest Little Golf Club
Cloghean, Co. Dublin
tel: (01) 840-1183; fax: (01) 840-1060
Tree-lined course exceptionally close to Dublin airport, earplugs sometimes required.

St. Anne's Golf Club
North Bull Island, Dollymount, Dublin
tel: (01) 833-6471
Links bordering Royal Dublin to the north, has recently been extended to eighteen holes.

* Grange Golf Club
Rathfarnham, Dublin
tel: (01) 493-2889; fax: (01) 493-9480
Designed by James Braid, just six miles from Dublin city-center near Dublin mountains.

Hollystown Golf Club
Hollywood Rath, Dublin
tel: (01) 820-7444; fax: (01) 820-7447
Public course twenty minutes from downtown Dublin.

City West Golf Course
Saggart, Co. Dublin
tel: (01) 458-8566; fax: (01) 458-8565
New public course designed by Christy O'Connor Jr., views of Dublin mountains.

Castle Golf Club
Rathfarnham, Dublin
tel: (01) 490-4207; fax: (01) 492-0264
Undulating south-side course designed by H. S. Colt.

* Hermitage Golf Club
Lucan, Co. Dublin
tel: (01) 626-8491
Fine old course bordered by majestic trees, River Liffey in play on tenth and eleventh holes.

Kildare, Westmeath and Offaly

* Curragh Golf Club
Curragh, Co. Kildare
tel: (045) 41238
Oldest golf club in the Republic, formerly Royal Curragh, with large membership from the army.

Kilkea Castle Golf Club
Castledermot, Co. Kildare
tel: (0503) 45156; fax: (0503) 45187
Course designed around castle which was built in 1180, River Greese in play on eight holes.

* Glasson Golf & Country Club
Glasson, Athlone, Co. Westmeath
tel: (0902) 85120; fax: (0902) 85444
Another new one from Christy O'Connor Jr., borders Lough Ree, almost exactly in the middle of Ireland.

* Mullingar Golf Club
Mullingar, Co. Westmeath
tel: (044) 48366; fax: (044) 41499
Lush inland course which is one of James Braid's better designs.

* Tullamore Golf Club
Tullamore, Co. Offaly
tel: (0506) 51757
One of the country's leading inland layouts (at least until the recent explosion of new developments), course dates from 1926 and was designed by James Braid.

Castlebarnagh Golf Club
Daingean, Co. Offaly
tel: (0506) 53384; fax: (0506) 53077
Peaceful and inexpensive parkland course in the heart of Ireland, about fifty miles west of Dublin.

Wicklow

* Charlesland Golf & Country Club
Greystones, Co. Wicklow
tel: (01) 287-6764; fax: (01) 287-3882
New course twenty miles south of Dublin, seaside, with views of Wicklow hills.

* Woodbrook Golf Club
Bray, Co. Wicklow
tel: (01) 282-4799; fax: (01) 282-1950
Clifftop course bisected by railway line, Christy O'Connor Jr. nipped a young Tom Watson here in the 1975 Irish Open.

Arklow Golf Club
Abbeylands, Arklow, Co. Wicklow
tel: (0402) 32492
Par-68 links with newly-installed irrigation system.

Delgany Golf Club
Delgany, Co. Wicklow
tel: (01) 287-4536; fax: (01) 287-3977
Hilly course with fine views of mountain and sea.

Laois, Carlow and Kilkenny

The Heath Golf Club
Portlaoise, Co. Laois
tel: (0502) 46533
Course built on commonage which golfers share with grazing sheep.

* Carlow Golf Club
Deerpark, Carlow, Co. Carlow
tel: (0503) 31695; fax: (0503) 40065
Often referred to as Ireland's finest inland course, testing layout designed by Tom Simpson.

Kilkenny Golf Club
Glendine, Co. Kilkenny
tel: (056) 65400
Pleasant, flat course which is undemanding until final four holes.

Wexford

Courtown Golf Club
Gorey, Co. Wexford
tel: (055) 25166; fax: (055) 25553
Parkland course (though very close to the sea) dating from the 1930s.

* Rosslare Golf Club
Rosslare, Co. Wexford
tel: (053) 32203
A traditional links dating from 1908 whose original architect is unknown, minutes from the international ferry port.

* St. Helen's Bay Golf & Country Club
Kilrane, Rosslare, Co. Wexford
tel: (053) 33669; fax: (053) 33803
Philip Walton's new seaside course of mixed links and parkland character with on-site accommodation available.

Waterford

* Tramore Golf Club
Newtown Hill, Tramore, Co. Waterford
tel: (051) 386170
Mature course designed by Captain H. Tippett of Walton Heath in 1936, most panoramic clubhouse view in Ireland.

Waterford Golf Club
Newrath, Waterford
tel: (051) 76748; fax: (051) 53405
Venerable course originally designed by Willie Park Jr. and extended by Braid.

* Waterford Castle Golf Club
The Island, Ballinakill, Co. Waterford
tel: (051) 71633; fax: (051) 79316
Situated on a private island accessible only by ferry, yet another five-star castle hotel with course attached, designed by Des Smyth.

* Faithlegg Golf Club
Faithlegg House, Co. Waterford
tel: (051) 382241; fax: (051) 382664
Another new layout in Co. Waterford, Paddy Merrigan design features some very undulating greens.

West Waterford Golf Club
Coolcormack, Dungarvan, Co. Waterford
tel: (058) 44343
Eddie Hackett design on banks of Brickey river with lovely backdrop of Comeragh and Knockmealdown mountains.

Northern Ireland

Derry and Tyrone

City of Derry Golf Club
Prehen, Londonderry
tel: (01504) 46369
Venerable club located two miles south of city center.

Roe Park Golf Course
Limavady, Co. Londonderry
tel: (015047) 22212; fax: (015047) 22313
Course which is now affiliated with upscale Radisson Roe Park hotel.

Strabane Golf Club
33 Ballycolman Rd., Strabane, Co. Tyrone
tel: (01504) 382271; fax: (01504) 382007
Eddie Hackett re-design just one mile from border with the Republic.

Belfast area

* Malone Golf Club
Dunmurry, Belfast
tel: (01232) 612758; fax: (01232) 431394
Belfast parkland course winding through lakes which is renowned for its conditioning, designed by Fred Hawtree.

* Belvoir Park Golf Club
Newtonbreda, Belfast
tel: (01232) 491693; fax: (01232) 646113
pronounced "Beaver," H. S. Colt design always in a battle with Malone for best Belfast layout.

Balmoral Golf Club
Lisburn Rd., Belfast
tel: (01232) 381514
Flat parkland course very close to Belfast city center with friendly atmosphere.

Shandon Park Golf Club
Shandon Park, Belfast
tel: (01232) 401856; fax: (01232) 402773
City course with views of Stormont, the seat of government prior to direct rule.

The Knock Golf Club
Summerfield, Dundonald, Belfast
tel: (01232) 483251
Tree-lined, heavily bunkered course designed by H. S. Colt.

Lisburn Golf Club
Lisburn, Co. Antrim
tel: (01846) 677216; fax: (01846) 603608
Lengthy Hawtree & Sons design ten miles southwest of Belfast.

Massereene Golf Club
Antrim, Co. Antrim
tel: (01849) 428096
Another Hawtree parkland layout, just three miles from Belfast international airport.

Whitehead Golf Club
McRae's Brea, Whitehead, Co. Antrim
tel: (01960) 353631
Undulating course at south end of Island Magee with exceptional views of the sea.

* Royal Belfast Golf Club
Craigavad, Holywood, Co. Down
tel: (01232) 428165
The oldest golf club in Ireland is the home of Belfast's elite, and extremely shy about visitors, but is possible to play by prior arrangement. Not a links, the present course was designed by H. S. Colt.

Holywood Golf Club
Nun's Walk, Demesne Rd., Holywood, Co. Down
tel: (01232) 423135; fax: (01232) 425040
Hilly course overshadowed by its neighbor Royal Belfast.

Down

* Clandeboye Golf Club
Newtonards, Co. Down
tel: (01247) 271767
Pretty thirty-six-hole complex with plenty of gorse for the wayward driver, "Dufferin" is the main course.

* Bangor Golf Club
Broadway, Bangor, Co. Down
tel: (01247) 270922
James Braid design, undulating course near Bangor town-center.

* Ardglass Golf Club
Ardglass, Co. Down
tel: (01396) 841219; fax: (01396) 841841
Seaside course with remarkable second hole whose tee is set on edge of precipice.

Kirkistown Castle Golf Club
Cloughey, Newtonards, Co. Down
tel: (012477) 71233; fax: (012477) 71699
James Braid revised this course overlooking the Irish Sea.

Spa Golf Club
Ballynahinch, Co. Down
tel: (01238) 562365
Parkland course which co-hosts annual "Heart of Down" tournament.

Downpatrick Golf Club
Downpatrick, Co. Down
tel: (01396) 615947
Undulating inland course, exceptional views from eighth fairway.

Bright Castle Golf Club
Bright, Downpatrick, Co. Down
tel: (01396) 841319
Long and wide-open course (7,100 yards from the tips), also has pitch-and-putt course.

Warrenpoint Golf Club
Warrenpoint, Co. Down
tel: (016937) 53695; fax: (016937) 52918
Scenic course with views of Mourne mountains and the Republic across Carlingford Lough, produced Ryder Cup player Ronan Rafferty.

LISTS

IRELAND'S BEST 18 HOLES

THE FOLLOWING IS A personal view of a dream eighteen-hole course chosen from the courses featured in this book. Our dream course is not overly long at 6,460 yards, but its par of 70 would be very difficult to match. We hope it will start as many arguments as it resolves.

1. **Portstewart #1 (Tubber Patrick), par 4, 425 yards:** Perhaps the best opening hole in links golf, with a dramatic descent from a gloriously elevated tee into an amphitheater of dunes.

2. **Tralee #2, par 5, 590 yards:** Some holes on this course are over-designed, but #2 is not one of them. Here Palmer and Seay have used Tralee Bay to great effect—creating a sweeping dogleg right with the beach as a constant hazard for the slice-prone. The Dingle Peninsula sits brooding on the horizon. Panoramic views of the entire course from the tee.

3. **Portsalon #3 (Strand), par 4, 356 yards:** A nineteenth-century masterpiece that weaves its way along Lough Swilly before the approach shot, which must be threaded between ancient rock outcroppings. The views over the Lough are as stunning as any at Pebble Beach or Turnberry.

4. **Royal County Down #4, par 3, 217 yards:** This oft-photographed hole is at its most glorious when the gorse is in bloom in early June. It is a beast at any time of the year, however, as the tee shot is all carry over the gorse until the cluster of eight bunkers in front of the hard, narrow green. The view from the back tee is the most gorgeous of all the vistas on the course.

5. **Mount Juliet #3, par 4, 385 yards:** Jack Nicklaus has taken advantage of the most wooded area on the estate to create a pretty and treacherous par 4. Played through a narrow opening in the woods to a green jutting out into a lake.

6. **Lahinch #6 (Dell), par 3, 156 yards:** This Old Tom Morris original is completely blind from the tee. The green is bordered by high dunes on all sides, a unique green placement which would never be copied today. On your first visit, there is nothing to do but aim for the white stone marker on top of the dune and hope. Also makes some people's Worst 18 list.

7. **Ballybunion Old #11, par 4, 449 yards:** "Don't be right, all of Ireland is to your left" was the advice we received when we first played this hole. How true. Downhill and bunkerless, the landing area for the drive progressively narrows between the dunes on the left and the sea. The second shot is played to a small green on a shelf with trouble on all sides.

8. **Ballybunion New #15, par 5, 476 yards:** One of the eeriest holes in golf, this par 5 is played over a crest of a hill into a bowl surrounded by the steepest sandhills you can imagine. The third shot is played to a green built high on a plateau. The unearthly solitude and strange terrain would make it a good location for the first Star Trek golf movie.

9. **Connemara #13, par 3, 215 yards:** There are so many wonderful par 3s in Ireland it is easy to become jaded, but this one is unlike any other. Set in its own rocky amphitheater, it requires a heroic drive over a wild jumble of stones, swamp and scrub. Play it from the back tees.

10. **Enniscrone #10, par 4, 338 yards:** A great links hole, a short downhill par 4 that scares and entices, charms and frustrates, all at the same time. Exquisite scenery off the tee, but the narrow, tilting landing area is intimidating and either the wind or the humps and hollows of the fairway conspire to throw many shots off-line and into the fearsome rough. A well-placed tee shot leaves just a wedge to a lovely, but tightly guarded green.

11. **Waterville #11 (Tranquillity), par 5, 496 yards:** Gary Player thought this was one of the best par 5s in the world. Almost bunkerless, this aptly-named hole sends you tumbling through a long, undulating chute lined with stately dunes. You feel cut off from the rest of the world amid the delightfully natural terrain.

12. **The European Club #17, par 4, 392 yards:** One of several holes at Pat Ruddy's masterpiece that provide a fairly generous landing area

(this time in a pretty valley), but demand an accurate second to a well-positioned, slightly elevated green protected by natural swales and a pot bunker.

13. **The Island #13 (Broadmeadow), par 3, 215 yards:** A wake-up call after meandering through the dunes of the first twelve holes at The Island. It is all carry over a half-moon shaped estuary. There is bail-out room to the left, but to reach the putting surface the water must be negotiated with a long iron or wood. Beyond the green the village of Malahide provides a lovely backdrop.

14. **Portmarnock #14 (Ireland's Eye), par 4, 395 yards:** The most elegant of Portmarnock's fine collection of par 4s, the line for the tee shot on this dogleg left is said to be "Ireland's Eye," an island poised on the horizon. The second shot is played over large bunkers to a plateau green that accepts only the most precisely played shot. English great Henry Cotton's favorite hole.

15. **Royal Portrush #14 (Calamity), par 3, 213 yards:** A treacherous and historic hole with a huge chasm of rough waiting to swallow any shot short or right of the green. Usually played into the wind. Bobby Locke got up and down from the depression to the front-left of the green in all four rounds of the 1951 British Open. This area thus became known as "Bobby Locke's hollow," and you are advised to keep it in mind, as it is the only conceivable bail-out area. The hole is said to be a source of inspiration for Pete Dye.

16. **Ballybunion Old #16, par 5, 490 yards:** The drive is everything on this dogleg, as it must be over 200 yards long and threaded through mountainous dunes in order to reach the fairway. The hole then turns inland for a second (if you are a very good driver) or third shot to a mercifully large green.

17. **Co. Sligo #17 (Gallery), par 4, 455 yards:** One of the toughest holes to par in all of Ireland, this severe dogleg sweeps uphill and to the left on the second shot. The green is large but slopes severely from the back.

18. **Killarney Mahony's Point #18, par 3, 197 yards:** "The best one-shot hole in the world," according to Henry Longhurst, and certainly one of the loveliest. A longish iron over a picture-perfect inlet to a green framed exquisitely by shrubs, flowers and a dramatic pine tree.

TOURNAMENTS OPEN TO VISITING GOLFERS

The Black Bush Causeway Coast Open is described in detail elsewhere in this book. While it is the premier handicapped tournament in Ireland, there are several other competitions open to amateur golfers for a modest entry fee. Unless otherwise stated, these tournaments are geared toward men only. You must produce acceptable proof of handicap to enter one of them. We have not played in most of these tournaments, so before you decide to plan a holiday around one of them, we would advise you to look into the details as much as possible.

BLACK BUSH CAUSEWAY COAST OPEN

Courses: Portstewart, Castlerock, Ballycastle, Royal Portrush
            (Valley course)
Dates: first week of June
Format: 72-hole Stableford competition for teams of three.
            Individual and daily prizes. Maximum handicap is 18.
Contact: John Dalzell, 155 Coleraine Road, Portstewart,
            Northern Ireland (01265) 832417; fax: (01265) 52174

HEART OF DOWN GOLF TOURNAMENT

Courses: Ardglass, Spa, Downpatrick
Dates: early September
Format: 54-hole Stableford competition, with the top 100 competitors from outside Northern Ireland playing a
            fourth round at Royal County Down. There is also a
            36-hole women's tournament, with a percentage of
            golfers playing a third round at Royal County Down.
            Maximum handicaps are men—20 and women—30.
Contact: Down District Council, 74 Market St., Downpatrick,
            Co. Down BT30 6LZ, Northern Ireland
            (01396) 612233; fax: (01396) 612350

WEST COAST CHALLENGE

Courses:	County Sligo, Strandhill, Bundoran, Donegal
Dates:	first week of September
Format:	72-hole Stableford competition for teams of three. Daily, individual and team prizes. Maximum handicap is 22.
Contact:	Bundoran Golf Club, Bundoran, Co. Donegal (072) 41302

ATLANTIC GOLF CLASSIC

Courses:	Galway, Galway Bay, Oughterard, Athenry
Dates:	first week of May
Format:	72-hole Stableford competition for teams of four. Women welcome. Separate overseas category. Maximum handicaps are men—20 and women—28.
Contact:	Frank Burke, c/o Rehab Group, Parkmore Industrial Estate, Galway (091) 751397

CELTIC INISHOWEN MIXED PAIRS

Courses:	Ballyliffen Old, Ballyliffen Glashedy, North West
Dates:	mid-June
Format:	four day tournament for couples, with 36-hole mixed pairs championship, 18-hole men's and ladies' singles and 18-hole mixed scramble. Maximum handicaps are men—24 and ladies—36.
Contact:	Eugene Corrigan, East Coast Golf, 6 College Rise, Drogheda, Co. Louth (041) 32881

EAST COAST CLASSIC

Courses:	Seapoint, Laytown & Bettystown, Dundalk, Headfort
Dates:	early May
Format:	72-hole Stableford competition for teams of four. Daily, individual and team prizes. Maximum handicap is 22.
Contact:	Eugene Corrigan, East Coast Golf, 6 College Rise, Drogheda, Co. Louth (041) 32881

Murphy's Irish Stout Dunmore East Waterford Golf Classic

Courses: Waterford, Waterford Castle, Tramore, Faithlegg
Dates: first week in May
Format: 72-hole Stableford competition for teams of four. Daily
             prizes, including Waterford crystal. Women welcome.
             Maximum handicaps are men—22 and women—28.
Contact: Charlie Boland, Candlelight Inn, Dunmore East, Co.
             Waterford (051) 383215; fax: (051) 383289

Carlsberg Tramore Golf Classic

Courses: Waterford, Waterford Castle, Tramore, Faithlegg
Dates: late September
Format: 72-hole Stableford competition for teams of four. Daily
             and individual prizes of Waterford crystal. Began in
             1995 as autumn complement to the successful
             Murphy's tournament. Women welcome. Maximum
             handicaps are men—24 and women—36.
Contact: Michael Bowe, Irish Golf Tours Limited,
             34 Sweetbriar Lawn, Tramore, Co. Waterford
             (051) 381728; fax: (051) 381961

Autumn Leaves Golf Classic

Courses: Waterford, Tramore, Faithlegg
Dates: mid-September
Format: 54-hole better-ball Stableford competition for teams of
             two. Players must be 50 years of age or older. Daily
             prizes. Women welcome. Maximum handicaps are
             men—24 and women—36.
Contact: Charlie Boland, Candlelight Inn, Dunmore East, Co.
             Waterford (051) 383215; fax: (051) 383289

South East Classic

Courses: Rosslare, St. Helen's Bay, Wexford, Enniscorthy
Dates: early October
Format: 72-hole Stableford competition for teams of four.
             Daily, individual and team prizes. Maximum handicap
             is 22.
Contact: Eugene Corrigan, East Coast Golf, 6 College Rise,
             Drogheda, Co. Louth (041) 32881

WORLD INVITATIONAL FATHER & SON EVENT

Course:	Waterville
Dates:	end of August
Format:	54-hole Stableford competition for teams consisting of father and son.
Contact:	Susanna Ryan, Carr Golf & Corporate Travel, 30 Upper Abbey St., Dublin 1 (01) 873-4244; fax: (01) 873-4091

KERRY HANDICAP GOLF CLASSIC

Course:	Killarney (Mahony's Point)
Date:	third Friday in September
Format:	Popular charity tournament with strong overseas entries featuring clinic and prize-giving by Ken Venturi. 18-hole Stableford competition for teams of four. Women welcome. Maximum handicaps are men—21 and women—28.
Contact:	Tony Darmody, KPFMH, Old Monastery, Killarney, Co. Kerry (064) 32742; fax: (064) 33370

GOLFER'S GLOSSARY

blow-in — an outsider

Bord Fáilte — the Irish Tourist Board

Bradshaw, Harry — Irish professional who, with Christy O'Connor, won the 1958 Canada Cup and ignited popular interest in golf

Bruen, Jimmy — legendary Irish golfer who was the John Daly of his day. Bruen used a loopy swing to hit the ball farther than any man alive, and in 1938 he caused a sensation at St. Andrews by equalling Bobby Jones's course record at the age of seventeen. When competitive golf returned after the Second World War, Bruen easily won the 1946 British Amateur, but then his career was derailed by a wrist injury. He was only twenty-six.

buggies — motorized golf carts, rare in Ireland except on new courses

camogie — version of hurling played by young women

caravan park — trailer park; very common next to seaside golf courses

Carr, Joe — three-time British Amateur champion, ten-time Walker Cup player, and captain of the Royal and Ancient in 1994. Arguably the most distinguished player Ireland has ever produced.

Carrolls Irish Open — the most important professional tournament held in Ireland each year; attracts top-flight field and massive crowds

clochan — a striking beehive-shaped stone hut (made without mortar), dating from the early Christian period

country member — golf club member who lives in another region of the country; popular way for Dublin players to join a golf club and get an official handicap

crack — good conversation

Dáil — the lower house of the Irish Parliament

dolmen — a prehistoric stone chamber formed by massive slabs of rock, dating to 2000 B.C.; used as logo for the European Club

Éire — Gaelic word for Ireland

293

European Community — economic and political association of European countries, which Ireland joined in 1973; several golf courses have benefitted from EC grants for tourism development

Fianna Fáil — most successful political party since independence; led for decades by Eamon de Valera

Fine Gael — led the first Free State government, but has spent more time in Opposition since then. Similar policies to Finna Fáil.

football — in the Republic often refers to Gaelic football; precursor to Australian Rules Football, it is a cross between soccer, basketball and rugby; in Northern Ireland, more often refers to soccer

fourball — a better ball competition between two teams of two golfers, or generally, four golfers each playing their own ball

fry — hot breakfast of eggs, meat and anything else that can go on the skillet

Gaeltacht — quickly vanishing areas of Ireland where Irish is still spoken by significant numbers; target of intensive government programs

gammon steak — ham steak, and a staple of Irish restaurants

Gardai — police force in the Republic

ghillie — fishing guide

golf chumann — golf course

grand — oft-used exclamation that is interchangeable with "lovely"

Hackett, Eddie — Ireland's foremost architect, has designed or remodelled over eighty courses

hurling — exciting, violent and popular sport that is similar to lacrosse but using large sticks known as hurleys

IRA — Irish Republican Army

jar — a pint of beer

Labour — political party in the Republic that has become a major player in recent years

links — golf course on sandy "linksland" next to the sea; notable for undulating terrain, the absence of trees, pot bunkers and firm fairways and greens

Loyalist — in Northern Ireland, a supporter of continued ties with Great Britain

Nationalist — a supporter of a unified Ireland; also Republican

Orange Order — Protestant associations of Loyalists formed to defend Northern Ireland's union with Britain; named after William of Orange, who defeated the Catholic James II at the Battle of the Boyne in 1690

O'Connor Jr., Christy — popular professional and architect known for his victory over Fred Couples in the 1989 Ryder Cup—he hit a pressure-packed 2 iron to four feet on the final hole

O'Connor Sr., Christy — uncle of Junior, best Irish player of the 1960s

parkland course — non-links course

petrol — gasoline

pint — the standard serving of beer, approximately 20 fluid ounces

pitch and putt — popular form of golf for beginners and the urban working class; holes are extremely short (less than a hundred yards) but the competition can be fierce

poteen — homemade liquor (usually very strong) produced in illegal stills and made from grain or potatoes

RTE — Irish national broadcasting system

RUC — Royal Ulster Constabulary; Northern Ireland's regular police force

sláinte — Irish for "to your health" or "cheers"

slata — Irish for the distance of one yard

soccer — in recent years the Irish soccer team has become a national preoccupation, twice qualifying for the World Cup, and with a famous victory over Italy in USA '94. This has disgruntled some supporters of Gaelic football. Northern Ireland has its own very competitive team.

snug — small, partitioned area in some older pubs for discreet conversations

Stableford — common form of competition in Ireland, based on awarding points for birdie, par, bogey, etc.

stout — rich and bitter black beer which is made from highly roasted malt; the most common brand is Guinness

takeaway — restaurant serving food to go

Taoiseach — prime minister of the Republic

tinkers — itinerant and materially poor group of people who traditionally travelled around Ireland mending tin kettles and pots; ethnically Irish, the Travellers (as they prefer to be known) are still visible today in roadside caravans, though official attempts are being made to provide permanent accommodation

trolley — a pull cart for golf clubs

Troubles — euphemism for violent unrest, used most recently in Northern Ireland since 1969 but also applied to the period after the First World War

tuition — golf lessons

twenty-six counties — the Republic of Ireland

UDA — Ulster Defence Association, a legal Protestant paramilitary organization in Northern Ireland

Unionists — much the same as Loyalists

GOLFER'S READING LIST
AND BIBLIOGRAPHY

The Irish have always held writers and poets in high esteem. From the bards of the early Celtic kings, to the learned Irish monks that educated Europe, to the poets and playwrights of the independence movement, to 1995 Nobel Prize-winner Seamus Heaney—Irish wordsmiths have been a potent force. Some argue that the introduction of the notorious censorship law in 1929 reflected how well the authorities (and the Catholic Church) understood the power of the written word. Today many Irish works that were once banned are considered national treasures, and a law passed in 1979 gave writers tax-free status. Here is but a brief sampling of (mostly) twentieth-century Irish writing.

ACCESSIBLE FICTION

Maeve Binchy's charming stories set in small-town Ireland are on international best-seller lists around the world. **Roddy Doyle's** affectionate and hilarious accounts of life in working-class Dublin have also made terrific movies; his books include *The Commitments*, *The Snapper* and *The Van*. The popular Victorian classic, *Some Recollections of an Irish RM*, by **E. O. Sommerville and Violet Ross** contains much lively and perceptive detail about rural life at the turn of the century. **David Hanly's** *In Guilt and in Glory* captures the spirit and contradictions of modern Ireland. The creator of *Dracula* is Irish, and some say the confrontation between peasants and debauched aristocrat in **Bram Stoker's** most famous story is full of revolutionary symbolism. Golf fiction is not yet a genre in Ireland, but **William Rocke** has done some pioneering with *Operation Birdie*—a fast-moving thriller about a fictitious IRA attack on a British Open at Turnberry.

MORE CHALLENGING FARE

A master of the short story, **William Trevor** writes exquisite and often heart-breaking stories that are usually set in his native Ireland. **John**

Banville's unsettling and sometimes bleak psychological novels rank among the best works of literature being produced in English today. **Brian Moore's** early novels, including *The Lonely Passion of Judith Hearne*, evoke the Belfast of his youth. The poems and essays of **Seamus Heaney**, winner of the 1995 Nobel Prize for Literature, have been deeply influenced by the Troubles in his native Northern Ireland; they often explore the relationship between art and society. Feel free to jump into **James Joyce's** *Ulysses*, but you might want to cut your teeth first on *Dubliners*, his famous and perfectly crafted group of short stories. **William Butler Yeats**—winner of the Nobel Prize in 1923—is one of the century's greatest poets and an important nationalist figure.

DRAMA

Take away Irish-born playwrights and you would leave a gaping hole in this century's English-language theater. The Irish influence starts with **George Bernard Shaw** and **Oscar Wilde,** and continues with the lyrical tales of **J. M. Synge,** the wrenching civil war plays of **Sean O'Casey,** the absurdist masterpieces of **Samuel Beckett,** and the more accessible, though equally penetrating dramas of **Frank McGuinness,** Ireland's best contemporary playwright. (Don't be put off by the titles of McGuinness's plays; *Observe the Sons of Ulster Marching Towards the Somme* and *Carthaginians* are exciting pieces of theater that illuminate Ireland's inner conflicts.) Reading plays is not everyone's cup of tea, of course, so keep an eye out for local productions of Irish plays, and definitely check out the lively theater scene in Dublin. Prices are reasonable and the quality is high.

HISTORY

Readable general histories of Ireland include John Ranelagh's *A Short History of Ireland* (Cambridge) and *The Oxford Illustrated History of Ireland* (Oxford), edited by R. F. Foster. *Ireland: A Concise History* (Thames and Hudson) by Máire and Conor Cruise O'Brien is well written and illustrated, but assumes prior knowledge of Irish affairs. Terence Brown's *Ireland: A Social and Cultural History 1922-1985* (Fontana) is much more interesting than it sounds. *A Traveller's History of Ireland* (Interlink) by Peter Neville is very accessible.

David Cannadine's *Decline and Fall of the British Aristocracy* (Yale) is a fascinating and exhaustive account of the demise of the landed gentry in Britain and Ireland. *The Great Hunger* (Hamish Hamilton) by Cecil Woodham Smith is a similarly definitive history of the Famine of the 1840s. *How the Irish Saved Civilization* (Bantam) by Thomas Cahill is an illustrated account of the golden age of Irish influence in Europe.

Early Irish Golf (Oakleaf) by William Gibson can be found in better bookstores in Ireland. It is a careful documentation of the development of golf in Ireland and should be of interest to those with a serious golf library. Robert Browning's 1954 classic, *A History of Golf: The Royal and Ancient Game* (A & C Black) contains some material on Ireland. Fans of Bernard Darwin could also peruse *The Golf Courses of the British Isles*. Herbert Warren Wind's famous article on Ballybunion, written in 1967, is reprinted in a collection of writings entitled *Following Through* (Ticknor & Fields).

CENTENARY BOOKS

If you fall in love with a specific course, and it's old enough, you might inquire whether the club has commissioned a special book to celebrate its one-hundredth anniversary. While the quality varies, most centenary books are well researched and make attractive and unique mementos. Many are labors of love, which we think gives them additional charm. There are centenary books on Ballybunion (written by John Redmond), Ballycastle (John Andrews, Michael Page and Tim Sheehan), County Louth (Charlie Mulqueen), County Sligo (Dermot Gilleece), Dooks (several authors), Killarney (Donal Hickey), Lahinch (Enda Glynn), Portsalon (several authors), Portmarnock (T. M. Healy), Portstewart (Bill Rodgers), Royal County Down (Harry McCaw and Brum Henderson), Royal Dublin (Liam Browne and Frank Chambers), Royal Portrush (Ian Bamford) and The Island (William Murphy).

GUIDEBOOKS

There are many excellent general guides to Ireland, and it would be pointless to list them all here. Browse in your local bookstore to find the one that suits you best. Most are terribly ill-informed about golf, however. The tourist boards have some attractive golf brochures that will help get your adrenaline going. Those who want a pictorial record of Irish golf should look for *Great Golf Courses of Ireland* (Gill & Macmillan Ltd.) by John Redmond, an attractive though not inexpensive coffee-table book.

Ireland, a Bicycle, and a Tin Whistle (McGill-Queen's University Press/Blackstaff Press) by David A. Wilson is an entertaining account of cycling around Ireland in search of traditional music. *Ireland's Pubs* (Penguin) by Sybil Taylor is an excellent exploration of pub culture, with detailed information on the most historic and worthwhile of Ireland's ten thousand pubs.

There are a myriad of general interest publications available from Bord Fáilte and the Northern Ireland Tourist Board. The most important are the comprehensive accommodation guides—*Ireland Accommodation Guide* and *Where to Stay in Northern Ireland*. The Irish Hotels Federation *"Be Our Guest"* guide is also useful, as it includes pictures of each of the listed hotels. So too does the Town & Country Homes Association *Bed & Breakfast Guest Accommodation* guide.

VIDEOS

One of the more interesting contemporary Irish film directors is Jim Sheridan, who made *My Left Foot, The Field* and *In the Name of the Father*. The latter film deals with the Troubles, as does Neil Jordan's *The Crying Game*.

The Commitments and *The Snapper* are wonderful adaptations of Roddy Doyle's comic novels, and there have also been outstanding film treatments of *The Dead* (the final story in *Dubliners*), *The Lonely Passion of Judith Hearne* and Maeve Binchy's *A Circle of Friends*.

Film buffs will enjoy *The Quiet Man,* starring John Wayne and Maureen O'Hara, and for a taste of the kind of scenery you will encounter on golf courses in the west of Ireland there's always *Ryan's Daughter*.

INDEX

accommodations 251–262
Adair, Rhona 185, 210–212
Adare Manor Golf Club 268
airlines 239
Alliss, Peter 273
Antrim, Glens of 206
Aran Islands 128–129
Ardglass Golf Club 282, 289
Arklow Golf Club 277
Ards Peninsula 206, 226
Armour, Tommy 203
Athenry Golf Club 290
Athlone Golf Club 271
Augusta National Golf Club 8, 28, 30, 34, 49, 58, 149, 168

Babington, Sir Anthony 195
Balfour, Lord Arthur 162–163
Ballesteros, Severiano 149, 165
Ballybunion Golf Club, New Course 37–39, 287
Ballybunion Golf Club, Old Course 3, 8, 14, 34–36, 60, 62, 66, 79, 81, 104, 119, 132, 134, 145, 201, 213, 233, 240, 287, 288
    graveyard at 34–35
    history of 15–21
Ballycastle Golf Club 124, 181, 193–196, 289
Ballykisteen Golf & Country Club 270
Ballyliffen Golf Club 272, 290
Balmoral Golf Club 281
Baltray (see County Louth Golf Club)
Bangor Golf Club 282
Barnes, Brian 188
Barton, Colonel B. J. 74
battle of the sexes 210

bed and breakfast (see accommodations)
beer 221–224
    Irish ale 223–224
    oysters and 223
    stout 221–223
Beaufort Golf Club 268
Beaverstown Golf Club 274
Belfast 205–206
Belmullet Peninsula 114–115
Belvoir Park Golf Club 280
Benbulben 110, 111, 130
Blarney Stone 69
Blasket Islands 59
Bligh, Captain William 162, 163
Bord Fáilte (Irish Tourist Board) 31, 46, 89, 91, 233, 263
Boner, Tony 106–108
Boyd, Kathleen 194–195
Boyne, Battle of the 227–228
Bradshaw, Harry 149, 233
Braid, James 2, 16, 75, 81, 97, 98, 99, 275, 276, 277, 282
Bright Castle Golf Club 282
Browning, Robert 10
Bruce, Robert of 194
Bruen, Jimmy 20, 233
budgeting 241–242
Bundoran Golf Club 140, 271, 290
Burke, John 49, 51
Burren, the 68

Campbell, Sir Guy 25, 45, 48
Campbell, Captain Willie 110, 111–112
Carlow Golf Club 278
Carne Golf Course 80, 114–121
Carr, Joe 135, 137, 186, 233

Carrick–a–rede rope bridge 207
Casey, Frank 74–75, 77, 97–98
Cashel 69
Cashen Course (see Ballybunion Golf
  Club, New Course)
Castle Golf Club 276
Castlebarnagh Golf Club 277
Castlerock Golf Club 181, 182,
  197–199, 289
Castlerosse, Lord 15, 23–26, 32–33,
  45–48
Castletroy Golf Club 269
Causeway Coast 206–207
Causeway Coast Open **179–183**,
  250, 289
Ceann Sibéal, Golf Chumann 3,
  58–61, 66, 67, 80, 233
Chaplin, Charlie 26, 253
Charlesland Golf & Country Club
  277
City West Golf Course 275
City of Derry Golf Club 280
Civil War 230–231
Clandeboye Golf Club 282
Clare, County 14, 68
Clonmel Golf Club 270
Colt, H. S. (Harry) 3, 75, 110, 112,
  162, 164, 166, 167, 184, 185,
  187, 198, 200, 201, 276, 280, 281
Combe, George 111, 200, 201
communications 242
Connemara 129
Connemara Golf Club 78, 79, 80,
  83, 115, **126–127**, 233, 287
  founding of **85–96**
Connery, Sean 123
Connolly, Jay 41, 42
Corballis Public Golf Course 274
Cork 69
Cork, County 68–69
Cork Golf Club 266
Cotton, Sir Henry 29, 40, 112, 150,
  288
County Longford Golf Club 272
County Louth Golf Club 8, 132,
  145, **152–156**, 232, 240

County Sligo Golf Club 72, 81,
  110–113, 232, 240, 288, 290
County Tipperary Golf & Country
  Club 269
Courtown Golf Club 278
cows 106–108
Craddock, Tom 274
Crenshaw, Ben 149
Cronin, Noel 26, 28, 41, 42
Crosby, Bing 45
Curragh Golf Club 276
currency (see budgeting)
Curtis, Margaret 185, 211
Cypress Point Golf Club 28, 49, 51

Daly, Fred 233
Dalzell, John 183
Darwin, Bernard 2, 164, 165–166,
  184, 185–187, 200, 202, 204
Deer Park Hotel & Golf Courses
  275
Delgany Golf Club 277
Derry (see Londonderry)
Dingle Peninsula 14, 58–59, 67
Doak, Thomas 42
Dobereiner, Peter 38, 53
Donegal 103, 130
Donegal, County 130
Donegal Golf Club 80, **102–105**,
  290
Dooks Golf Club **62–65**, 66, 213
Doolin 68
Douglas Golf Club 266
Downpatrick Golf Club 282, 289
drinking 220–225
Dromoland Castle Golf Club 269
Dublin 132, 173
Dundalk Golf Club 273, 290
Dunfanaghy Golf Club 272

Easter Rising 230
Enniscorthy Golf Club 291
Enniscrone Golf Club 80, **122–125**,
  233, 287
European Community 7, 115, 234

European Golf Club, the 22, 29–32, 132, 168–172, **287–288**
Ewing, Cecil 112

Faldo, Nick 47, 80, 103
Faithlegg Golf Club 279, 291
Famine, the Great 74, 215, 229–230
Faulkner, Max 186, 188
Feherty, David 234
Fernhill Golf Club 267
Floyd, Raymond 28, 44
food 215–219
    breakfast 216
    dinner 217
    ethnic 218–219
    lunch 216–217
    menus 217
    snack 219
    vegetarian 219
Ford, Doug 28
Forrest Little Golf Club 275
Fota Island Golf Club 267

Gaeltacht 58, 67, 128
Galway 128
Galway Bay Golf & Country Club 270, 290
Galway Golf Club 270, 290
Garvey, Philomena 212
Giant's Causeway 181, 185, 207
Gibson, Charles 49, 51
Giffin, Des 189, 191
Gilroy, Thomas 152, 153, 163
Glasson Golf & Country Club 276
Gleeson, Bridget 212
Golf in the Kingdom 7, 138
Golfing Union of Ireland 3, 82, 153, 178
Gourlay, Molly 3, 16, 34, 153
Gow, A. G. 189, 190
Grafton Street (Dublin) 174
Grange Golf Club 275
Greenore Golf Club 273
Guinness Brewery 174

Hackett, Eddie 3, 10–11, 26, 37, 40, 42–43, 58, 60–61, 76, **78–84,**
    89–92, 97, 98, 99, 102–104, 114, 120, 122–123, 125, 126–127, 146, 148, 163, 268, 270, 271, 274, 279, 280
    courses of 79–81
Ha'Penny Bridge (Dublin) 173
Harbour Point Golf Complex 266
Hawtree, Fred 45, 46, 47, 146, 271, 280, 281
Headfort Golf Club 290
Heath Golf Club, the 278
Hermitage Golf Club 276
Hervey, Frederick 198
Hewson, Lionel 54
Hezlet, Major C. O. 195
Hezlet, May 185, 210–212
Higgins, Liam 30
Hillery, Dr. P. J. 51
Hillsborough 206
Hilton, Harold 133–134, 147, 210
Hollystown Golf Club 275
Holywood Golf Club 282
Hope, Bob 28, 45
hotels (see accommodations)
Howth Golf Club 275

Independence, War of 49–50, 224, 230–231
Irish Tourist Board (see Bord Fáilte)
Island Golf Club, the 107, 132, **143–146,** 241, 288
itineraries 243–250

Jacklin, Tony 186
Jones, Bobby 8, 9, 11
Jones, David 48
Jones, Robert Trent 3, 10, 14, 37–39, 82, 233, 268
journey planning 238–263
Joyce, James 173, 174, 175–176

K Club (see Kildare Hotel & Country Club)
Kells, Book of 173–174, 227
Kerry, County 14, 66–67
Kerry, Ring of 14, 66, 80

Kildare Hotel & Country Club 140,
  160–161
Kilkea Castle Golf Club 276
Kilkee Golf Club 269
Kilkenny Golf Club 278
Killarney 24–25, 45–47, 66
Killarney Golf & Fishing Club 14,
  23–26, 45–48, 64, 66, 142, 213,
  232, 233, 240, 288, 292
Killeen Course (see Killarney Golf &
  Fishing Club)
Killorglin 67
Killorglin Golf Course 268
Kinsale 69–70
Kirkistown Castle Golf Club 282
Knock, Chapel of 129, 136
Knock Golf Club, the 281

Lahinch 50, 68
Lahinch Golf Club 2, 14, 49–52, 79,
  81, 107, 140, 232, 240, 287
Langer, Bernhard 112, 149, 161,
  165, 274
Laytown & Bettystown Golf Club
  273, 290
Lee Valley Golf Club 267
Leitrim, Earl of 73
Lemmon, Jack 28
Letterkenny Golf Club 271
Limerick 67
Limerick County Golf & Country
  Club 268
Limerick Golf Club 268
links courses, characteristics of 7–11,
  79–81, 179, 182
Links Portmarnock, the 274
Lisburn Golf Club 281
Lisdoonvarna 58
Locke, Bobby 10, 186, 187, 288
Londonderry 207
Longhurst, Henry 2, 25, 33, 36, 288
Luttrellstown Castle Golf & Country
  Club 274
Lynch, James 128
Lyons, Peter 153–154
Lyttle, David 198

Macdonnell, Sorley Boy 193
Macgillycuddy's Reeks 45, 48, 58,
  66
Mackenzie, Alister 3, 49, 51–52,
  266, 270
Mahony's Point Course (see
  Killarney Golf & Fishing Club)
Malahide Golf Club 274
Mallow Golf Club 267
Malone Golf Club 280
Mangan, Michael 114–118, 121
Massereene Golf Club 281
McAndrew, Liam 114, 116–118, 120
McCarthy, Paddy 16
McCarthy, Patrick 16
McCarthy, William 16, 18, 34
McCready, Max 149
McKenna, James 49
Merrigan, Paddy 272, 279
Mickelson, Phil 149
Moher, Cliffs of 68
money (see budgeting)
Monkstown Golf Club 267
Moran, Michael 164
Moriarty, John 14, 16, 17–21, 37,
  39
Morris, Old Tom 2, 3, 14, 16, 49,
  51–52, 73, 75–76, 80, 97, 98, 99,
  104, 200, 201, 287
  vs. Rhona Adair 210
Mount Juliet Golf Course 140, 142,
  157–159, 286
Muirfield (Honourable Company of
  Edinburgh Golfers) 79, 104
Mulcahy, Jack 22, 23, 26–29, 32–33,
  41, 43, 89, 91
Mullingar Golf Club 276
Murphy, Bob 188
Murvagh (see Donegal Golf Club)
Muskerry Golf Club 268

Narin & Portnoo Golf Club 72,
  106–109
National Gallery (Dublin) 174
National Museum (Dublin) 174
Natterjack Toad 63, 64

Newcastle 201, 206
Nicklaus, Jack 3, 78, 82, 83, 140, 157, 158, 286
Nixon, Richard 27
North West Golf Club 272, 290
Northern Ireland Tourist Board 263
Nuremore Hotel & Country Club 273

O'Brien, Michael 53–54
O'Connor, Christy (Jr.) 58, 60, 234, 267, 270, 275, 276, 277
O'Connor, Christy (Sr.) 43, 149, 167, 233, 271
Olazabal, Jose Maria 149
O'Neill, Tip 28
O'Regan, Jim 122–124
O'Sullivan, Bernard 58
O'Sullivan, Dr. William 45–47, 64
Oughterard Golf Club 270, 290
oysters 223

Palmer, Arnold 10, 14, 53–57, 82, 83, 140, 150, 160–161, 233
Park, Mungo 149
Park, Willie (Jr.) 189, 190, 279
Pebble Beach Golf Links 28, 56, 76, 79, 100
Penal Laws, the 228
Pickeman, W. C. 134, 147, 148
Player, Gary 28, 287
Portmarnock Golf Club 3, 8, 79, 81–82, 145, 147–151, 154, 172, 212, 213, 233, 240, 288
one–hundredth anniversary of 133–138
Portrush 180, 181, 184–185, 190
Portsalon Golf Club 2, 100–101, 130, 140, 286
history of 73–74, 76–77
Portstewart 179, 181, 189–190
Portstewart Golf Club 107, 179, 181, 189–192, 240, 286, 289
pubs 220–221
Puck Fair 67

Rafferty, Ronan 234, 283
Rathlin Island 194
rental cars 239–240
ring forts 59, 66
Robinson, Mary 213
Roe Park Golf Course 280
Rosapenna Golf Club 2, 72, 80, 97–99, 130, 140
history of 73–77
Ross, Donald 155
Rosses Point (see County Sligo Golf Club)
Rosslare Golf Club 278, 291
Royal Belfast Golf Club 281
Royal County Down Golf Club 3, 9, 79, 134, 172, 178, 189, 200–204, 211, 213, 240, 286
Royal Dublin Golf Club 81, 132, 143, 145, 162–167, 213, 232, 240
Royal Portrush Golf Club, Dunluce Links 2, 10, 79, 134, 147, 178, 181–182, 184–188, 189, 191, 211, 232, 240, 288
Royal Portrush Golf Club, Valley Course 181, 188, 289
Ruddy, Pat 7, 22–23, 29–33, 80, 168–172, 235, 272, 274, 287
Ryan's Daughter 53, 56

St. Albans, Duke of 74, 75
St. Andrews (Old Course) 3, 8, 9, 23, 28, 34, 49, 79, 112, 113, 134, 166
St. Anne's Golf Club 275
St. Helen's Bay Golf & Country Club 278, 291
St. Margaret's Golf & Country Club 31, 139, 141, 213, 274
St. Patrick 206, 226–227
Sarazen, Gene 46
Savalas, Telly 28
Sayers, Ben 197, 198
Seapoint Golf Club 273
Seay, Ed 53–57, 160–161
Shandon Park Golf Club 281
Shannon Golf Club 269

Shell's Wonderful World of Golf 46
Simpson, Tom 3, 8, 16, 18, 34, 35, 152–155, 278
Slieve Donard 200, 206
Slieve Russell Hotel Golf & Country Club 140, 141, 272
Sligo 110–111, 129–130
Smyth, Des 234, 268, 270, 273, 279
Snead, Sam 27, 28, 150, 233
Spa Golf Club 282, 289
Spring, Dr. Arthur 268
starting times 240–241
Steel, Donald 49
stout (see beer)
Strabane Golf Club 280
Strandhill Golf Club 271, 290
Swift, Jonathan 173, 174, 228
Sybil Head 58–59
Synge, J. M. 129

Taylor, J. H. 2, 81
telephone calls 242
Temple Bar (Dublin) 175
The Field 129
The Quiet Man 129
The Van 218
Thomas, Dave 273
Thomastown 159
Tippett, Captain H. 279
Tralee Golf Club 53–57, 233, 286
Tramore Golf Club 279, 291
Troubles, the 26, 28, 72, 98, 108, 179–180, 182, 202, 233–234
Tuam Golf Club 271
Tullamore Golf Club 277

Ulster Folk and Transport Museum 206
Ulster Way 207

Vardon, Harry 2, 75, 80, 81, 97, 98, 99, 201, 271
Venturi, Ken 28, 292

Waldron, Peter 80, 83, 85–96, 126
Walton, Philip 234, 269, 278

Warrenpoint Golf Club 282
Water Rock Golf Course 267
Waterford Castle Golf Club 279, 291
Waterford Golf Club 279, 291
Waterville 26, 28–29, 40–42
Waterville Golf Links 14, 22, 26–29, 40–44, 60, 62, 66, 80, 82–83, 240, 287, 292
Watson, Tom 2, 15, 20, 39, 112, 113, 277
West Waterford Golf Club 279
Westport Golf Club 233, 271
Westward Ho! Golf Club 51
Wexford Golf Club 291
whiskey 224–225
Whitehead Golf Club 281
Wind, Herbert Warren 2, 7–8, 15, 34, 36
Woodbrook Golf Club 277
Woodstock House Golf & Country Club 269
Woosnam, Ian 149

Yeats, Jack 111, 129, 161
Yeats, William Butler 110–111, 129–130, 173, 174
Youghal Golf Club 267

About the Authors

Richard Phinney is an award-winning writer and documentary producer whose assignments have taken him to more than two dozen countries. He is a member of the Golf Writers' Association of America.

Scott Whitley is a Toronto-based lawyer and writer. He has also worked as a sports broadcaster on television and radio.

Bill Russell is a San Francisco-based illustrator whose work has been featured in the *New York Times*, the *Wall Street Journal*, *Esquire* and many other publications.

We Welcome Your Comments

We have gone to great lengths to ensure that this edition of *Links of Heaven* is as accurate as possible. We would be delighted to learn what you think about the book, and about any changes, additions and deletions you would like to see in future editions. Please write to *Links of Heaven*, Baltray Books, Corporate Center, 812 Proctor Ave., Ogdensburg, NY 13669 or to Box 4902, Station E, Ottawa, Ontario, K1S 2J1.

Need More Copies?

Links of Heaven makes a perfect gift. For additional copies of this book we encourage you to see your local bookseller. In the United States and Canada you can also phone toll free at 1-800-250-2295 and order by credit card. There will be a $1.75 shipping charge per book plus applicable taxes.

Those of you in Britain, Ireland and the rest of the world can order by mail—send your credit card information (name, number and expiry date) to Baltray Books, Box 4902, Station E, Ottawa, Ontario, Canada, K1S 2J1. Or you can send an international postal order or a check in U.S. dollars drawn on a U.S. bank. Send $19.95 plus $2.85 shipping per book (surface mail).